The Art and Business
of Champagne

The Art and Business of Champagne

DAN GINSBURG

McFarland & Company, Inc., Publishers
Jefferson, North Carolina, and London

Library of Congress Cataloguing-in-Publication Data

Ginsburg, Daniel E., 1956–
    The art and business of champagne / Dan Ginsburg.
        p.   cm.
    Includes bibliographical references and index.

    ISBN 0-7864-2225-4 (softcover : 50# alkaline paper) ∞

    1. Champagne (Wine).   2. Sparkling wines.   3. Wine and wine
making.   4. Wine industry.   I. Title.
TP555.G54   2006
641.2'224 — dc22   2005034168

British Library cataloguing data are available

On the cover, clockwise from right: ©2006 PhotoAlto;
©2006 PhotoSpin; oldmapsbooks.com; ©2006 PhotoSpin

Manufactured in the United States of America

McFarland & Company, Inc., Publishers
    Box 611, Jefferson, North Carolina 28640
        www.mcfarlandpub.com

To René Collard

Table of Contents

Preface

THE WORD CHAMPAGNE BRINGS many images to mind. Jet-setting couples at an elegant reception. A romantic evening. Sports teams celebrating a championship. A lavish wedding reception. Perhaps most of all, revelers ushering in the New Year.

Beyond the images, however, the word champagne signifies some of the world's greatest wines—those made only in the Champagne region of France, using only grapes grown in that region. Only those wines are real champagne. Making champagne is a complicated process, and making quality champagne is vastly more difficult. This is the art of champagne.

However, champagne is also a business. In 2003, champagne producers had total sales of 293,308,769 bottles. In financial terms, this represents sales of well over three billion dollars. While not a huge business by modern standards, champagne is by no means a cottage industry.

A tiny part of those 293 million bottles were produced and sold by a small company located in the village of Ay, Champagne De Meric. Since 1997, I have been the majority owner of Champagne De Meric. I have been studying champagne for fifteen years, lived in the Champagne region, and spent countless hours tasting champagne from hundreds of different producers, so this is not just an investment for me—it is a passion.

Most books on the subject of wine are written by wine journalists and critics. Although these professionals are highly knowledgeable, they are by definition outsiders and lack inside access to what really happens in the wine business. However, as outsiders they can view their subject somewhat objectively. While they have their own preferences and prejudices, they are generally not strongly attached to a particular brand or producer.

There are, however, a number of interesting books written by wine producers who are insiders to the industry. They know all of the trade secrets, both positive and negative. On the other hand, it's hard for them to be objective, and books by producers are generally their story or the story of their winery.

I decided to write this book in 2001, while living in Champagne. My original idea was to write a totally objective book about champagne and the Champagne region, discussing who were the top champagne producers in terms of quality, the methods they used to achieve excellent results, and the history of the wine and the region. However, I soon found out that it was next to impossible not to repeatedly refer to my winery when discussing the various key points of the production process. I then shifted the focus to my story and the story of my winery, Champagne De Meric. However, I found this focus too limiting because I wished to discuss both the wine-making and business aspects of the champagne industry as a whole, not just my company, and to present a picture of the Champagne region.

Not being able to choose between the two approaches, I decided to pursue both. In this book, I attempt to give the reader an inside look into the world of champagne. The primary focus is on the wine, how it is made, and how it is sold, but I also attempt to provide an overview of the region and its history.

Before going any further, I want to call the reader's attention to a style point. Both the wine and the region bear the name champagne. However, the region, Champagne, is capitalized. The wine, champagne, is in lower case.

This book is divided into two parts. Part I, "Lessons of an American in Champagne," presents the key lessons I have learned about champagne and how we've applied these lessons in recreating Champagne De Meric. This is partly a personal history of how I learned about champagne and how I ended up owning a champagne winery. The primary focus, however, is on the art and business of champagne. The keys to quality — viticultural methods, vinification methods, and aging — are discussed in depth. Also covered are the problems and opportunities on the business side, including the most painful part of our business, cash flow.

Part II, "The World of Champagne," is a guide to champagne and Champagne. The history of the wine, including an in-depth discussion of past vintages, is a key element of this part. I also provide short profiles of many of the wine-producing villages in the Champagne region, along with an overview of what it is like to live in Champagne. Although Champagne is not a major tourist destination, it is well worth visiting, and a visitor's guide is included in this part. Most importantly, I profile my twenty favorite champagne producers (not including Champagne De Meric), along with a number of other brands worth getting to know.

I decided to write this book for a number of reasons. One is that the public's knowledge of and appreciation of champagne is much less than that their understanding of other fine wines. Champagne is too often viewed as a generic product, with no great difference between producers. In reality, however, champagne is a complex wine, and the difference between producers can be enormous, in terms of both style and quality. In addition, many wine connoisseurs are familiar with the more famous vineyard areas of Bordeaux, Burgundy, and the Napa Valley, but few know the difference between the various regions of Champagne, to say nothing of the nuances of the different grand cru villages such as Ay, Bouzy, or Avize. So while there have been some excellent books written about champagne, the public's education is far from finished. I hope this book contributes to the knowledge base.

Another goal of mine is to clear up some common misconceptions about champagne. Much of what has been written about champagne focuses on the glamour and romance of champagne as a wine. Discussions of quality are somewhat generic and focus more on the universal aspects of winemaking in Champagne rather than on what separates a good champagne from an outstanding one. In this book I discuss the specific and sometimes technical elements that make a great champagne and present an overview of the business side of the champagne industry. I discuss the many positive aspects of the champagne business, but I also present a few problems that affect those of us in the business and, ultimately, champagne consumers. Every industry has problems, and it is my opinion that a frank and forthright discussion of these problems is by no means a negative reflection on the product. In fact, I feel that only a strong, successful industry like champagne can be open and transparent with consumers. We may not be perfect, but I believe champagne is the greatest wine in the world. We have a great deal to be proud of, and nothing to hide.

A third reason I decided to write this book is to debunk certain myths about what makes champagne a great wine. The two things that seem to catch the fancy of the public and many journalists are the blending process, whereby still wines are blended together before the bottling and second fermentation, and the turning of the bottles prior to getting them ready to sell (rémuage, or riddling in English). Although both of these tasks are certainly necessary and important parts of the process, they are by no means the key factors. However, because both of these operations are visual and perhaps a bit mysterious, many producers tend to emphasize these operations rather than focus on the real keys to quality, which will be discussed in the following pages.

Another motivation was to tell the story of my winery, Champagne De Meric. As the only American owner of a champagne winery, I believe I bring a unique perspective to the business. Because we have completely changed our production process, product line, and business methods since my arrival, I've had to get intimately involved in nearly all aspects of the champagne business. I'm proud of what we've accomplished and believe it makes an interesting story.

Perhaps the most important motivation for this book, however, was to pay tribute to those who've taught me about champagne. I've heard it said that there are no new ideas in the world, and certainly nothing I've done for Champagne De Meric has been new. Each step has been based on what I have learned from others.

I have been pleasantly surprised by the generosity many champagne producers have shown me by giving me their time and sharing with me their knowledge and philosophy. And while I have learned from many people, most of what I know about champagne has come from one man: René Collard.

I've devoted a whole chapter to René Collard, so I won't steal my own thunder by telling his story at this point. However, René has become my closest friend and professor, and I owe him a huge debt of gratitude.

Finally, let me say that I express some strong opinions in this book. Some of my fellow producers and some wine professionals may disagree with some of these opinions, and some of my opinions may cause some controversy. However, if I can stir some debate and add to the body of knowledge about champagne, I will be quite satisfied.

Dan Ginburg
Ay, France
Fall 2005

Introduction:
Champagne Basics

BEFORE WE DISCUSS THE TOPIC of champagne in depth, let's take a moment to review some basic facts about champagne production. For those not familiar with the champagne process, this introduction will serve as background for the subjects we will discuss. For those familiar with the subject, it will serve as a refresher course.

The first and perhaps the most important point is that champagne is wine. Of course everyone knows this, but how many times have you heard someone, perhaps a waiter or a host, say, "Would you prefer wine or champagne?" Yes, champagne is different from still wine, just as red wine is different from rosé, rosé is different from white wine, and sweet dessert wines are different from dry wine. Each is a different category of wine, and each category has its own nuances and methods of production, but when all is said and done the basic principles of wine and winemaking hold true for each and every category.

Champagne starts off as a still wine. However, unlike the grapes for most still wines, champagne's grapes are not harvested, crushed, and then pressed; they are simply harvested and quickly pressed. This is because two of the three main champagne grapes (pinot noir and pinot meunier) are black grapes, and crushing or delayed pressing would put the juice in contact with the grape skins, which would add unwanted color and tannins. Even in the case of chardonnay, which is a white grape, extended contact with the skins will make the juice less clear and add certain characteristics considered less desirable for champagne.

Another important point is that champagne is only champagne if 100 percent of the grapes are grown in and the wine is produced in the Champagne region of France. Of course sparkling wine is made in many places, including Alsace and the Loire Valley in France as well as Germany, Spain, England, Russia, North and South America, Israel, and even India. However, the term champagne refers specifically to sparkling wine from the Champagne region.

Unfortunately, in the United States the term champagne is often used generically to mean any sparkling wine. This circumstance is partly due to a strange court case a number of years ago in which it was found that one couldn't trademark or protect the name of a place. However, part of the confusion comes from makers of sparkling wine looking to ride the coattails of champagne — that is, to take advantage of the mystique and notoriety of the product.

Using the term champagne for a wine that is not really champagne is not permitted in Europe. However, sparkling wine producers in the United States are allowed to use the term champagne as long as it is modified by the state in which it is produced (i.e., California champagne, New York State champagne, Michigan champagne, etc.). This is an ongoing source of debate in trade talks between the United States and the European Union, and I believe that one day the European position will prevail. However, I'm less concerned with this issue than most of my fellow champagne producers since I've found that serious wine drinkers and connoisseurs understand the difference between sparkling wine and champagne.

We'll discuss grape quality, viticultural methods, and vinification methods in depth in future chapters. To continue with the basics, however, let's look at how a still wine becomes a sparkling wine.

In the case of still wine, once the wine has aged to a level satisfactory to the winemaker, the wine is bottled as is and will not be opened again until the end consumer decides to drink it. However, this is not the case with champagne. At the time of bottling, a mixture of sugar and yeast, called the "liqueur de tirage," is added before the bottle is sealed. This mixture will produce a second fermentation, this time in the bottle. Because the carbon dioxide gas that is a by-product of the fermentation can't escape from the bottle, bubbles will form and stay in the wine. This is called the "prise de mousse." Dead yeast cells will form sediment called the "depot."

By law champagne must age in the bottle at least 15 months before being sold. We will discuss this topic in depth in a coming chapter. However, once the decision to sell the bottle is reached, it is necessary to remove the sediment from the bottle. This is done using two processes: remuage, the process of moving the depot into the neck of the bottle, and dégorgement, the process of opening the bottle to remove the depot. We'll discuss the specific methods that can be used to perform these operations later, but it's important to understand that the carbon dioxide trapped in the bottle produces tremendous pressure, the equivalent of six times the pressure of the earth's atmosphere. Once the depot is in the neck, this pressure will force the depot out once the bottle is opened during dégorgement. The liqueur de dosage, a mixture of wine and sugar, is added to replace the small amount of wine lost during the dégorgement.

The amount of sugar added will determine how the wine is classified. It is measured by the number of grams of sugar per litre in the dosage. This can be a bit confusing because a normal bottle of champagne is 750 ml, or three-fourths of a litre, but because bottles come in many sizes, using a volume of sugar per litre is a way to standardize the measurement.

If no sugar or almost no sugar is added, the wine is classified as ultra brut. If the dosage is equivalent to less than 14 grams of sugar per litre, the wine is classified as brut. The word brut implies that the champagne is extremely dry, which is not always the case because a dosage of 14 grams per litre isn't all that dry. However, these terms came into vogue when sweeter champagnes were the style, so the term is relative. The vast majority of all champagne sold today is classified as brut.

Next on the list is extra sec or extra dry, which is up to 20 grams per litre. A more accurate description of this style by today's standards would be semi-sweet. The best example of an extra dry champagne is Moët White Star, which, the last time I checked, is sold only in the United States.

The next category is sec, which has a dosage of up to 35 grams of sugar per litre. Sec actually means dry, but a 35-gram dosage is far from fitting that description. One very rarely sees a sec champagne anymore — in fact, I've never tried one.

A more common category of champagne is demi-sec, which contains a dosage of 35 to 50 grams of sugar per litre. This is actually a very sweet wine. Demi-sec champagne is generally a dessert wine. I know some real champagne connoisseurs who enjoy demi-sec champagnes very much in place of a Sauterne or a late harvest dessert wine.

The sweetest category is doux, which has a dosage of more than 50 grams of sugar per litre. Doux means sweet, and these wines are that and then some. A few producers, most notably Moët, offer a doux champagne.

As you can see, there are different levels of sweetness to suit different palates. I personally like only brut and ultra-brut champagnes, so that is all we make at Champagne De Meric. We do, however, provide a demi-sec version on a custom-order basis for our better clients if they have a special occasion and prefer a demi-sec to another dessert wine. All told, our demi-sec production is between one and two cases per year.

I mentioned that a standard champagne bottle is 750 ml, or three-fourths of a litre. Like most things in the champagne business, the size of the bottle is strictly regulated. In addition to the standard 750-ml bottle, there are eight different legal bottle sizes used for champagne. The smallest is the quart, which contains 187 ml. A demi-bouteille, or half-bottle, contains 375 ml. A magnum contains 1.5 litres, the equivalent of two bottles. A Jeroboam contains three litres, the equivalent of four bottles. A Methuselah is the equivalent of eight bottles, or six litres. Less common are the Salmanazar (nine litres or 12 bottles) and the Balthazar (12 litres or 16 bottles). The largest size, the Nebuchadnezzar, is the equivalent of 20 bottles (15 litres). All sizes larger than a Methuselah are fairly rare, although the Nebuchadnezzars were somewhat in vogue during the period leading up to the millennium. You'll notice that the larger sizes are all named after biblical kings. I assume this reflects the physical or moral stature of these leaders rather than their drinking capacity.

In addition to different bottle sizes and different sugar levels, there are a number of different champagne styles based on the grapes used. Most champagnes are a mixture of the juice from pinot noir, pinot meunier, and chardonnay grapes. The proportion of each will vary greatly by producer. Although there is no official designation for this style, it is often referred to as a classic champagne, or a nonvintage brut.

The second most common style of champagne is a blanc de blancs. This literally means "white of whites," a reference to the fact that only the white chardonnay grapes are used in this style. What I've found interesting is that some people who don't care for chardonnay-based still wines enjoy blanc de blancs champagnes very much because the taste is very different.

A third common type of champagne is a rosé champagne. What distinguishes a rosé is not the type of grapes used (this varies widely by producer) but the pale red color. This color usually comes from the addition of red wine made from pinot noir or pinot meunier grapes from the Champagne region, but some producers arrive at the rosé coloring using maceration, or extended skin contact with the black grapes. The advantage of blending in red wine is that it is easier to control the coloring, while rosés using maceration may vary widely in coloring from year to year.

Less common are blanc de noirs champagnes, which are made using only the juice from black grapes. Actually, many smaller producers in certain parts of Champagne, particularly récoltant-manipulants, make a blanc de noirs due to a lack of chardonnay grapes, but these wines are seldom labeled blanc de noirs. Some traditionalists argue that a true blanc de noirs is made using exclusively pinot noir rather than a mixture of pinot noir and pinot meunier.

Two other types of champagne, vintage and cuvée prestige, deserve mention. These categories are not based on the type of grapes used. Rather, vintage champagnes are champagnes made using only grapes from a single year. Most champagnes are a mixture of the juice from two or more years, and traditionally producers make a vintage champagne only after a year of high quality.

Cuvée prestige champagnes are positioned as luxury blends and are generally the best product a producer has to offer. These are usually (but not always) vintage champagnes and are generally aged longer than the rest of the product line. The best-known cuvée prestige champagnes are Dom Pérignon from Moët & Chandon and Cristal from Roederer, but today most producers have something that falls in the cuvée prestige category. Catherine de Medicis is the cuvée prestige offered by Champagne De Meric, and Champagne Baron Martin is introducing Cuvée Louis XVII, named after the lost dauphin, in 2006.

Another champagne basic worth mentioning is the cork. Corks are a controversial subject in the wine world today because a certain number of bottles will be tainted by TCA, a fungus sometimes found on cork. Although TCA is harmless, it will give the wine an unpleasing odor and will add bitterness to the taste.

Champagne corks are generally of higher quality than corks used for still wine. This is necessary because of the pressure inside the bottle. Although I have no proof of this, it is my belief that TCA is less common in champagne than in many other types of wine because of this higher quality cork.

A champagne cork actually has three parts: two solid pieces of top-quality cork at the bottom that are close to the wine itself, called rondelles, and the larger top portion made from many pieces of cork glued together. This top part is merely for shape and has no contact with the wine.

You may have noticed that after the cork is removed, the shape of the bottom part will vary widely by bottle. Some corks flare out at the bottom, giving them a shape resembling a mushroom, while others conform to the shape of the neck of the bottle. This is generally a function of the length of time between the disgorgement by the producer and the uncorking of the bottle by the consumer. Corks with a mushroom shape have usually been disgorged very recently, and in this case the wine could probably benefit from a few more months of bottle age. Of course, if you only bought one bottle, by the time you see the shape of the bottom of the cork it is too late!

Another item worth mentioning is the muselet, the wire cage that is used to hold the cork in place in a champagne bottle. This device was invented by Adolphe Jacqusson in 1844, and it has proved far more effective in holding the cork than the string that was used before that time for this purpose. The muselet helps protect the wine by ensuring a tight seal, and the wine lover by making it easier (and safer) to uncork the bottle.

Finally, it is important to understand the organization of the champagne industry. To begin with, there are five categories of producers and marketers of champagne: négociant-manipulant (NM), récoltant-manipulant (RM), coopérative-manipulant (CM), récoltant-coopérative (RC), and marque auxiliare or marque d'acheteur (MA).

An NM is a champagne producer who buys some or all of the grapes needed for production. A négociant's key jobs are sourcing grapes (negotiating) and using these grapes to produce champagne (manipulating). An RM is a grower (vigneron) who produces his or her own champagne. Growers must perform each and every step themselves, from growing the grapes to vinifying the wine to labeling the bottles. An RM is only allowed to purchase a maximum of 5 percent of the grapes for their champagne, and the few who use this allowance generally purchase red wine made from champagne grapes (either pinot noir or pinot meunier) to use in a blend to create rosé champagne. A CM operates in much the same way as an NM, except the grapes come from members of the cooperative rather than from totally independent growers. The RC code usually means that a member of the cooperative has chosen to take some or all of his or her payment for the grapes in bottles of champagne produced by the cooperative. In most cases, these bottles are made in large quantity from the grapes of many members rather than from the grapes supplied by any specific member or group of members. An MA can be a private label or a buyer's own brand (very popular in U.K. mass retailers) or finished bottles purchased by a marketer and labeled to his or her specifications. Bottles marked MA are not produced by the marketer and are usually purchased from a CM or a large NM.

More than two-thirds of the champagne production is sold by négociant-manipulants. However, this group owns less than 20 percent of the vineyards in Champagne. The relationship between NMs and growers is an important dynamic in the business.

Now that we've covered the background, let's move on to the lessons I've learned as proprietor of Champagne De Meric.

Part I

LESSONS OF
AN AMERICAN
IN CHAMPAGNE

1. Choose Your Teachers Well

THERE IS A NEVER-ENDING RIVALRY between the residents of Reims and Epernay regarding which city has the right to call itself the champagne capital of the world. Of course, this is all theoretical due to the geographic organization of France. The regions, such as Champagne, Bordeaux, and Alsace, represent the older system, while today the country's administration is divided into departments. The regions are still used to define wine boundaries and tourism, and these regions overlap the boundaries of multiple departments. In the case of Champagne, the region includes all of the Marne department, most of the Aube, part of the Aisne, and a very small part of the Haut-Marne and Seine et Marne departments. Each of these departments has its own capital and system of administration, as first organized by Napoleon.

So although there is no true capital of Champagne, Reims and Epernay both claim to be the spiritual capital — the world center for champagne wine. These claims are based on the fact that each houses an impressive array of cellars, and the majority of the major champagne producers are based in either Reims (Mumm, Veuve Clicquot, Charles Heidsieck, Piper Heidsieck, Krug, Pommery, Roederer, Ruinart, and Taittinger) or Epernay (Moët & Chandon, Boizel, De Castellane, Marne & Champagne, Alfred Gratien, Mercier, Vranken, Perrier Jouët, and Pol Roger).

However, in choosing a capital the focus should be on the quality of champagne, not on the number of bottles produced, and although there are some high-quality producers in both Reims and Epernay, we must look elsewhere for the spiritual capital. One could make a case for some of the most famous champagne-producing villages — Ay, Sillery, Avize, Cramant, or Bouzy, for example — or for Hautvillers, where Dom Pérignon lived and plied his trade. With all due respect to these towns and their residents, I believe the true spiritual capital of Champagne today is a place probably unknown to most readers—the tiny village of Reuil.

Reuil is located in the heart of the Vallée de La Marne, twelve kilometers west of Epernay. It is much easier to find this charming village, however, than to pronounce its name. At first glance, one might try something like "rooeyl," but in reality it is closer to "roy," with a very guttural French "R." Like most non-natives, I never did get it exactly right.

Why do I give Reuil such distinction? Because in Reuil one can find René Collard, proprietor of the champagne that bears his name. René Collard is a unique individual in Champagne today, a perfectionist who puts quality before all else. When it comes to champagne, he is the grand master.

I first met René Collard quite by chance, one Sunday in the spring of 1995. I had been a frequent visitor to the Champagne region for five or six years and made a habit of visiting producers to learn as much as possible. On this occasion, I was in Champagne by myself for the weekend, having lunch in a restaurant in Epernay. I had brought along a French magazine on the subject of champagne and was reading an article about aged champagne. (We'll discuss the concept of aging champagne in another chapter.) The article focused on the best-known brands, but at the end of the article the writer mentioned that there was a small producer in Reuil who sold older vintages of his champagne, including 1969, 1975, 1976, and 1979. I had already learned enough about champagne to know that these were great vintages, and finding a producer selling vintages more than fifteen years old was something quite rare indeed.

After finishing lunch and waiting until two o'clock (lunch time in Champagne is noon until two, and everything is closed except restaurants), I drove out to Reuil to see if I could buy a few bottles. I arrived to find René Collard eating a late lunch, and we agreed that I should return at three o'clock, which I did. René had just finished his meal and was drinking a glass of champagne from an old, unlabeled bottle. He offered me a glass, which I gladly accepted.

This glass opened a new world for me. It was the best champagne I ever tasted, and it turned out to be 1961 Champagne René Collard. His associate and companion, Liliane Nominé, then arrived, and the three of us shared a bottle of 1969 Champagne René Collard, which was perhaps even better than the 1961. We also talked about champagne for a long time (with some difficulty because my French wasn't that great and René is a bit hard of hearing), and I was fascinated with his knowledge of every aspect of viti-

René Collard and Liliane Nominé (courtesy Champagne De Meric).

culture and winemaking and his generosity in sharing that knowledge. I had found the ideal teacher.

I saw René and Liliane on most of my subsequent visits, and we became friends. We spent a great deal of time together over the next few years, and I had a chance to taste his champagne from great vintages such as 1943, 1945, 1947, 1949, 1955, 1961, and 1964.

Much of what became the plan for Champagne De Meric is a result of things I learned from René Collard. We spent many hours discussing every aspect of the champagne process, from planting vines to growing grapes, from fermentation to aging. At the same time, I taught René a few things about marketing and finance. For example, he was selling his champagne at a price far too low for the quality, and I convinced him to raise his prices to a more realistic level for the older vintages.

René Collard is a champagne purist. He believes that champagne, when all aspects of the viticultural and production process are done correctly, is the greatest wine in the world. However, he has watched as an increasing number of producers have sacrificed quality for short cuts requiring less time and labor. To give the reader a complete picture of this great man, I feel it is important to relate his background.

René Collard was born in Reuil on September 15, 1921. (Coincidentally, or perhaps not coincidentally, 1921 is considered one of the great champagne vintages of the twentieth century). The third generation in a family of champagne growers, he found that he had an aptitude and an affinity for champagne at an early age, and in 1934, at the age of thirteen, he left school to study and work under his father, Georges Collard. He also spent a year as an apprentice at Champagne Gauthier in Epernay.

Once René had proven his capabilities and dedication, his father gave him a small parcel of vines (seventeen ares—a bit less than one-half acre). René produced his first champagne in 1943, not a very auspicious year in French history. (As an aside, the period from 1938–1944, as the Nazis came to dominate Europe, was a fairly dismal period in virtually every European wine region, while 1945, after the fall of Hitler, was probably the greatest vintage of the twentieth century all throughout Europe). Because a surface of seventeen ares was not sufficient to earn a living, René also worked as a photographer. He saved his entire production from 1943, and he is still enjoying the remaining bottles today. I've tasted René Collard 1943 on a number of different occasions, and it is superb.

Although he left school early, René Collard remained an avid student, especially in regard to all things connected with champagne. He studied and learned the traditional methods of his father and practiced them well. René promised his father that he would always follow the traditional methods and never sacrifice quality for efficiency or profit. It is a promise that he has always honored.

In addition to his father, the other great mentor in the life of René Collard was Raoul Lamaire, a close friend and outstanding champagne producer from the neighboring village of Damery.

Georges Collard, father of René Collard (courtesy Champagne René Collard).

René Collard in his favorite place — his cellars (courtesy Champagne De Meric).

The Lamaire family is a famous family of growers in the region. In fact, Raoul Lamaire's father was one of the leaders of the famous protests of 1911 in Champagne, when the growers rose up against the fraudulent practices of négociant-manipulants (NMs) who purchased less-expensive grapes from other regions to produce their "champagne." These protests turned violent in Ay and helped lead to the system of Appellation d'Origine Controlée (AOC) in Champagne and throughout France.

Raoul Lamaire was a staunch traditionalist and was disturbed by the trend away from the traditional methods that had already begun in the 1950s. He had no children to pass his vines along to, so when it came time to dispose of his vines and cellars, he chose to sell them to someone he felt would carry on his tradition — René Collard.

In the meantime, René Collard had begun to acquire additional parcels of vines to expand his holdings. By 1959 he had amassed about five hectares (twelve acres) in Reuil. After acquiring the 1.5 hectares from Raoul Lamaire, René Collard was able to produce champagne from a total surface of 6.5 hectares — 5 hectares went for Champagne René Collard, and 1.5 hectares for Champagne Raoul Lamaire.

In 1986, René began to turn vines over to his son Daniel, who had formed the company Collard-Chardelle (Daniel's wife is also from a family of vignerons and also has vines). The last year that René Collard harvested and produced champagne was 1995.

Today, René Collard is receiving the recognition that he deserves. He has had six different vintages rated ninety or above by the Beverage Testing Institute of Chicago and has been the subject of feature stories in the wine press throughout Europe. Four of his vintage champagnes and his nonvintage Carte D'Or are on the prestigious wine list at Les Crayères in Reims, and Champagne René Collard appears on many other top wine lists in France. He is well known to true connoisseurs of champagne.

Although René Collard has been by far my most important teacher on the subject of champagne, he has not been my only one. I've learned a number of things from the Besserats, especially on the subject of pressing grapes. I have also learned a great deal from such excellent champagne producers as Olivier Bonville, Daniel and Nadia Duval, René and Nicole Goutorbe, Philippe Aubry, Reynald Leclaire, Maurice Vesselle and his wife, and René Severin. I've also learned a great deal by visiting such excellent larger producers as Bollinger, Krug, and Alfred Gratien.

I have been focusing on those who taught me the art of champagne, and they have been invaluable. For the business side, I have talked with many people but followed the advice of very few. In addition to my advertising background, I've been involved in a number of other business ventures, and I brought this knowledge with me to the champagne business. Although I have learned a great deal about the business aspects of champagne, most of this knowledge has come from the school of hard knocks, my experience with Champagne De Meric.

As the reader will see in the following chapters, there are a tremendous number of decision points in the champagne process. If one's goal is truly quality, one must make the right choice at each of these points. I learned from René Collard how to make the best decision each step of the way. I have tried to make many of these same decisions as we have changed how Champagne De Meric is made, although there is still at least a lifetime of work to do before I could truly emulate René's methods and approach his results.

2. It's All in the Grapes

During the 1990s, the phrase "it's the economy, stupid" came into vogue in America as a way to remind politicians that, although there are many issues important to voters, everything is secondary to the economy. Without a good economic situation, nothing else really matters.

The same concept applies to the making of champagne (or any wine for that matter)—without good grapes, nothing else matters. Although a producer using good grapes will not necessarily produce a superior quality champagne, even the best producer can accomplish little without grapes of good quality. This may seem obvious because wine is essentially fermented grape juice. However, in today's world, where the focus is on technology and production processes, many people seem to forget the importance of top-quality grapes. This includes many wine producers.

This focus on wine technology is especially true today in the English-speaking world. I'm sure most of you have encountered what wine critic Kim Caffrey calls "techno-bourgeois-elitist-yuppy-bores" who try to show their sophistication by waxing poetic about the latest "hot" wine and describing all of the technical details of fermentation and production (for some reason, these people have decided that the speed and temperature of the fermentation of this special wine are details we are dying to know). However, you'll rarely hear these people discussing the grapes, where they come from, or how they were grown.

The most important lesson I've learned as a champagne producer is that it is truly all in the grapes. Many other things have an impact on the quality of champagne, but the real secrets to success when attempting to produce a top-quality product are (1) the grapes, (2) the grapes, and (3) the grapes.

19

In Champagne, there are three primary grapes: two black grapes (pinot noir and pinot meunier) and one white grape (chardonnay). Each of these grapes has different characteristics, and all are ideal for the production of champagne either singly or in combination. Here is my capsulized version of the characteristics of each of these three grapes.

Pinot Noir. This black grape is immensely popular today and is most often associated with the Burgundy region and, in the new world, with Northern California and Oregon. Pinot noir is normally used to make red wine, but for champagne, pinot noir (like pinot meunier) is gently pressed to make white wine, avoiding prolonged contact between the juice and the skins. Pinot noir is usually described as producing wines of character. Putting this another way, champagnes with a heavy pinot noir content tend to be rich wines with a depth of bouquet and flavor.

Chardonnay. This is a white grape and is best known for producing still wine in Burgundy and in California. The Champagne region is just north of Burgundy, so it is not surprising that the two regions share the same grape varieties. Chardonnay tends to be more acidic than the other champagne grapes and makes a crisp, fresh wine that is overly tart when young but develops a richness with age.

Pinot Meunier. This is the Rodney Dangerfield of the wine world — it doesn't get any respect. Pinot meunier has the reputation of being a step (or two) below pinot noir and chardonnay, producing wine that matures early and does not conserve well. The reality is very different, however. Pinot meunier produces a very fruity juice that is flavorful and easy to drink when it is young and gradually takes on exceptional depth and flavor as it ages.

Over the last few years, I have been privileged to drink great pinot meunier–based champagnes from such great vintages as 1945, 1949, 1955, 1961, and 1964, and I can assure you that these were wines of exceptional depth and flavor. They were among the greatest champagnes that I have ever tasted and were still wonderful and lively after decades. Curiously, pinot meunier is not widely grown outside of Champagne.

More than 99 percent of all grapes used in champagne are one of these three varieties. All are capable of making a great champagne, singly or in combination. Reaching this potential, however, is by no means easy or automatic. Let's examine the key issues and factors involved in top-quality grape production.

Terroir

The three champagne grapes can be grown in many locations around the world. Champagne methods are used by many sparkling wine producers in various locations. So what makes champagne so special? The terroir.

Terroir is a French concept with no precise English equivalent. It has become a widely used term in wine circles, but it is often misunderstood. Simply put, terroir is a combination of all of the factors and growing conditions provided by nature: the soil, the temperature, the wind, the amount of rain, the elevation, the amount of sunshine, and even the direction in which the grapes face the sun (exposure).

In the case of the Champagne region, there are a number of specific conditions worth noting. About seventy million years ago, the entire area was an inland sea, and the fossils of billions of prehistoric sea creatures have given the region a chalky subsoil with a reservoir of water underneath. This chalky soil provides a challenging environment for the vines; they must work extremely hard to produce fruit, which tends to limit the quantity of grapes produced (this is referred to as the yield). In general, the lower the yield, the higher the concentration (and thus quality) of the grape juice.

The weather is also worth mentioning. The Champagne region receives an average of 1,650 hours of sunshine per year. This is greater than 20 percent less than Bordeaux (2,069 hours) and far less than many of the sunnier, new world wine regions. This leads to an extended period of maturation for the grapes, which helps balance the acidity and sugar levels. The region is also influenced by both an oceanic climate and a continental climate, which leads to reduced fluctuation in temperature between the winter and summer. I've often remarked that there are two seasons in Champagne — winter and August — and in some years (such as 2004), August weather doesn't last very long.

At the same time, there are a lot of destructive natural forces at work that limit yields. Spring frosts during flowering are not uncommon (frosts in Champagne can occur until mid–May), nor are powerful localized hailstorms. Needless to say, these weather catastrophes serve to limit the size of the crop. For example, the harvest of 2000 ended up providing grapes of above-average quality despite a particularly cool, sunless August. The good quality was due to two factors: two or three weeks of very sunny weather immediately before the harvest and three late spring/early summer hailstorms that destroyed a significant portion of the grapes on the vine in villages such as Ay.

Rainfall is also an important factor. The vines need rain, and the Champagne region receives an average of approximately two hundred days of rain per year. Even during dry periods, the soil retains water and the subterranean reservoirs of water provide a reserve. There is no artificial irrigation necessary (or allowed) for the vines in Champagne.

The terroir varies in the different areas of the region approved for growing Champagne grapes. The Appellation Law of 1927 limited the surface for growing grapes to be used in making champagne to thirty-four thousand hectares (approximately eighty thousand acres) of specified land, and this law still governs the region. The land approved for growing grapes falls into four main areas: the Montagne de Reims in the Marne department; the Côte des Blancs in the Marne department; the Vallée de La Marne, primarily in the Marne but extending into the Aisne department, which lies to the north and west of the Marne department; and the Côte de Bar in the Aube department, which is south of the Marne department.

Each of these areas has its own specific terroir and, in fact, each village (cru) and even each section of each village has a specific microclimate. The Montagne de Reims is at a higher elevation, has a deep sublayer of chalk, and is best known for producing pinot noir grapes. Both Ay and the town in which I lived, Chigny-Les-Roses, are in the Montagne de Reims. The Côte des Blancs is more level; has dense, chalky soil; and, as the name implies, this area is known for chardonnay grapes. Unlike other areas that emphasize one grape but include all three, it is difficult to find anything other than chardonnay in the Côte des Blancs. The Vallée de La Marne has higher levels of sand in the soil, is at a lower elevation, and is more susceptible to frost, making it ideal for pinot meunier. Finally, the Côte de Bar, as well as most of the Aube department (which contains more than 20 percent of the total vineyards in Champagne) has soil with a heavy concentration of marl and is best known for pinot noir.

One of the advantages of being a négociant-manipulant (NM) is that one can purchase grapes from different villages, each with their own unique terroir. Because our objective was to maximize quality, evaluating and upgrading our existing grape supply was my top priority.

One of the most useful tools to evaluate the different terroirs of Champagne is a ranking of the various champagne-producing villages called the échelle des crus. This concept was originally developed in 1911, and the current system was put in place in 1945.

In today's system, each cru is given a numerical score of between 80 percent and 100 percent. This score, at least in theory, sets the price that NMs and cooperatives will pay for each kilo of grapes. For example, in 2000 the "official" price per kilo, as agreed by representatives of NMs and growers, was four euros. Under this concept, growers who are selling grapes from crus with a rating of 100 percent would receive 100 percent of this price, four euros per kilo. Growers selling grapes from a cru with a rating of 80 percent would receive 80 percent of this price, or 3.20 euros. The rating scale of the crus is reviewed every few decades (the last time was in 1985).

There are three main categories of crus: grand cru (rating of 100 percent), premier cru (rating between 90 percent and 99 percent), and others (rating between 80 percent and 89 percent). There are 17 grand crus (including Ay, which was a factor in my decision to invest in De Meric), 38 premier crus (plus the pinots from grand cru Chouilly and the chardonnay grapes from grand cru Tours-sur-Marne), and well over two hundred other crus.

As an evaluation tool, the échelle des crus system is far from perfect. First of all, it is based on the concept of all things being equal in weather conditions during a particular year and in viticultural methods used, and this is never the case. In addition, different parcels in each cru have different microclimates, which leads to large differences in the grapes. I feel that some of the ratings are flawed because the Vallée de La Marne tends to be underrated (for example, such excellent crus as Reuil, Damery, Venteuil, and Mardeuil, all of which have excellent southern exposure and produce grapes of very high quality, easily merit premier cru status). On the other hand, I believe that some crus in the Montagne de Reims are overrated.

Despite these drawbacks, the échelle des crus is a useful system, and at this point it is certainly the best objective tool that we have. Table I presents the échelle des crus, the rating of each village. It is interesting to note that all of the premier crus and grand crus are in the Marne department, and only a total of five crus in the Aisne and Aube departments have ratings higher than the minimum 80 percent.

Table I. The Échelle des Crus

Crus	Échelle (%)	Crus	Échelle (%)
MARNE		(white)	87
Allemant (black)	85	Baslieux-sous-Châtillon	84
(white)	87	Bassu	85
Ambonnay	100	Bassuet	85
Arcis-le-Ponsart	82	Baye	85
Aubilly	82	Beaumont-sur-Vesle	100
Avenay	93	Beaunay	85
Avize	100	Belval-sous-Châtillon	84
Ay	100	Bergères-les-Vertus (black)	90
Barbonne-Fayel (black)	85	(white)	95

Crus	Échelle (%)	Crus	Échelle (%)
Bergères-sous-Montmirail	82	Cormicy	83
Berru	84	Cormontreuil	94
Bethon (black)	85	Cormoyeux	85
(white)	87	Coulommes-la-Montagne	89
Bézannes	90	Courcelles-Sapicourt	83
Billy-le-Grand	95	Courjeonnet	85
Binson-Orquigny	86	Courmas	87
Bisseuil	95	Courtagnon	82
Bligny	83	Courthiézy	83
Bouilly	86	Courville	82
Bouleuse	82	Cramant	100
Boursault	84	Crugny	86
Bouzy	100	Cuchery	84
Branscourt	86	Cuis (black)	90
Breuil (Le)	83	(white)	95
Brimont	83	Cuisles	86
Brouillet	86	Cumières	93
Broussy-le-Grand	84	Damery	89
Broyes (black)	85	Dizy	95
(white)	87	Dormans (Try, Vassy,	
Brugny-Vaudancourt	86	Vassieux, Chavenay)	83
Cauroy-les-Hermonville	83	Écueil	90
Celle-sur-Chantemerle (black)	85	Épernay	88
(white)	87	Étoges	85
Chantemerle (black)	85	Étrechy (black)	87
(white)	87	(white)	90
Cernay-les-Reims	85	Faverolles	86
Cerseuil	84	Fèrebrianges	85
Châlons-sur-Vesle	84	Festigny	84
Chambrecy	83	Fleury-la-Rivière	85
Chamery	90	Fontaine-Denis (black)	85
Champillon	93	(white)	87
Champlat-Boujacourt	83	Germigny	85
Champvoisy	84	Givry-les-Loisy	85
Châtillon-sur-Marne	86	Grauves (black)	90
Chaumuzy	83	(white)	95
Chavot-Courcourt	88	Gueux	85
Chenay	84	Hautvillers	93
Chigny-les-Roses	94	Hermonville	84
Chouilly (black)	95	Hourges	86
(white)	100	Igny-Comblizy	83
Coizard-Joches	85	Janvry	85
Coligny (black)	87	Jonchery-sur-Vesle	84
(white)	90	Jonquery	84
Congy	85	Jouy-les-Reims	90

Crus	Échelle (%)	Crus	Échelle (%)
Lagery	86	Pourcy	84
Leuvrigny	84	Prouilly	84
Lhéry	86	Puisieulx	100
Loisy-en-Brie	85	Reims	88
Louvois	100	Reuil	86
Ludes	94	Rilly-la-Montagne	94
Mailly-Champagne	100	Romery	85
Mancy	88	Romigny	82
Mardeuil	84	Rosnay	83
Mareuil-le-Port	84	Sacy	90
Mareuil-sur-Ay	99	Sainte-Euphraise	86
Marfaux	84	Sainte-Gemme	84
Merfy	84	Saint-Gilles	82
Méry-Prémecy	82	Saint-Lumier	85
Les Mesneux	90	Saint-Martin-d'Ablois	86
Le Mesnil-le-Hutier	84	Saint-Thierry	87
Le Mesnil-sur-Oger	100	Sarcy	83
Mondement	84	Saudoy (black)	85
Montbré	94	(white)	87
Montgenost (black)	85	Savigny-sur-Ardre	86
(white)	87	Selles	84
Monthelon	88	Sermiers	89
Montigny-sous-Châtillon	86	Serzy-et-Prin	86
Montigny-sur-Vesle	84	Sézanne (black)	85
Morangis	84	(white)	87
Moslins	84	Sillery	100
Moussy	88	Soilly	83
Mutigny	93	Soulières	85
La Neuville-aux-Larris	84	Taissy	94
Nogent-L'Abbesse	87	Thil	84
Oeuilly	84	Tours-sur-Marne (black)	100
Oger	100	(white)	90
Oiry	100	Tramery	86
Olizy-Violaine	84	Trépail	95
Orbais l'Abbaye	82	Treslon	86
Ormes	85	Trigny	84
Oyes	85	Trois-Puits	94
Pargny-les-Reims	90	Troissy	84
Passy-Grigny	84	Unchair	86
Pévy	84	Vandeuil	86
Pierry	90	Vandières	86
Poilly	83	Vauciennes	84
Pontfaverger	84	Vaudemanges	95
Port-à-Binson	84	Venteuil	89
Pouillon	84	Verneuil	86

Crus	Échelle (%)	Crus	Échelle (%)
Vert-Toulon	85	Vitry-en-Perthois	85
Vertus	95	Vrigny	89
Verzenay	100	Marne (autres crus)	80
Verzy	100		
Villedommange	90	AISNE	
Ville-en-Tardenois	82	Canton de Condé-en-Brie	
Villeneuve-Renneville	95		
Villers-Allerand	90	Barzy-sur-Marne	85
Villers-aux-Noeuds	90	Passy-sur-Marne	85
Villers-Franqueux	84	Trélou-sur-Marne	85
Villers-Marmery	95	Autres crus du canton	83
Villers-sous-Châtillon	86		
Villevenard	85	AISNE (other crus)	80
Vinay	86		
Vincelles	86	AUBE	
Vindey (black)	85	Villenauxe-la-Grande (black)	85
(white)	87	(white)	87
Viopreux	95	Other crus of the Aube	80

Viticultural Methods

Second only to terroir in importance are viticultural methods, or what the producer does with his or her terroir. The true goal of any great wine is to provide the full expression of the terroir in which the grapes are grown. This is why great Bordeaux wines such as Chateau Lafite Rothschild, Chateau Margaux, and Chateau Haut Brion have been cherished by connoisseurs for centuries. The wine is different each year, but the different vintages are held together by a common style that expresses their terroir. It is as if the wine becomes a vehicle to experience the bounty of nature.

Producing top-quality grapes cannot be a massive industrial project but instead must be a personal, hands-on labor of love. The vigneron must not only have the experience and know-how to achieve success but also be willing to work hard at it. He or she must be in the vines on a daily basis to see how the grapes are progressing and to detect any problems. Old-time farmers say that, if you listen, the earth will speak to you. When it comes to viticulture, I believe this is especially true. It was certainly true for René Collard.

How does one measure the quality of viticulture? There are a number of methods. An easy one is visual. Do the grapes look healthy? Are they ripening? Is there mold or mildew (common problems in the Champagne climate)? Are the vines well cared for (good color, leaves cut back to ensure that the grapes receive exposure to the sun)? Is the earth healthy with good topsoil, or hard and crusty (less nutrients and a prime target for erosion)? I'm not an expert in agriculture, but it is often easy to judge quality just from taking a tour of the vineyards even if one is not an expert.

During the harvest period, we use a number of methods to judge the quality of grapes: their appearance, their smell, their size, and their taste. We also measure acidity and pH levels, but due to the difficult climate in Champagne perhaps the best barometer is the degree of sugar (potential alcohol) in the grapes. (In the United States, we use the Brix system, and 1 degree Brix = 0.55 degrees on the European scale). The final product, after the second fermentation, is generally 12–12.5 percent alcohol, so it is desirable to start with a good level of sugar in the grapes (ten to eleven degrees is a good range).

There are three general approaches to viticulture: biologique, culture raisonnée, and systematic treatment. Biologique is the equivalent of organic farming — using only natural products in the vineyards. Culture raisonnée involves using chemical pesticides, fungicides, and herbicides but in limited quantities to treat specific problems. Systematic treatment involves regular use of chemical products.

Unfortunately, and despite what you may have read, systematic treatment is still commonly used in virtually every wine region in the world. Some growers (including some in Champagne) will systematically spray chemical products on their vines regardless of whether any problems are present. Aside from the negative impact on the environment and the vines, this makes no economic sense. These chemicals are expensive, and using them for no reason costs money.

Why do some growers use systematic treatment? Because they are afraid of losing a part of their crop to disease, insects, and bad weather, and some chemical company sales people play on these fears to promote increased chemical use. I have often heard growers discuss the few bad years when the crop suffered major damage as a justification for their systematic treatment methods. In fact I remember visiting a vigneron in mid–August 1998, one of the hottest, driest months in the Champagne region in many years. Despite this, the grower had just finished treating the vines for mildew, something that occurs only when there is too much rain. When I asked him why he was doing this, his response was, "There's no problem now, but who knows about tomorrow?"

This attitude is the equivalent of taking antibiotics on a daily basis because it's possible to catch a disease in the future, an absurd concept. Yet when I provided this analogy to the grower, he responded, "Yes, I understand what you are saying, but the risk of crop reduction is too great."

The true traditional method of viticulture is to use biologique (organic) methods—the methods of René Collard. Organic methods require a very different approach to working in the vines. Yes, one treats problems. Mildew can be treated with a natural product (copper sulphate), as can odium (sulfur). Sulfur can also be used for insect problems because it will drive insects away. Organic methods are also about preventing problems before they start. Other plants can be put in the vicinity of the vines to attract insects away from the vines. More time can be spent in the vines to cut away leaves that block sunlight and hold dampness and moisture. Rather than using herbicides to eliminate grass between the vines, the grass can be cut or plowed under five to seven times a year to nourish the earth. All of this requires more work, however, and may lead to missing the appellation maximum from time to time. However, it will also lead to better quality grapes and better wine.

In the same family as organic methods are biodynamic (biodynamique) methods. Biodynamic agriculture, based on the teachings of Rudolph Steiner, includes many of the basics of organic practices. However, biodynamic methods also incorporate lunar cycles for determining when to perform such key operations as planting, trimming vines, and harvesting. Biodynamic agriculture focuses on revitalizing the soil, the key to all agriculture, and its complicated formulas for agriculture and viticulture management have been proven more effective and far less harmful than the chemical-based "modern" agriculture. I highly recommend reading Nicolas Joly's excellent book *Wine from Sky to Earth* to learn more about these methods.

Between the organic methods and systematic methods lies culture raisonnée. Practitioners of this method view chemical products like prescription drugs—they can be of help if used when absolutely necessary but are best avoided if not needed.

Most of the better growers in Champagne have practiced these methods for many years. Recently, however, this concept has taken on added importance. In a survey conducted in France at the end of the year 2000, 73 percent of respondents said it was necessary to promote and adopt culture raisonnée in all agriculture. As a result of this public sentiment, the Comité Interprofessionnel du Vin de Champagne (CIVC) has been heavily promoting this philosophy and is beginning to put pressure on growers. Three crus, including Chigny-Les-Roses where I lived, were selected for a pilot program for the use of culture raisonnée in 2000. Unfortunately, there were no specific guidelines or rules, and I did not observe much difference in methods (if anything, the use of chemicals increased as we endured a year of difficult weather until September).

The CIVC came out with written guidelines for culture raisonnée in the first half of 2001, and growers are being bombarded with messages about the benefits of this system. The objectives of these guidelines (référentiel) are to "treat vines when it is necessary, and only when it is necessary" and to "maximize the use of natural methods." Philippe Feneuil, former President of the Syndicat Général des Vignerons, expressed confidence that the majority of growers will cooperate and that culture raisonneé will soon be the method of viticulture of the Champagne region.

The move toward culture raisonnée is definitely a major step in the right direction. For the better growers, culture raisonnée is nothing new, and few changes in their methods will be necessary. For some growers, however, these guidelines represent a real change for the better.

The Harvest

The third area with an important effect on the quality of the grapes is the harvest, known as "les vendanges." Although most wine lovers are aware that the harvest is a time-consuming and labor-intensive undertaking, few are aware of its important impact on the quality of the grapes that are used in champagne.

The first important element is when the harvest is conducted. Like many elements associated with the making of champagne, the starting date of the harvest is strictly regulated. Each year the CIVC conducts tests throughout the region to determine how the grapes are progressing in order to set the dates for the harvest. No harvesting can take place before the date specified, which will vary by area, by cru, and, in some cases, by grape variety. Table II shows the opening dates for the 1999 harvest in the Marne department by cru and by grape variety.

Table II. Opening Dates for 1999 Harvest

Cru	Chardonnay	Pinot Noir	Meunier
Ambonnay	09/18	09/18	09/18
Avenay Val d'Or	09/18	09/18	09/18
Avize	09/14	09/18	09/18
Ay	09/16	09/16	09/16
Baslieux sous Châtillon	09/20	09/20	09/20
Baye	09/20	09/23	09/20
Bergères les Vertus	09/15	09/18	09/18
Bethon	09/17	09/20	09/20
Bézannes (Murigny)	09/20	09/20	09/18

Cru	Chardonnay	Pinot Noir	Meunier
Bison et Orquigny	09/18	09/18	09/18
Bisseuil	09/15	09/17	09/17
Boursault	09/18	09/22	09/18
Bouzy	09/18	09/18	09/18
Châlons sur Vesle	09/20	09/18	09/20
Chamery	09/20	09/20	09/18
Champillon	09/20	09/20	09/20
Châtillon sur Marne	09/23	09/23	09/20
Chavot Courcourt	09/20	09/22	09/20
Chigny les Roses	09/17	09/20	09/20
Chouilly	09/16	09/18	09/18
Coizard Joches	09/20	09/23	09/20
Coligny (Val des Marais)	09/15	09/18	09/18
Congy	09/20	09/23	09/20
Cormontreuil	09/17	09/20	09/20
Cormoyeux	09/22	09/22	09/20
Courjeonnet	09/20	09/23	09/20
Couvrot	09/16	09/18	09/18
Cramant	09/16	09/18	09/18
Cuis	09/18	09/18	09/18
Cumières	09/15	09/17	09/15
Damery	09/15	09/18	09/17
Dizy	09/20	09/20	09/18
Dormans (Soilly)	09/22	09/22	09/20
Epernay	09/20	09/20	09/18
Etoges	09/20	09/23	09/20
Etrechy	09/20	09/18	09/18
Ferebrianges	09/20	09/23	09/20
Festigny	09/20	09/22	09/20
Fleury la Rivière	09/18	09/21	09/20
Germaine	09/22	09/23	09/22
Germigny	09/22	09/22	09/18
Givry les Loisy	09/20	09/23	09/20
Grauves	09/20	09/18	09/18
Gueux	09/21	09/22	09/20
Hautvillers	09/16	09/18	09/16
Igny Comblizy	09/20	09/22	09/20
Jonchery sur Vesle	09/22	09/22	09/20
Loisy sur Marne	09/20	09/20	09/20
Louvois	09/18	09/18	09/18
Ludes	09/17	09/20	09/20
Mardeuil	09/15	09/19	09/17
Mareuil le Port	09/20	09/22	09/20
Mareuil sur Ay	09/16	09/18	09/18
Mesnil sur Oger (Le)	09/15	09/18	09/18
Montigny sur Vesle	09/20	09/20	09/20

Cru	Chardonnay	Pinot Noir	Meunier
Mutigny	09/19	09/19	09/19
Nanteuil la Forêt	09/20	09/26	09/22
Oeuilly	09/18	09/20	09/18
Oger	09/15	09/18	09/18
Oiry	09/16	09/18	09/18
Orbais l'Abbaye	09/20	09/20	09/20
Pierry	09/20	09/20	09/18
Puisieulx	09/20	09/20	09/20
Reims	09/21	09/22	09/20
Rilly la Montagne	09/17	09/20	09/20
Saint Martin d'Ablois	09/22	09/22	09/20
Sillery	09/20	09/20	09/20
Taissy	09/17	09/20	09/20
Tauxières Mutry	09/18	09/18	09/18
Tours sur Marne	09/18	09/18	09/18
Trépail	09/18	09/20	09/20
Vaudemanges	09/16	09/20	09/20
Vert Toulon	09/20	09/23	09/20
Vertus	09/15	09/18	09/18
Verzenay	09/20	09/20	09/20
Verzy	09/18	09/20	09/20
Ville sous Orbais (La)	09/20	09/20	09/20
Villers Allerand	09/17	09/20	09/20
Vinay	09/21	09/22	09/19
Voipreux	09/16	09/18	09/18

The CIVC also sets a minimum for the acceptable degree of sugar for grapes during the harvest. This level applies to each marc of grapes pressed (a marc is four thousand kilos of grapes, the unit that is used in a traditional press in Champagne). This level generally is between eight and nine degrees, depending on the weather conditions that year.

Unfortunately, in my opinion, the CIVC sometimes allows the harvest to start too early. An extra week or two, or even a few days, can have an extremely beneficial effect on the ripening of the grapes, and riper grapes will have higher sugar levels. At De Meric, we made a study of the results of the grapes that we pressed from 1990 to 1999, and we found that the average marc we pressed at the end of the harvest was one degree higher than the average marc we pressed at the beginning of the harvest. This is a major difference in quality.

I stated earlier that the CIVC sometimes allows the harvest to start too early, and the evidence of the De Meric experience backs this up. Of course, adverse weather conditions during the harvest will occasionally reward those who start early, but in general the best vignerons, especially the récoltant-manipulants (RMs) who must live with the quality of their harvest, often wait before they begin harvesting their vines. René Collard feels that the harvest often starts two weeks too early, citing the lunar cycle as evidence. Regardless of whether it's a few days or one or two weeks, the early harvest sometimes leads to a minimum level that to me is unacceptable. It is extremely difficult to make good champagne using grapes with a sugar level below nine degrees, and ten to eleven degrees is the best range.

In addition to when the grapes are harvested, how they are harvested is also extremely important. All harvesting in Champagne is done by hand, and the use of harvest machines is forbidden.

The rule against machines exists for three reasons. The first is a mechanical one — harvesting machines tend to bruise or break a portion of the grapes. This is not necessarily a huge problem in the case of chardonnay grapes, but both pinot noir and pinot meunier are black grapes that are used in Champagne to make white wine. The bruising of these grapes will add pigments from the skin to the juice, causing unwanted coloring of the wine. Some claim that advancements in machine quality will make it possible to refine the harvest machines to avoid this problem; however, others are skeptical.

The second reason to pick by hand relates to quality. Unlike in Bordeaux, where grape clusters tend to be sorted after picking, grape cluster selection in Champagne is made when the grapes are still on the vines. No two vines are exactly alike, and often the grapes on one vine are mature and ready to pick, while the grapes on the neighboring vine need another week or more to mature. In fact, there are often major differences between different clusters on the same vine. Hand picking can allow for strict selection both in terms of ripeness and in terms of the health of the grapes. Unripe clusters can be left to ripen, and diseased clusters can be eliminated during the harvest. This necessitates a lot of time for harvesting because each row of vines must be worked a number of times to constantly select the clusters ready for harvesting.

Traditionally the harvest was a very social affair, as each grower recruited his or her family and friends to harvest the grapes. This group was supplemented with migrant workers from the region and other parts of France, and by and large the same people worked the harvest year after year.

Today, however, this has changed. It has become very difficult to find people to work the harvest, despite a relatively high unemployment rate in France. The harvest today tends to be performed by a wide variety of people, including students looking for an adventure, migrant workers from Eastern Europe, unemployed workers, and the remnants of the traditional group rather than by a close-knit group. There is less commitment to the grower and subsequently less effort made in the selection process unless the grower closely supervises the process.

The French government has made the problem even worse with a well-meaning but misguided set of employment regulations. Their goal is to put the unemployed in France to work during the harvest, and this is logical. However, unemployed workers will lose their unemployment benefits during the time they are working the harvest, and due to the relatively high unemployment stipend, the small amount of money that can be earned from working the harvest is not considered worthwhile given the physically exhausting nature of the work. To force the growers to hire the unemployed, there are rules against hiring retirees or state employees on vacation, and a heavy surtax is imposed on the salaries of foreign workers. This leaves the growers scrambling to find people, and it is becoming more and more difficult simply to find enough workers to harvest the grapes, regardless of the quality of their work. Local interests are lobbying the government to loosen these restrictions, and hopefully these efforts will bear fruit.

The final argument against using harvesting machines is that their use will have a negative impact on the image of champagne. The harvest season is the peak time for tourism in the region, and the sight of thousands of people picking the grapes is certainly more pleasing and romantic than machines in the field.

As you can see, there are a tremendous number of factors to consider in the quest for top-quality grapes. When I arrived on the scene at De Meric, the company could count on a series of grape contracts in Ay and the surrounding area. However, the company was subcontracting most of the vinification, which included exchanging their grapes for a larger quantity of grapes of lesser quality to increase production and to have an adequate amount of chardonnay for blending. The best grapes were saved for the Catherine de Medicis, which was (and is) an excellent champagne, but all of the other products needed to be upgraded.

Of course, it was necessary to eliminate the practice of subcontracting production, which will be discussed in the next chapter. That still left me with the task of evaluating our current supply and determining what we needed for the future.

At the time we had contracts with growers in Ay and the surrounding villages for approximately four hectares (about 9.5 acres) of pinot noir. These were four-year contracts through the end of 1999, which is the standard in Champagne. Most of these vignerons had been selling grapes to the Besserats for generations. However, the champagne business was going through a premillennium boom, which culminated in record sales of 327 million bottles in 1999. NMs were furiously searching for grapes, and an increasing number of growers were keeping their grapes to make their own champagne. In this type of competitive environment, I felt we could not count on automatic loyalty from the growers.

Most of the vignerons under contract to De Meric had small parcels, typically ten to twenty ares, the equivalent of between one-quarter and one-half acre. Looking at the historical records, I learned that, on average, the majority of these growers produced grapes of high quality, which was encouraging. There were, however, a few exceptions.

Because our current supply was 100-percent pinot noir, I was left with two choices: change our style of champagne because we had no chardonnay or pinot meunier to use in making our wines, or find more grapes. In addition, I needed to increase our supply in order to have adequate grapes to continue producing our old product (now Champagne Baron Martin) as well as the new and improved Champagne De Meric.

One of the key elements in the strategic plan was to use only premier cru and grand cru grapes to make Champagne De Meric. Although the échelle des crus system is not perfect, it is the best thing we have to work with. In addition, I wanted to label our products as premier cru or grand cru to help demonstrate the quality of our grapes to the market. In Champagne, to call a champagne grand cru, it must contain 100-percent grand cru grapes. To call a champagne premier cru, it must contain 100-percent premier cru and grand cru grapes. Similarly, champagne must be made uniquely from grapes from the region, and a blanc de blancs champagne must be made using only white grapes (chardonnay). This is in contrast to California, for example, where a varietal wine (such as pinot noir or cabernet sauvignon) need only contain 75 percent of the named varietal, and one can use an appellation, such as Napa Valley or Stag's Leap, as long as 85 percent of the grapes come from that appellation.

I knew the effort of improving our supply of grapes would require some work, but it turned out to be much more difficult than I had envisioned. I started this quest in 1998, and 2002 was the first year I was completely satisfied with the quality of our grape supply. Of course we made progress each year, but there were some bumps along the road.

One of the odd things about my partners was that despite being in the business for five generations, virtually all of their connections were with fellow NMs rather than the grower community. This is actually fairly typical of NMs, and I believe it is a vestige of an outdated "class system" in which vignerons were considered simple farmers who were inferior to the sophisticated NMs. The reality is quite different, and I've generally found vignerons to be much more knowledgeable and quality oriented than NMs. Anyway, it turned out that I actually had more grower contacts based on my years of visiting various RMs than the Besserats did, so I ended up playing the key role in this recruitment process.

The primary focus in 1998 and 1999 was to add to our supply of quality grapes because our existing contracts had two years to run. We were successful in acquiring a good supply of grand cru chardonnay through a friend of a friend who is a wine broker (courtier). We then added some organic pinot meunier and chardonnay from a grower in Cumières that I knew. All of these were one-time transactions on the free-market, and purchasing grapes on the free market is expensive. It is hard to generalize, but I've found that free-market grapes cost at least 10 percent and up to 20 percent more than grapes from the same cru under contract. This is logical because the grower takes far more risk on the free market than with a contract. However, the growers that we worked with on the free market were all quality growers, and because we hoped to convert these relationships to contractual ones at a future date, the extra cost was a necessary part of our recruiting investment.

At the same time, I visited most of the RMs whose champagne I enjoyed to explore the possibility of working together. My rationale was that because these RMs produced great champagne from their grapes, these were the type of grapes I was looking to put into Champagne De Meric. We also tried advertising in *Champagne Viticole*, a magazine targeted to

The festival of Saint Vincent, patron saint of the wine growers (courtesy Champagne De Meric).

winegrowers. We didn't expect much in the way of response from our ads (and we didn't get anything worth discussing), but we felt it was a way to build name recognition with-in the community.

I also put together some ideas for building loyalty from our current growers. I felt the company had taken these vignerons, who I view as our most important partners, for granted, and I proposed a series of relationship-building meetings and an annual party every January 21, the evening before the day of the patron saint of winegrowers (Saint Vincent). Before we had a chance to put any of these plans into action, however, our largest grower (more than 60 percent of our grapes) died suddenly. He was fairly young and a very nice person, so this was quite a tragic event in Ay. Most of the land he had worked was still owned by his father, who decided to lease the land, a common practice in the region. We were fortunate that he chose the Goutorbe family, one of the best RMs in Champagne, and René and Nicole Goutorbe agreed to continue to work with us. The net result was that the quality of the grapes we were buying improved a great deal under the care of the Goutorbes.

In the end, we lost some of our old growers but gained some outstanding new partners, including some of my friends and contacts. The net effect was that our quality improved each year. By the 2000 harvest, we had a reliable supply of grapes from quality growers from Ay (grand cru), Avize (grand cru), Cramant (grand cru), Oger (grand cru), Mareuil-sur-Ay (premier cru), and Mutigny (premier cru). The average rating on the échelle des crus for these grapes is higher than 97 percent, or the same as the grapes used in the ultra-expensive Roederer Cristal.

We have also developed a supply of good quality nonpremier cru grapes, including some organic grapes. Beginning with the 2002 harvest, these organic grapes are being used to make our new blanc de noirs, which will be discussed in a later chapter. The nonorganic grapes, along with some of the "lesser" premier cru grapes, can be sold or used to make our second brand, Baron Martin.

Having grapes cultivated by top-quality growers from highly rated terroirs was one of our key goals. To further motivate our vineyard partners, I put into place a special bonus system, offering significant bonuses based on the degrees of sugar in the grapes. This gives our partners an additional incentive to maximize quality.

We have made a great deal of progress in improving the quality and quantity of our grapes. Of course we continue to look for additional quality partners, but now we are working from a solid base. There are major economic implications to our strategy, both in the cost of our raw materials and in the price of our wine, which will be discussed in a future chapter.

Obtaining quality grapes is our most important job. One can't make good champagne from bad grapes. One can, and some producers do, make mediocre champagne from good grapes. Lesson 3 is how to avoid this mistake.

3. Respect Tradition

IF YOU VISIT AS MANY CHAMPAGNE producers as I have, you'll find that each and every one claims to use traditional methods. Whether a small, family operation, or a giant factory producing millions of bottles per year, all claim to ensure quality by using traditional methods in the production of their champagne. In fact, you'll even get this speech from marque d'acheteur (MAs), who have nothing to do with the bottles they are marketing, but they still claim to use traditional methods.

In fairness, there is a great deal of truth to this claim if one looks at champagne in comparison to other sparkling wines. Certain traditional methods, such as grape varieties, how the vines are trimmed, and the method of the second (in the bottle) fermentation, are indeed the traditional methods because this is mandated by the Comité Interprofessionnel du Vin de Champagne (CIVC.) However, some traditional methods important to quality have fallen by the wayside in the search for speed and efficiency.

This whole discussion may seem a bit strange to some readers. After all, if one follows the wine trade press, there seems to be an endless effusion over the wonders of modern winemaking technology and its benefits for wine drinkers. Of course, some technological innovations in wine making, such as temperature control, are clearly of benefit. Furthermore, technological advances such as tractors, elevators, and forklifts bring improved efficiency with no impact at all on the wine itself. These are all good things and positive developments.

However, a number of modern changes, at least in Champagne, have a definite effect on the quality of the wine, and the effect is *not* positive. Let's examine a few of the traditional methods that should be preserved.

Pressing

As soon as the grapes are harvested, they are brought to the press. As mentioned earlier, the standard unit of pressing is one marc, or 4,000 kilos of grapes. The majority of presses are for one marc, although there are also presses for 2,000 kilos and some larger presses for multiple marcs.

Pressing is a precise and time-consuming business by nature. Because two of the three champagne grapes are black and champagne is a white wine, the pressing must be done carefully and gently to avoid prolonged contact between the juice and the skins. It generally takes between 2½ and 4 hours to press each marc, depending on the method used. The four-hour method uses a traditional press.

A traditional press in Champagne is a vertical press. It can be either round or square — this has no real effect on the quality or the operation. The grape clusters are placed on the floor of the press that is made from oak. The top of the press, also made of oak, consists of two flaps, which fold down to match the size and shape of the lower portion of the press. The grapes are held in by removable wooden sides. Although the press is operated by a motor, the pace is slow and oriented to gravity.

As the grapes are pressed, the juice flows into holes that lead to two tanks: one for the cuvée (the first 20.5 hectolitres of juice) and a second for the taille (the second 5 hectolitres of juice). That is all of the juice that can be used to make champagne — all other juice, called the rebeche, must be delivered to a distillery and is used (along with the grape skins) to make products such as marc de champagne (a medium quality brandy), ratafia (a somewhat sweet aperitif), mustard, vinegar, rubbing alcohol, and industrial products. Some of the better presses vary this routine a bit by adding the first litres of juice to the taille or rebeche based on the idea that these first litres are more likely to contain a higher concentration of the chemical products discussed in the last chapter.

The 25.5-hectolitre limit is fairly recent. The old limit was 26.66 hectolitres. The reduction was a commendable move by the CIVC to increase quality. Under the old limit, there was a première taille and a deuxieme taille. The deuxieme taille was eliminated with the reduction in quantity.

The cuvée and taille are often translated into the "first pressing" and "second pressing" by journalists. Although this does convey the general idea, it is a bit misleading. The number of pressings can vary (four to five is the average), and the key is how much juice can be pressed. As each pressing is complete, the press is opened, and two or three people with pitchforks start the backbreaking work of turning the grapes on the press to prepare for the next pressing.

Putting the grapes into a traditional press (photograph by John Hodder/Collection CIVC).

Many producers have abandoned the traditional vertical press in favor of a horizontal press. The reason is simple — horizontal presses are quicker, less labor intensive, and consequently less expensive. In fact, the most modern versions are totally run by computer — an entire pressing operation can be run by one person who merely presses a button and monitors the machines to make sure nothing breaks down.

I remember when I first moved to France, one of our neighbors invited us during the harvest to visit the local cooperative, which is part of the giant cooperative CVC. This cooperative markets under many brand names; Nicolas Feuillatte is the most well known. Our neighbor beamed proudly as he showed us the ultra modern structure all run by machine — there were only two or three people manning this massive pressing operation. We smiled politely as we were given a tour, but in fact we were a bit shocked because this was a factory operation that was no different than a plant making cars or washing machines.

Aside from the fact that horizontal pressing operations lack the charm of the traditional press, there are quality differences between the different types of presses. Although both horizontal and vertical presses come in many different models, there are two principal types of horizontal presses:

A traditional press in operation (photograph by John Hodder/Collection CIVC).

hydraulic presses and pneumatic presses. The hydraulic models press the grapes between two metal plates, and the more sophisticated pneumatic presses use inflatable membranes to more gently crush the grapes.

It is felt by many professionals that the pneumatic technology is equal in quality to the traditional press design (few would disagree that the hydraulic models are inferior). However, I prefer the traditional vertical design. To me, the key advantage of the traditional press is not the degree of pressure as some have written, because I do not believe that there is a significant difference in this area, but the act of turning the grapes from every marc four or five times when using the horizontal method. This helps ensure that all of the grapes are equally pressed and that the best juice is extracted from each grape.

When I first became involved in Champagne De Meric, Christian Besserat owned two presses in Ay. Naturally, we had him press most of our grapes from the Ay area (grapes from other villages were pressed close to their vineyards, because long transportation of grapes during the harvest can

have a negative effect on quality). However, some of our key vigneron partners prefer to do the pressing themselves, and most primarily use vertical
presses. So when Christian offered to sell us these presses (along with the
very "fragile" building housing them) in 2002, I declined the offer. René
Goutorbe has an excellent pressing operation, and it makes more sense for
us to work with him and focus our investment elsewhere.

Vinification

At the end of the pressing, we are left with a large quantity of very
expensive grape juice known as the moût. Like all wines, this juice must be
fermented to convert the sugar into alcohol and the juice into wine. This
wine, known as vin clair, is fermented separately by grape variety and, in
many cases, by cru. I won't bother with the technical details of the first fermentation because this information is available in almost any wine book.
However, two key points are worth noting.

The first is that the fermentation must be carefully controlled to maintain a proper temperature. Although this is less of a problem in Champagne
than in warmer wine regions since the base temperature of the wine is lower,
it is still an issue. Temperatures too high or, as can happen in Champagne,
too low will stop the fermentation process, leading to unwanted residual
sugar and unstable wine.

The second is that the yeast used to inoculate the moût and begin fermentation must be native to the Champagne region. This is not the case in
most wine regions, where there are no restrictions.

A very important issue relating to vinification is the process of chapitalisation. This is the process of adding sugar to the moût to allow the vin clair
to reach the desired level of alcohol. This is necessary if the moût has a degree
of sugar less than 10.5. Although chapitalisation is not allowed in many wine
regions, it is in Champagne. This is because, due to the climate, it is usually
impossible for even the best growers to reach the necessary degree of sugar.

Now let me tell you a closely guarded secret: Some négotiant-manip-
ulants (NMs) and cooperatives prefer grapes with lower degrees of sugar
as long as they can meet the CIVC minimum for the year. The reason for
this is economics. During the fermentation process, the volume of wine
increases. One hundred kilos of sugar creates an additional 66 litres of wine.
Because purchasing sugar is far less expensive than purchasing champagne
grapes, a producer can increase production at a relatively low cost. In fact,
I know of one large NM who told of being able to add the equivalent of
more than 100,000 bottles in a single year purely due to chapitalisation.

There are also some other key issues regarding the vinification process that affect quality and, unfortunately, these are areas where traditional methods seem to be going by the wayside. The most important one is in what type of material the wine is fermented and stored.

Traditionally, wine was made and aged in wood, usually either small oak barrels called tonneaux or fût chênes or large oak vats called foudres. Like all wine, the vin clair for champagne must go through the process of racking to remove the sediment from the wine, and this is more labor intensive with wood, especially the small barrels. In addition, wood is a porous material, and a producer will lose a small percentage of the vin clair during the fermenting and aging process due to evaporation and absorption. Barrels must be topped off, a process called ouillage. Losing even three to five percent of the wine is a problem when the grapes are as expensive as they are in Champagne.

To improve efficiency, producers gradually turned to large vats to produce and age the vin clair. These vats were originally ceramic or tile, although today most vats are stainless steel.

There is nothing wrong with stainless steel vats; one can make an excellent champagne using this material. However, fermenting and/or aging the vin clair in oak adds a richness that one cannot get from stainless steel. Unlike some still wine producers who use new oak barrels each year to add certain flavors to the wine, champagne producers have traditionally used aged oak barrels, which add the richness without overpowering the wine.

Although you will see a few oak barrels in many champagne houses, these are usually either solely for show or are used to make one special cuvée. Very few producers use oak for a significant portion of their vin clair. I know of only about a dozen, but these are among the top producers of champagne in terms of quality.

Another key decision for every producer is whether to facilitate a secondary fermentation, called malo-lactic fermentation. We will discuss this subject in the next chapter.

There are two other processes worth discussion: sterile filtration and tartrate stabilization. Sterile filtration is a method of further clarifying and stabilizing the wine by passing it through a rigorous filtering process. Although this is effective and has the side benefit of removing any residual sugar that may remain and certain microbes, it also removes positive elements that help give the wine character and flavor. We originally performed a light filtration, but since then we have eliminated this step entirely.

Tartrate stabilization is a process for removing potassium and tartaric acid from the wine. This is considered desirable by many producers because, if the bottle is subsequently refrigerated at a low temperature by the consumer,

The author in front of one of the De Meric foudres (courtesy Alexandre Verguet).

these minerals can combine to form KHT, a crystalline substance. Although these crystals have no impact on the wine, consumers who aren't familiar with them (which probably includes almost everyone who over-refrigerates champagne) often regard this as an impurity in the wine. Tartrate stabilization is done by using a process called cold stabilization (passage au froid) in which the wine is chilled to below freezing temperatures for up to several weeks to promote the formation of KHT, and then removing these crystals either by racking or filtration.

The problem is that these subzero temperatures shock the wine, which often diminishes the flavor. René Collard is very much against this process, and I have discontinued its use at Champagne De Meric.

Some of you may have been waiting for a discussion of the great art of blending. If you read the wine press or have visited a large champagne producer (grande marque), you doubtlessly have heard that this is the key to the champagne process. In fact, a visit to one market leader begins with a film that depicts an artist mixing his paints and compares this to the artistry of the blending process. As George Gershwin once wrote, however,

The author (left) greets two of the top sommeliers in the world, Werner Heil (center) and Gérald Guillotin, at the annual De Meric vin clair tasting (courtesy Alexandre Verguet).

"It ain't necessarily so." Let's separate the reality of blending from the marketing hype.

Known in French as the assemblage, blending takes place after the first fermentation and usually shortly prior to bottling. This step is the mixing of vin clair from the different grape varieties and different crus. In this step the raw materials—the different types of vin clair—are assembled to create the final product. It is indeed an important step because the different grapes and different crus have different taste characteristics, and these have an effect on the final product. However, the blending is not as unique, as mysterious, or as critical to quality as is popularly thought.

First of all, most wines are blends. Even most of the varietal wines made famous in California are blends—a wine labeled cabernet-sauvignon is only required to contain 75 percent cabernet-sauvignon. Virtually all the great red wines of Bordeaux are blends of grapes such as cabernet-sauvignon, merlot, cabernet franc, and petit verdot. Although the concept of blending grapes from different microclimates is a bit less common, it is widely used in some new world regions. However, when one thinks of great wines such as those of Bordeaux, one thinks of the grapes and the terroir, not the assemblage. Why should it be different for champagne?

Regarding the difficulty of blending, this process is indeed something that requires some expertise. For example, although I participate in this process at De Meric, the final decision is made by our chef de caves. This process is complicated due to the fact that these professionals are judging still wine (vin clair) to determine the ultimate make-up of a sparkling wine. In fact, it really does sound like a Herculean task.

In reality, the key decision for the composition of the champagne is made when the grapes are purchased. At five euros per kilo of grapes, no one is throwing any of the vin clair away, so it is really a question of allocation of the various types of vin clair by product (nonvintage, vintage, cuvée prestige, blanc de blancs, etc.). Although each producer has his or her own style, one can enjoy and appreciate quality champagnes of many different styles. The blending process determines style rather than quality. The key factor is the quality, not the style.

In fact, if we examine the importance of different factors in determining the actual quality of a champagne, I would have to rate blending a very distant fourth. My ranking, based on a scale of 100 percent, would be as follows: grapes 65 percent, vinification 20 percent, aging 10 percent, blending 3 percent, and other (cork quality, etc.) 2 percent. Of course, this is not exactly a precise scale and anyone could quarrel with these numbers, but the concept — grapes come first, followed by vinification methods and aging — is irrefutable.

An argument put forth by some to emphasize the importance of blending is that although blending is less critical for vintage champagnes and cuvée prestige products, it is critical to the creation of the brut nonvintage, which accounts for the vast majority of the bottles produced and sold. The concept is that nonvintage champagne must taste the same every year and that blending is the key to achieving this goal. In addition to blending the different grape varieties and crus, reserve wine (vin clair) from previous years is added to balance out the characteristics of the current vintage.

There are, unfortunately, a few problems with this argument. First of all, wine is a natural rather than manufactured product. Nature differs each year. No matter how much blending one does, the wine produced each year will vary. Although the use of reserve wine will somewhat neutralize the yearly differences, very few producers use a significant amount of reserve wine (an exception is Krug, which claims to use up to 40 percent reserve wine). At De Meric, we use about 15 percent reserve wine, which is fairly typical, and 15 percent is not enough to change nature. For that matter, 40 percent is not enough to change nature.

Furthermore, the whole idea of trying to make the wine taste the same each year makes no sense. Why should this be a goal for champagne when it is not a goal for any other wine? All great wines have their specific styles to reflect the terroir and the grapes used. For example, the wines of Chateau

Lafite Rothschild vary a great deal from the wines of neighboring Chateau Cos D'Estournel. Each of these wines has a style that does not change. It doesn't need to be forced or manipulated. The exact taste, however, varies from year to year. This is nature.

Finally, one of the most important methods used to attempt to have the same taste each year has nothing to do with blending. Some producers use a heavier dosage (more sugar added) to, in essence, mask the true taste of the wine. Using stronger flavors such as a bit of cognac in the liqueur d'expédition also aids in creating a consistent taste. Top-quality champagnes do not need a heavy dosage or a strong liqueur; it is only the mediocre champagnes that must mask the true flavor of their wine.

Blending is important to create a style, and this blending will be slightly adjusted each year to ensure that style. It is something that is done, but it is by no means a critical factor.

It is interesting to understand blending in the historical context. The whole concept that blending is such a key element in champagne is a relatively recent one. In fact, Cyrus Redding, one of the first and one of the greatest wine writers, wrote in his classic book *A History and Description of Modern Wines*, published in 1833, "Mixtures are not often made of the effervescing wines. They generally remain the pure production of the spots the names of which they bear."

The exaggeration of the importance of blending has even entered the realm of folklore. Most people believe that the process of making sparkling wine was invented by Dom Pérignon, a Benedictine monk who lived from 1638 to 1715, while he served as cellarmaster at the Abbey of Hautvillers, a small town near Epernay. However, like the myth that Abner Doubleday invented baseball, it has been disproved in more recent times. Sparkling wine was not invented by anyone but began as a naturally occurring process. However, unlike Doubleday, who had no connection with baseball, Dom Pérignon did play an important role in the development of champagne by refining champagne production methods. He is also credited with inventing the blending process, which, according to one scholar, "lies at the base of all great champagnes made today." In reality, Dom Pérignon's position as the "father of champagne" is well merited by his refinement of many methods, not a discovery of blending.

Finally, each producer must decide how long to age the vin clair before beginning the process of converting it to champagne. By law this process cannot begin before the January following the harvest. This process involves mixing the vin clair with a yeast/sugar mixture called the liqueur de tirage and putting it into bottles. This liqueur de tirage is responsible for bringing on the second fermentation that produces the famous bubbles.

Some producers, especially the mass producers and large cooperatives, start this process as early as possible. There are two reasons for this. As will be discussed in the next chapter, the minimum time the wine must remain in the bottle before it can be disgorged and sold is strictly regulated. Therefore, the sooner one can bottle the wine the sooner one can "start the clock running." The second reason is one of logistics. A huge operation requires time for the bottling, even with modern sophisticated equipment. Therefore, starting early gets the process moving.

However, it is best to wait until the spring before beginning the bottling. The vin clair will improve during these additional months, leading to a better champagne. Aging is extremely important to the quality of champagne, and we will explore this topic in the next chapter.

Improving our vinification was a major part of the strategy for re-creating Champagne De Meric. This is an area that we can totally control and something that has a major impact on quality.

The first step was to move away from subcontracting the vinification process. As I related earlier, this was one of my most important conditions for investing in the company. By 1999 we had taken all production in-house with the exception of rosé champagne, a product that we discontinued in 2003. Rosé is not a major priority for us, and we feel that we are better served by eliminating rosé rather than selling a subcontracted or ordinary product.

As an aside, there are a few different ways to subcontract production. One used by most of the large producers is to buy grapes from cooperatives and have the cooperative both press and vinify the moût. Another method is to simply purchase vin clair from cooperatives or other producers, which in essence is no different than buying the grapes and having the cooperative do the vinification. Another method is to provide the moût to another producer who combines this with other juice for vinification and bottling and then returns the bottles for aging, disgorging, etc. This is what Champagne De Meric did for most of their products. Another method is to contract with another producer whose abilities you respect to use his or her own grapes for vinification and bottling and then have the bottles delivered for aging, etc. This is what we did in the case of the rosé product. The final possibility is to purchase bottles "sur latte," finished bottles aged 15 months or more, to be disgorged and labeled.

The goal was to perform each stage of our production process in such a way as to ensure maximum quality. In addition, I decided to completely replace our existing product line, with the exception of our cuvée prestige Catherine de Medicis. This plan was expensive to execute, but vinification is a critical aspect in the job of a NM and I felt the investment was justified.

World-famous chef Gérard Boyer (right) and the author at the annual vin clair tasting for Champagne De Meric (courtesy Alexandre Verguet).

The most important decision was the type of fermentation vessels to use. Following the advice of René Collard, my decision was to age and vinify two-thirds of our wine in oak for Champagne De Meric and the rest in stainless steel. However, working with barrels is much more labor intensive than working with stainless steel, so we decided to start with one-third oak and work our way up to the goal. We were quickly able to achieve a 50/50 balance, and we are moving toward our goal of two-thirds oak. The vin clair for Champagne Baron Martin continues to be vinified in stainless steel.

The entire vinification project has required constant investment. Between the stainless steel vats and the barrels (we have a mix of 3,500-liter French oak foudres and 228-liter French oak tonneaux) and the associated equipment, we have invested well over $100,000, primarily in the tonneaux and foudres. In addition, the company ended up buying the building that housed the cuverie (originally we rented it from the Besserat family), an additional $50,000 investment. Because of the labor-intensive nature of fermenting and aging wine in wood, our labor costs have also gone up significantly, and, of course, the evaporation process costs us up to 5 percent of our vin clair each year. All of this adds up quickly for a small, struggling company.

One advantage of the oak barrels, however, is that we don't need to worry as much about the moût becoming too hot during the fermentation process in these barrels. There are two reasons for this: (1) Wood is porous, allowing some heat to escape, and (2) these barrels are relatively small (our largest foudre holds 3,500 liters), and by the laws of physics smaller containers do not get as hot as larger ones due to the surface/volume ratios.

Temperature control is an issue for the stainless steel cuves, however. We have installed a system (water cooling) to ensure that the temperatures do not climb too high. Fortunately, the mild climate in Champagne allowed us to opt for a simpler system than one would have to use in a warmer wine region such as the Napa Valley.

When the company subcontracted production, the bottling was generally done in late February or early March. We continued this practice at first because we were eager to get our new products into our cellars, but we now bottle in late May.

Remuage/Dégorgement

The second fermentation takes place shortly after the bottling is finished. Bottles are stacked on their side, or sur latte, and put into the cellars. The chalky soil of Champagne is ideal for storing the wine, because a deep chalk cellar will maintain a temperature of between nine and 11 degrees centigrade with very little variation by season. This is especially important for champagne, which is a fragile wine and can be damaged as a result of too high a temperature or any significant temperature variation.

We have a series of excellent cellars under our cuverie building at De Meric. We also have an excellent cellar built into a hillside near our office that we rent.

The second fermentation generally takes between four and six weeks. After this fermentation is finished, the vin clair is transformed into a sparkling wine, champagne. Of course the wine is still very acidic and "green" and, as will be discussed in the next chapter, the bottles must be aged in a sur latte position for some time before the wine is ready to drink.

One of the important results of the second fermentation is the creation of a deposit in the wine referred to as the depot, or the lees in English. The lees are extremely important for the development of the champagne, and the most important part of the aging process occurs when the lees are still

The cuverie of Champagne De Meric (courtesy Champagne De Meric).

in the bottle. However, the lees, which consist mainly of dead yeast cells, are not very attractive and give the wine a cloudy hue. Therefore, this deposit is removed to make the champagne ready for drinking.

The first step in the process of removing the lees is to gather all of this sediment into the neck of the bottle. The bottles are usually sealed using a crown cap and a small plastic insert called a bidule. The goal is to capture all of the sediment in the neck of the bottle for removal. Until the 1960s, bottles were sealed with a cork and metal clasp (liège et agrafe) after bottling, but the crown cap and bidule have generally replaced the liège et agrafe method. This is one case where moving away from the traditional method has not lowered quality. In fact, it may actually have helped quality, because it removes the possibility of a bottle being ruined by a bad cork during or after the second fermentation.

At one time, the sediment was gathered in the neck simply by turning the bottle upside down and letting gravity do the rest. However, it was found that this method was not wholly effective. Some of the sediment would cling to the glass, which in addition to the aesthetic problem sometimes led to a partial continuing of the fermentation process after the rest of the sediment was removed.

A solution was discovered in the early nineteenth century by Veuve

Clicquot, legendary matron of the house bearing her name. She found that gradually tilting the bottles from their side (sur latte) to an upside down position (sur pointe) was an effective method of shifting all of the sediment into the neck. This action is called remuage.

This process was greatly aided by adding an additional motion, sharply giving the bottles a quarter turn to the right and to the left on a daily basis during the tilting process. A special board with holes cut at a 45-degree angle, called a pupitre, was a further enhancement because it speeded up the remuage process and made it more precise. It generally takes about three weeks to completely move the sediment to the neck if the bottles are turned twice daily.

This process moves quite quickly. In fact, a skilled remueur can, at least in theory, turn up to 60,000 bottles in a single day (of course, one can't work at this level on a daily basis). However, even with outstanding remeuers, this is a very labor-intensive and consequently expensive process. Therefore, producers began to look for ways to save time and effort.

This search eventually led to the development of the gyropallet, a mechanized method of performing the remuage process. The gyropallet is in essence a large metal case in which many bottles are placed, and the entire case is turned in such a way to roughly mirror the process of remuage by hand. Before the gyropallet, other systems allowed cases to be turned by a hand crank or motor, but the gyropallet is fully automated. Virtually every large champagne producer and a number of the smaller ones use the gyro-pallet today. Although you will see pupitres if you visit a large producer, these are at most for the company's cuvée prestige and often, like wood barrels, are merely for show because people are fascinated with the remuage process. Almost 300,000,000 bottles of champagne are produced each year, and if the major producers really still did the remuage by hand, you can be sure that unemployment in the Champagne region would be virtually non-existent.

This is another area where tradition has gone by the wayside. The key question, however, is what effect this change has on the quality of the champagne.

Most producers argue that the gyropallet does not have any effect at all on quality. However, there are a significant number of professionals who disagree. Although they acknowledge that the gyropallet is well designed, they believe this machine cannot totally duplicate the effectiveness of remuage by hand.

For Champagne De Meric, the remuage of every bottle is done by hand. Christian Besserat believes this produces better results than the gyropallet. I have never made a study of this, but his theory is that some of the bottles

Pupitres in the cellars of Champagne De Meric (courtesy Champagne De Meric).

in the middle of the gyropallet may retain a small amount of sediment. In addition, performing the remuage by hand fits in with our overall philosophy of ensuring quality in every bottle by preserving traditional methods.

Our final area for exploration in this chapter is the dégorgement (disgorging), the process of removing the sediment from the bottle. After the remuage is complete, the sediment is concentrated in the neck of the bottle. When the crown cap is removed, the pressure in the bottle will expel the sediment and the bidule. However, the key is to accomplish this task while losing only a minimal amount of the wine from the bottle. Each bottle is then topped off with the liqueur d'expédition, which is primarily a mixture of wine and sugar. The amount of sugar determines whether the champagne is ultra brut (no sugar), brut (less than 15 grams per liter), or one of the sweeter styles.

Originally dégorgement was done totally by hand. Because a bottle of champagne contains five to six atmospheres of pressure and the cap shoots off when opened, this is a difficult, precise, and sometimes dangerous task. Over the years a machine for disgorging was developed, and this has been further enhanced by moving the neck of the bottle through a freezing saline solution to freeze the sediment and make it easier to eject.

Rémuage by gyropallette (photograph by Valérie Dubois/Collection CIVC).

I know producers who use each of these methods. Some small producers, such as Champagne Duval-Prétrot, still disgorge each bottle by hand. Some use a machine but do not freeze the neck of the bottle, and most producers use the saline solution. I love to watch a bottle being disgorged by hand — it is a fascinating process. We used to point out in our marketing materials that De Meric disgorged bottles "à la vollée," without freezing the necks. However, the truth is that I have seen no evidence that the method used to disgorge bottles has any effect on quality.

As the reader has seen, there are many details in the champagne process. Although the quality of the grapes is the most important factor in determining the quality of a champagne, the production methods discussed here make a major difference.

I feel that our plan of choosing higher quality, more labor intensive traditional methods is one of the things that separates Champagne De Meric from the vast majority of champagne producers today. While the industry is searching for new, labor saving methods, we are reaching back to the traditional methods that made champagne the "wine of kings." We'll discuss the economic and marketing implications of this strategy in future chapters.

I don't necessarily believe in tradition for tradition's sake. If we can improve our efficiency, I'm all for it. We upgraded our computer systems in 2001 and 2002 and look to be as efficient as possible. If the price for greater efficiency is a decrease in quality, however, then I feel that price is too high for Champagne De Meric.

4. Patience Is a Virtue

Wᴇ ʜᴀᴠᴇ ᴇxᴀᴍɪɴᴇᴅ ᴛᴡᴏ ᴏꜰ the elements essential to producing a great champagne — top-quality grapes and the use of superior vinification methods. The third key element, aging, is in many ways the easiest to achieve because it takes no special skill or knowledge. However, it takes a great deal of patience, and as I've learned through my association with Champagne De Meric, it puts a huge strain on the producer's financial resources.

Most wine connoisseurs are familiar with the concept of aging red wines. Better quality red wines — especially the great red wines of Bordeaux — take a number of years to mature and often decades to reach their full potential. In his outstanding reference work *The Great Vintage Wine Book*, Michael Broadbent relates that the 1870 Lafite Rothschild, considered one of the greatest wines in history, was not highly regarded when it was young and took more than 50 years to mature. I was fortunate enough to taste this wine in 2001, and it is still outstanding.

There is also a need to age champagne to reach the product's full potential. Although there are no tannins such as one finds in red wine, champagne takes on a richness with age, as the acidity is softened and the tart green taste yields to nutty, toasty aromas and flavors.

You may well ask what this has to do with the making of champagne. After all, red wines are sold by the producer relatively young, and it is up to the consumer to decide whether to age the wine and for how long. This is not the case, however, with champagne. The period of beneficial aging for champagne is *before* disgorgement, while the lees are still present. Although champagne does age after disgorgement, the wine is quite fragile and generally should be drunk within three years of disgorgement unless stored under absolutely ideal conditions, such as the cellars of the producer. If the bottle stays in the cellars of the producer and if the producer has good, deep chalk cellars (not all do), the wine can last for years after disgorgement.

Because beneficial aging precedes disgorgement, the aging process must take place *before* the bottle is sold. Compare this to the situation for still wine. If we say that one prefers to drink all wine 10 years after the harvest, the vast majority of the aging for a still wine (seven to nine years) will take place in the consumer's cellar, and the producer will have been paid for his or her efforts. In the case of champagne, however, the vast majority of the aging (eight to nine years) will take place *before* disgorgement, in the cellars of the producer. The producer will receive no compensation for his or her work and no return on investment until the bottle is actually sold. Although virtually all of the costs of production (grapes, labor, and bottles) will be paid within a year of the harvest, no revenue will be forthcoming for a number of years. As stated earlier, this is extremely hard on cash flow, because the process repeats itself year after year.

To ensure at least some degree of aging, the Comité Interprofessionnel du Vin de Champagne (CIVC) has mandated that nonvintage champagne must age at least 15 months before disgorgement and vintage champagne must age for three years. This rule is one of the most strictly enforced in the Champagne appellation and is almost never violated.

The CIVC polices this rule by conducting periodic, unannounced audits. Verifying the minimum age for a vintage champagne is relatively easy — one knows which harvest it is from, and it is only necessary to verify the date of the tirage (bottling). In the case of nonvintage champagnes, the inspectors must carefully check the paperwork regarding when various batches were bottled and verify that the quantities match.

How important is aging champagne? I believe it is critical. This is because champagne is a complex wine, and it takes time to bring out this complexity. Exactly how much time is a subjective decision, but I've never had a truly great champagne that had not been aged at least seven years before disgorgement, and most of my favorite champagnes have been aged ten years or more.

One of the many misconceptions proliferated by "experts" is that champagne is not a wine that ages well. Nothing could be further from the truth, as long as the bottle has not been disgorged. It is true, however, that champagne does not have the long life span of red wine. I would be extremely surprised, for example, to find a drinkable, no less outstanding, champagne from 1870. However, I have been fortunate enough to have tasted four excellent bottles of 1907 Heidsieck Monopole. This wine was part of the cargo of the Swedish schooner Jönköping that was sunk by a German submarine 20 miles off the Finnish coast during World War I. This cargo rested at the bottom of the sea in ideal storage conditions— no light, high pressure, and a constant cold temperature of around 4 degrees Celsius—for 82 years. Although many of the bottles were damaged, those that survived were excellent (although highly dosed, as was the style at the time).

If one likes aged champagne, salvaged shipwrecks are not a very reliable source of supply. I've also had bottles, all recently disgorged, from 1914, 1921, 1928, and 1929, and all were quite good, although the 1914 had lost most of its mousse. I've also had many recently disgorged or ideally stored bottles from the 1940s, 1950s, and 1960s, and most were outstanding. A few high-quality producers still market champagne from the 1970s, and René Collard offers the outstanding 1969 vintage.

Obviously, most champagnes available on the market today are not 10 to 20-plus years old. Nor can they be. It is unrealistic to expect producers to hold their product for this length of time. However, this doesn't mean that merely meeting the legal minimums is acceptable. A producer must find a middle ground.

There is some talk of increasing these minimums, which would be a very positive step because 15 months is usually not adequate to produce a true quality champagne. Unfortunately, the fact is that many producers begin disgorging bottles after 15 months. If you visit a producer, especially a large one, they will tell you they age their nonvintage product three years, but this is rarely true. Because there is no vintage on the bottle, it is impossible for the consumer to verify the truth, and even wine writers seem to take producers at their word. The only thing that one can be fairly well assured of is that the legal minimums are being respected. This is why increasing these minimums would be a positive move.

How long should champagne be aged? What is a good middle ground? This is where one needs to put champagne into two classes. One class contains the basic products— brut nonvintage and nonvintage blanc de blancs and rosé. The other classes are the top-of-the-line products— vintage champagnes and the various cuvée prestige products. There is a major difference in the price of these classes of products, in how one should evaluate them, and in how long they should age.

The basic class is dominated by the brut nonvintage product. In fact, the entire champagne market is dominated by this product. Brut nonvintage represents between 80 percent and 90 percent of the sales of almost every major champagne producer. It is the least expensive product in every producer's line and is designed for everyday drinking, although it is not necessarily consumed this way. Traditionally, the brut nonvintage product was the calling card of a producer, the product that represented the producer's philosophy, and the product on which his or her reputation was based. I still hear this statement from time to time, but it is no longer true due to the decrease in the quality of the brut nonvintage product. Today much of the brut nonvintage champagne is sold quite young, and the best grapes are usually not used for the brut nonvintage product because these are reserved for the top-of-the-line class.

Brut nonvintage champagne is a volume product today, and the majority is distributed through mass merchants such as supermarkets. Although nonvintage blanc de blancs and rosé are more expensive and made in smaller quantities, they also tend to be young, mass-produced products.

Today, a producer's calling cards are his or her top-of-the-line products. These are the products that get the best grapes and the most care and attention from the wine maker. Sales in this class have grown, especially for the well-known cuvée prestige brands. These products can be two to five times more expensive than the brut nonvintage, and even if they represent a relatively small percentage of the number of bottles sold, they are an important contributor to the producer's annual turnover and profit.

As mentioned earlier, the legal minimums are 15 months for nonvintage products and three years for vintage products. I would like to see this increased to two years and five years, respectively.

One critical decision that directly affects aging is whether the wine undergoes malo-lactic fermentation. Malo-lactic fermentation is a major issue for wine producers, especially in Champagne. This is a secondary fermentation in which harsh malic acid, which is present in all grapes, is converted to softer lactic acid. This fermentation softens the wine and adds a buttery flavor.

The issue is whether to encourage or avoid this fermentation during the production process. This is extremely important because malo-lactic fermentation reduces acidity in the wine, and an early malo-lactic fermentation will result in a more rapid aging process in the bottle. This can be good or bad. If the champagne will be aged on the lees only a short time, malo-lactic fermentation will make the wine more drinkable. However, if the champagne is aged for a long period of time, malo-lactic fermentation limits its potential and results in a wine that is tired and worn out before it reaches its full maturity.

Because the majority of champagne produced is nonvintage and is often aged not much more than 15 months on the lees, malo-lactic fermentation is used by the vast majority of champagne producers. This makes sense. A good rule of thumb is that if the champagne will be aged less than three years, it is best to encourage malo-lactic fermentation. If the champagne will be aged five years or more, it is best to avoid malo-lactic fermentation. Between three and five years is a judgment call.

However, most producers routinely encourage malo-lactic fermentation regardless of how long they will age the wines. Unfortunately, however, it is becoming harder and harder to find champagnes aged four years or more, so perhaps malo-lactic fermentation is no longer a major issue. However, for those producers still willing to properly age their vintage and cuvée prestige champagnes, the decision regarding malo-lactic fermentation is still important.

Because we are on the subject of aging top-of-the-line champagnes, this is probably a good time to discuss the concept of a champagne vintage. For most quality still wines each bottle is, at least in theory, from a specific year's harvest and labeled accordingly. Therefore, each year is a vintage year. Because most of champagne is nonvintage, a mixture of two or more years, vintage labeling is reserved for excellent years in which good weather conditions produce grapes of better than normal quality. At least that is the traditional concept.

If one looks back over the post World War II era, vintage champagne has been produced in approximately half of the years. Of course, not all vintages are equal. Certain years, such as 1945, 1949, 1952, 1955, 1959, 1961, 1964, 1969, 1976, 1982, 1985, and 1990, have been great years, producing truly outstanding champagne. These were outstanding years for quality throughout the Champagne region, and even lesser quality producers were able to make very good champagne. Other vintage years, such as 1966, 1973, 1975, 1979, 1983, 1988, and 1989, have been quite good but not classic years such as the aforementioned group. Depending on the grower and the cru, many of these champagnes are outstanding, but some can be disappointing.

During the 1990s, the number of vintage years has increased. Because there is no uniform policy regarding what constitutes a vintage year, each producer must make his or her own decision about whether to bottle a part of the harvest as a vintage champagne. However, the regulations require that the decision must be made at the time of bottling — if a bottle is declared nonvintage, it cannot be later reclassified, even if it contains only juice from a single harvest. As discussed earlier, vintage champagnes must be aged longer, so producers carefully consider whether to declare a vintage. In addition, most producers use only their best juice in the vintage and cuvée prestige products, which serves to limit quantity somewhat.

The increase in the number of vintage years is not necessarily a bad thing. First of all, declaring a vintage forces the producer to age the bottles to be vintage dated for three years, which is better than 15 months. In addition, a year may be a vintage quality year in certain crus and a very mediocre year in others. Récoltant-manip-ulants (RMs) and small négociant-manipulants (NMs), who use a smaller number of crus than the mass producers, can sometimes produce excellent champagne in years not generally highly regarded. For example, 1991 was considered a fairly mediocre year in the Champagne region as a whole, but it was quite a good year in certain crus, most notably Cramant and Avize, and 1994 was not generally a vintage year but was good in certain crus in the Vallée de La Marne.

Setting a policy for aging has been my most difficult task. The decisions to invest in quality regarding grapes and vinification have been quite expensive, but the biggest impact is in the profit/loss accounts. Because we are a private company and I am the majority owner, I have felt comfortable trad-

The flagship of Champagne De Meric, Grande Réserve Sous Bois (courtesy Champagne De Meric).

ing off short-term financial results for long-term benefits. In the case of aging, however, the primary impact is in the area of cash flow. Any step that negatively impacts cash flow not only affects the reports but forces me as the major shareholder to write a check to keep the company in a liquid position. This is harder to take lightly than a dismal profit/loss account.

If I were making the decision totally on quality, I would age our basic products at least five years and our top-of-the-line products much longer (10-plus years). This is what René Collard does.

Unfortunately, this would involve virtually stopping sales of the De Meric brand for a two-year period while still continuing to pay for purchasing grapes and all overhead costs. Given that no bank in their right mind would finance such a scheme, the burden would fall solely on me to provide what would amount to at least *an additional two million dollars in working capital,* with no real hope of recouping this investment. Although I am somewhat of a champagne purist, I am not a fanatic.

Therefore, we've been forced to compromise, just like every producer this side of René Collard. We've tried to limit these compromises to the basic class because this represents most of our volume and, therefore, the major burden on cash flow.

We currently have two De Meric products in the basic category: our Grande Réserve Sous Bois (the first of our new products) and our Blanc de Blancs Sous Bois. We now begin disgorging the Grande Réserve after 36 months, and most of the bottles are aged four to five years. The Blanc de Blancs Sous Bois is aged at least three years, and the current bottling has been aged four years.

In the case of the top-of-the-line products, one current vintage (1993) has been aged for ten years, the other (1996) for seven, and our current version of Catherine de Medicis was bottled fourteen years ago (1990). Our minimum aging for any vintage is six years, and we won't even consider disgorging a bottle of Catherine de Medicis before seven years.

This may not sound all that impressive to many readers because some

major champagne houses claim to age their products as long as we do. You'll notice, however, that only a few (most notably Bollinger, Krug, and Charles Heidsieck) make these claims in writing. One of our projects for the future is to begin adding bottling and disgorgement dates to many of our bottles. We don't currently have the proper equipment for this operation, but it is something we plan to do in the future, at least for the products labeled in small quantities for which the logistics are a bit easier.

Now that we've covered the basics of champagne making in general and the making of Champagne De Meric in particular, it's time to focus on the market.

The top of the line at Champagne De Meric, Catherine de Medicis (courtesy Champagne De Meric).

5. The Business of Champagne
Is Business

U P TO THIS POINT, we have primarily concentrated on the artistic side of champagne. Now let's turn our attention to the business side. We'll start by examining the overall marketplace, including how much champagne is sold, who is selling it, and where it is sold.

As mentioned earlier, champagne is a three billion-dollar business, with more than 293 million bottles sold in 2003. Table III shows the recent evolution of sales by type of producer. You'll notice that sales dropped sharply after the millennium but are again slowly increasing to normal and sustainable levels.

Table III
Bottles Sold by Year by Type of Producer

	Négociants	Cooperatives	Récoltants	Total
1997	192,709,896	21,985,224	54,344,491	269,039,611
1998	204,975,456	26,811,534	60,671,102	292,458,092
1999	221,902,403	26,102,524	79,074,315	327,079,242
2000	168,256,621	19,190,016	65,784,323	253,230,960
2001	172,250,744	23,250,920	67,111,786	262,613,450
2002	195,114,444	24,697,296	67,839,635	287,651,375
2003	197,779,350	68,357,860	27,171,559	293,308,769

One of the nice things about having a market share of under 0.02 percent is that we don't have to spend a great deal of time worrying about how our competition will react to us. We could double our sales and still not show up on the industry radar. However, it is important for us to understand the marketplace and its trends.

There are roughly 4,000 true champagne producers, which does not include sub-brands, récoltant-cooperatives (RCs), or marque d'acheteur (MAs). Only 272 of these are négociants. However, as Table III demonstrates, approximately two-thirds of annual champagne sales are attributable to négociants, and more than 85 percent of all bottles exported from France are sold by négociant-manipulants (NMs).

The NM category is dominated by a small number of producers. In 2000, the top ten NMs accounted for 83 percent of all NM bottles sold and 86 percent of total revenues in the NM category. The top 20 NMs accounted for 94 percent of the bottles and 95 percent of the revenues in the category. In fact, a few large conglomerates dominate the champagne field. The largest, LVMH (Moët-Hennessy-Louis-Vitton) sold 50 million bottles in 2000, which represented more than 22 percent of the total worldwide champagne sales that year. Table IV shows the 13 largest champagne groups and their 2000 sales. LVMH sold Champagne Pommery to the Vranken group in early 2002.

Table IV
Largest Champagne Groups (Based on 2000 Sales)

Group	Principal Brands	Bottles Sold (In Millions)
LVMH	Moët et Chandon, Mercier, Ruinart, Pommery, Veuve Clicquot, Canard Duchène, Krug	49.62
Marne et Champagne	Burtin, Marne & Champagne, Lanson, Besserat de Belfont, Massé	17.96
Vranken Monopole	Charles Lafitte, Charbaut, Barancourt, Vranken, Demoiselle, Germain, Heidsieck Monopole	10.40
Laurent Perrier	Laurent Perrier, De Castellane, Salon, Delamotte	8.48
Allied Domecq	Mumm, Perrier Jouët	8.39
Remy Cointreau	Piper Heidsieck, Charles Heidsieck, Bonnet	8.23
Groupe Coopératif Alliance Champagne	Jacquart, Veuve Devaux, Pannier	7.45
Groupe Coopératif Centre Vinicole de la Champagne	Nicolas Feuillatte	6.82
Boizel B.C.C.	De Venoge, Chanoine Frères, Abel Lepitre, Boizel, Philipponnat, Alexandre Bonnet	6.53

Group	Principal Brands	Bottles Sold (In Millions)
Martel	GH Martel, Mansart Baillet, De Noiron	6.20
Duval Leroy	Sedi Champagne, Duval-Leroy	5.97
Taittinger	Taittinger, Irroy, Saint-Evremont	4.29
Roederer	Louis Roederer, Théophile Roederer, Deutz	4.04

SOURCE: Banque de France

This type of consolidation is typical in most industries around the world today, from wine to automobiles. Whether the trend is a positive one or negative one for business in general is a subject I will leave to others. In regard to the champagne industry, however, I find it troubling. The most important decisions that affect product quality for an NM are which grapes to purchase, which vinification methods to use, and how long to age the bottles. Buying better grapes, using superior vinification methods, and aging champagne must be viewed from a long-term perspective, however, and large corporations, especially those listed on the stock exchange, tend to be short-term (quarter-to-quarter results) oriented. Also, it is much safer to make a good, standard champagne with strong marketing support than to strive to make an excellent champagne that may not be immediately well received by a largely unsophisticated mass market.

On the subject of the market, let's look at where champagne is sold. Table V shows the number of bottles sold from 1997 to 2003 in France, the rest of the European Union, and in other markets.

Table V
Champagne Sales by Type of Producer by Market
(Number of Bottles)

	France	European Union	Other Countries	Total
Négociants	93,317,725	65,320,470	39,141,155	197,779,350
Récoltants	63,848,106	3,333,823	1,175,931	68,357,860
Cooperatives	16,868,016	7,409,627	2,893,916	27,171,559
TOTAL 2003	174,033,847	76,063,920	43,211,002	293,308,769
TOTAL 2002	175,000,710	71,510,179	41,161,532	287,672,421
TOTAL 2001	164,522,817	65,062,535	33,109,962	262,695,314
TOTAL 2000	149,626,415	64,181,378	39,401,753	253,209,546
TOTAL 1999	190,449,776	87,045,816	49,543,471	327,039,063
TOTAL 1998	178,965,956	73,374,906	40,079,068	292,419,930
TOTAL 1997	165,154,959	67,760,369	36,124,283	269, 39,611

As you can see, France represents approximately 60 percent of the global market for champagne. This has been true for many years.

Table VI shows the principal export markets and the number of bottles sold from 1999 to 2003.

Table VI
Principal Export Markets
(Number of Bottles Sold)

	2003	2002	2001	2000	1999
U.K.	34,465,159	31,689,580	25,076,435	20,433,640	32,261,232
U.S.A.	18,957,031	18,227,280	13,701,967	19,268,837	23,700,839
Germany	12,053,665	11,386,703	12,824,724	14,235,737	17,496,865
Belgium	9,143,810	9,002,153	7,433,331	7,320,681	10,753,197
Italy	8,506,287	7,951,166	7,031,437	8,239,536	9,431,994
Switzerland	5,596,549	5,825,576	6,177,999	6,518,658	8,658,165
Japan	5,013,705	4,006,523	3,560,029	3,174,914	3,946,155
Netherlands	2,575,838	2,618,997	2,246,436	2,122,547	3,443,679
Spain	2,158,056	1,998,770	1,830,439	2,035,983	1,731,055
Australia	1,659,441	1,225,724	892,615	1,434,895	1,686,231
Canada	1,188,726	1,094,627	681,454	1,070,878	2,462,938
Sweden	958,973	972,204	790,409	944,272	1,099,399
Ireland	692,851	723,397	628,593	566,067	918,692
Austria	679,037	757,424	773,250	722,437	865,803
Denmark	639,475	753,099	673,172	903,283	1,156,762
Luxemburg	621,952	664,046	593,425	615,143	685,614
Brazil	551,833	402,324	375,616	653,136	746,398
Portugal	515,395	562,054	403,855	612,520	574,406
Hong Kong	501,921	483,139	519,515	506,035	572,739
Singapore	450,835	518,099	826,604	929,777	900,089
New Zealand	407,801	370,510	241,420	298,750	499, 417
Mexico	371, 132	276, 566	265, 418	319,443	335,951
Russia	357,735	301,974	249,698	163,434	140,415
Greece	351,612	340,422	254,690	299,873	335,951
Finland	286,581	290,815	249,956	237,981	364,867

Approximately 75 percent of the sales of Champagne De Meric are to the export market. Our key markets were Belgium and the United Kingdom. However, the United States and Germany have joined Belgium as our leading markets, while our sales in the United Kingdom have declined. The United Kingdom is a key target market for 2005.

I expect our reliance on the export market to grow in the coming years. It's not that we are ignoring the French market — after all, France is the dominant marketplace for champagne — but our niche of making champagne from superior quality grapes and using the best vinification methods is more unique in the export market, where we are competing against a limited number of producers, than in the French market, where all products are available.

Historically, our main competition in the export market has come from other small NMs. However, with our new products and new positioning, I believe we will also compete with some of the grandes marques. Competing with these producers isn't easy, so it is important to understand their position in the marketplace.

Let's start by defining who are the grandes marques. Without going through the entire history of these producers (if you are interested in this subject, you should read Tom Stevenson's excellent book *World Encyclopedia of Champagne and Sparkling Wine*), this category contains the largest and best-known NMs, formerly called the Syndicat des Grandes Marques de Champagne. This group officially existed between 1964 and 1997, when it disbanded to be reborn as the broader based Union des Maisons de Champagne, of which we are a member. However, the concept of a grande marque existed before 1964, and the concept still exists today.

At the time of the disbanding of the Syndicat des Grandes Marques de Champagne, the membership included the following NMs: Ayala, Billecart-Salmon, Bollinger, Canard Duchêne, Deutz, Gosset, Hiedsieck & Co. Monopole, Krug, Lanson, Laurent-Perrier, Mercier, Moët & Chandon, Mumm, Joseph Perrier, Perrier-Jouët, Piper-Heidsieck, Pol Roger, Pommery, Roederer, Ruinart, Salon, Taittinger, and Veuve Clicquot. These producers represent more than 80 percent of the champagne sales outside of France.

Although the Syndicat des Grandes Marques de Champagne no longer exists, the term grande marque is still in common usage and the member houses wear the designation as a badge of honor. However, quality was not a requirement for membership in the syndicat. In fact, according to Tom Stevenson, the quality issue was what led to the dissolving of the syndicat. In 1991, *Wine & Spirits* magazine in the United Kingdom did a survey of the grandes marques on quality and whether there should be quality standards for admission to and continuing membership in the syndicat. Bollinger was the only producer to respond with an unqualified yes. As a follow-up, in March of 1992 Bollinger published its excellent document "Bollinger Charter of Ethics and Quality." This document defines where the grapes used in Bollinger's champagnes come from, the vinification methods, and the length of aging (at least three years). The late Christian Bizot, at the time the head of Bollinger, then called on his fellow members to produce similar documents and to adopt quality standards. This call was met with deafening silence, although a few of the producers later introduced more vague, watered-down versions of the charter. This led to a rift among the members and, according to Stevenson, the undoing of the Syndicat des Grandes Marques de Champagne.

In terms of quality, the Grandes Marques are a very diverse group, in essence a microcosm of Champagne. This category includes some great producers and some very good producers, but also some mass producers making good, average-quality champagne. Although some wine journalists would probably disagree, my view is shared by many in the Champagne region who are knowledgeable about the subject, including restaurateurs who are forced to keep certain grandes marques on their wine list solely because of the reputation of these brands.

Why are even the lesser quality grandes marques still held in such high esteem, especially in the United States and the United Kingdom, where they are considered the "haut de gamme" of champagne? There are many reasons, including strong advertising, good public relations with journalists, sponsorship of image-enhancing events, and excellent design and packaging. Another reason is that they are indeed the biggest and best-known brands and therefore benefit from what was once called the IBM syndrome. (The saying in the early 1980s was that no one was ever fired for choosing IBM because there is an implied guarantee of quality in choosing a market leader.) Another important reason for the elevated reputation of the grandes marques has been their ability to sell the idea that the key to champagne quality is blending and, because they have more grapes from more crus, they have superior blending possibilities. Of course, there is the history of these brands.

Most of the grandes marques have been around for a long time — Moët was founded in 1743, Ruinart traces its roots back to 1729, and Mumm was founded in 1827, to name just a few. More important, the large houses were indeed at one time the standard of excellence. Part of the reason for this is that relatively few growers made their own champagne until the twentieth century and, more important, as NMs, the grandes marques could truly choose the best grapes to use in making their champagnes. I still hear stories from older vignerons of seeing the heads of the grandes marques in the vineyards during the harvest, examining each basket of grapes to make sure it met their standards.

Unfortunately, all of this has changed. Today, some of the large grandes marques are primarily volume driven, looking for ever-increasing sales and production. They need grapes to achieve volume, and most can't afford to set overly strict standards as long as the grapes meet Comité Interprofessionnel du Vin de Chanpagne (CIVC) minimums. As the head of one large NM remarked recently to one of my friends, "If I hear that a grower has 50 ares (a little over an acre) in the Aube (which contains almost exclusively crus ranked 80 percent, the bottom of the scale) and is looking for a contract, I'm in my car on my way to see him in five minutes." This is a long cry from the selectivity of yesterday.

You may have the impression that I think the large grandes marques and other mass producers have no interest in quality. This is not the case, and some of these producers employ some very talented and serious professionals. In fact, some of my favorite producers—Krug, Bollinger, Salon, Roederer, and Deutz—are grandes marques. When one produces 10,000,000 or 20,000,000 bottles per year, however, industrial methods and less selectivity are almost obligatory, and quality is bound to suffer. This is why the top-of-the-line category discussed in the last chapter is more representative of the talents of the largest producers because these products are bottled in somewhat smaller volumes. Although I do not really enjoy the very standard champagne from these large producers, their products meet the needs of most casual champagne drinkers who make up the bulk of the market.

Competing with these well-entrenched brands is extremely difficult. They are universally known, and most champagne drinkers don't even know that alternatives exist. Therefore, to survive, a small producer like Champagne De Meric must have a clearly defined market niche to overcome the total lack of name recognition. Small producers also must offer better value than the large brands to motivate both consumers and the trade.

A key part of our strategy was my analysis that there were really only three market niches in champagne that offered any potential: be a part of one of the international groups, such as the grandes marques; remain small and produce unique, high-quality champagne; or produce good champagne at a price well below the primary competition. Being part of a large group was not an attractive or even realistic option for Champagne De Meric. Competing on price alone is contrary to my business philosophy. Besides, low price is primarily a category for récoltant-manipulants (RMs), who have land and don't buy grapes, or cooperatives, who generally work on small margins. Therefore, the only logical solution was to focus on quality to differentiate ourselves.

We've already discussed how we improved our champagne. Now we will discuss the marketing process for our new products.

6. The World Won't Beat a Path to Your Door Just Because You Make a Better Champagne

I AM A GREAT BELIEVER THAT, at least to some extent, beauty is in the eye of the beholder. Everyone has somewhat different taste in wine, depending on both their individual sensory make-up and their past experiences. The fact that a reviewer in a wine publication considers the 1982 Chateau Talbot to be far superior to the 1982 Chateau Brane Cantenac, to use a real example, doesn't mean that you or I will have the same view.

At the same time, I agree with wine critic Matt Kramer that there is an absolute standard of quality. This is not a question of whether a wine deserves a rating of 91 or 89 or 79 points but a basic standard by which to judge wines—flavor, complexity, finish, etc. Certain wines are quality wines and one can debate their relative merits, and certain wines are not.

To develop one's standard for wine, one needs a certain amount of wine-tasting or wine-drinking experience. If the only types of sparkling wine I had ever tasted were Gallo's Andre and Champagne De Meric, it wouldn't be surprising that I had a pretty high opinion of our product. However, my concept of quality is based on a great deal of tasting experience as well as my own personal preferences.

Overall, I have found that the wine market in Western nations is a relatively knowledgeable one. Of course, the majority of the population in any country has little knowledge or interest in wine, but there is a large segment in most Western countries with a good knowledge base. The same holds true for wine writers and professionals in the food and wine industry. Wine is an important part of Western culture, and it is getting more and more serious attention.

Unfortunately, however, I have not found this to be true for all categories of wine, especially the champagne category. This is why I referred to a "relatively unsophisticated mass market" when discussing exports. Even many food and wine professionals seem to have little knowledge of champagne. To give just one of many examples of this, one of my favorite restaurants in the Napa Valley offers food and wine pairing, matching wines by the glass with the cuisine. The sommelier, who is quite knowledgeable, presents each wine and explains why he has chosen it, where the grapes come from, and one or two interesting anecdotes about the producer. The exception, however, is the glass of champagne or sparkling wine that starts the meal, which arrives like a generic product with no explanation.

This reflects the way most people perceive champagne. Champagne has the image of being a drink for celebration only. Many believe it is something for a party or perhaps an aperitif, but it is not a serious wine. Because of this, critics tend to spend little time on champagne.

The champagne industry itself helps perpetuate the image of champagne as the drink of celebration. Many of the large producers promote various sporting events and present large bottles of champagne to the winners. Although there is nothing wrong with this, it would be better if some of these efforts were redirected to educate the public that champagne is a wine, not a symbol of celebration. That champagne has an image problem is supported by the fact that, according to analysts, sales of champagne went down dramatically in the United States. following the 2001 terrorist attack on New York and Washington, primarily because people didn't feel right celebrating in the aftermath of a national tragedy. No similar reservations were expressed about other types of wine.

Another factor in the lack of understanding about champagne is that champagne producers, especially the large ones, tend to put much more effort into packaging than producers of top-quality still wines. When one focuses on the beautifully designed bottle or the magnificent box it comes in, one is apt to forget the truly important aspect — the wine in the bottle. One seldom sees a top producer of still wine with this focus on packaging. They prefer to focus on the wine in the bottle.

Perhaps most important, the champagne industry does little to help or educate wine writers. In fact, the opposite is usually true. Producers often do their best to portray the champagne process as some mystical ritual and imply that details of the producer's specific methods are some type of proprietary secret. When one goes to Bordeaux or Napa Valley, for example, producers are willing to share the details of grape selection, which grapes are used each year, and production methods. In the Champagne region, producers, especially the largest ones, give out little real information. Their tours, even those given to professionals, are entertainment, with automated trains, slick film presentations, and witty commentary. When one leaves, one realizes that the producer has mainly talked in generalities, providing a good generic overview of the champagne process, a nice visit to the cellars, a discussion of "blending artistry," and claims of quality with little in the way of specifics to support these claims.

Even some of the smaller producers are guilty of being less than open. They discuss the generalities of champagne production rather than focusing on what makes their product special. Today at Champagne De Meric we also provide a general overview, but our focus is on our key points of difference.

All these factors have contributed to downplay the image of champagne as a serious wine. To me this is a shame because I believe champagne is the world's greatest wine.

Fortunately, there is a knowledgeable segment of the market, connoisseurs looking for better quality champagne rather than standardized products from well-known producers. This is the market niche we are targeting for Champagne De Meric. One must live in the real world, however, and recognize that most champagne buyers do not fit into this segment. They are looking for a bottle for a celebration and although they want reasonably good quality, they are not interested in exploring the nuances of champagne. Because the Appellation d'Origine Controlée (AOC) regulations guarantee that most champagne will be of at least good quality (although not necessarily more than this), mass-market consumers have many acceptable choices. For the once-a-year champagne drinker, a very standardized taste is not a problem.

Initially, my attention was almost totally focused on the quality improvement program for Champagne De Meric. However, when we introduced Grande Réserve Sous Bois in the fall of 2001, we found that although we attracted many new customers, we lost some of our old customers who were used to, and preferred, the somewhat standard nonvintage brut (Brut Sélection) that the company had been marketing.

One point I should clarify is that when I discuss clients in the export market, I am generally referring to importers. Although in France we mainly sell direct to restaurants, wine shops, and private clients, in other European markets we sell to an importer, who then sells to restaurants and wine shops in his local area. The United States is more complicated due to an outdated set of regulations that will be the subject of the next chapter.

Because the connoisseur segment is small, it is difficult to rely totally on this niche, especially given the investments we have made and the generally poor cash flow of the champagne business. This is where our second label, Champagne Baron Martin, fits into our strategy. Christian Besserat's grandmother came from the Martin family, and this brand has existed for many years. Rather than just use this label for a few customers, we decided to revitalize the brand and use it to provide very good quality, standard champagne for the broader market at a bargain price. Because the De Meric brand was expected to cover our overhead, we could afford to have very attractive pricing for Champagne Baron Martin.

The Baron Martin brand had been ignored for quite some time. The labels were unattractive, and brut nonvintage (Brut Sélection) was the only product that existed. There was no promotional material, and few people knew that the brand still existed.

Our first move was to create an image and product line for Champagne Baron Martin. We changed the name of Brut Sélection to Réserve Du Baron and added a rosé, to be known as Rosé Du Roi (the king's rosé). We redesigned the labels to feature the attractive family crest. Because the Martin family is a famous noble family in France, we positioned Champagne Baron Martin as "The Wine of the Nobility."

We relaunched the brand in late 2003. We are marketing Champagne Baron Martin to those looking for a very good quality, reasonably priced champagne similar in style to many of the large producers. We plan to introduce a cuvée prestige product for Baron Martin in 2006. It will be a limited edition of 500 bottles. It is far too early to judge whether Champagne Baron Martin will be successful, but to date the product has been well received.

Developing the marketing plan and product line for Champagne De Meric has been much more difficult and expensive. We've already discussed the tasks of sourcing top-quality grapes and adding superior vinification equipment. This was all done for the De Meric line, although some of these grand cru and premier cru grapes are used to make Réserve Du Baron.

As I've discussed, part of the new plan was to completely change our product line. We did this but were left with the task of continuing to sell our current inventory while waiting for the new products to acquire sufficient age to be introduced on the market. We had lots of exciting news to communicate to clients and potential clients, but until we were ready to introduce the new products we were forced to continue the status quo. Our marketing efforts consisted primarily of servicing our existing clients, following up when potential clients contacted us, and planning for the future. Therefore, I will focus my comments on our marketing program for the "new" Champagne De Meric, which officially began in June 2001 at the world's most important wine fair, Vinexpo in Bordeaux.

The positioning of Champagne De Meric had been that of a traditional, family champagne house. However, although the Besserats remain minority partners, this is no longer a family business. More important, as discussed earlier, almost all champagne producers position themselves as traditional houses. The old positioning was in essence a parity positioning and therefore of no value when competing against better known brands with greater resources.

Our new positioning focuses on our two key product features: exclusive use of grand cru and premier cru grapes and the extensive use of oak barrels. The new products are part of a "sous bois" (under or on wood) line, and the words "sous bois" will appear in the names of most products. The benefits delivered by these features are better quality and, to the connoisseur, the ability to demonstrate a more discriminating taste than someone who merely buys a well-known, mass-produced brand.

Selling a lesser known, upscale brand of champagne is a challenge to us and, consequently, to our clients. Therefore, it is critical that we seek importers who truly believe in our concept and our product because they will have to communicate our message to their clients. We also need to give them plenty of support. As part of this effort, one of my partners, Eike Wolff, developed a very professional brochure to tell the story of Champagne De Meric and our product line. We also developed a short video on Champagne De Meric. Both Kirsten Neubarth, who replaced Patrick Besserat as our managing director in 2001, and I make ourselves available to spend time with our clients to help open doors and communicate our message. Kirsten has also been an

The author and Champagne De Meric Managing Director Kirsten Neubarth enjoy a short break at Vinexpo in Bordeaux (courtesy Champagne De Meric).

exhibitor at wine fairs in London and Germany as well as Vinexpo in Bordeaux, and this has been a key method of introducing our products and recruiting new clients. The fact that Kirsten is fluent in French, German, and English is a huge benefit for the company.

Part of our strategy is to use product introductions to allow us to build some excitement and resell our overall positioning. In 2003 we introduced our second sous bois product, our premier cru Blanc de Blancs Sous Bois. In 2004 we introduced our 1996 vintage, the last of our vintage champagnes before we switched to the sous bois line. In 2005 we introduced our grand cru blanc de blancs. In future years we will also introduce our first sous bois vintage (1999), our next bottling of Catherine de Medicis, and the product that I am most excited about, our blanc de noirs. The product is made exclusively from biodynamic grapes and vinified and aged in small oak barrels.

As I'm sure the reader can tell, my heart is in Champagne De Meric, not Champagne Baron Martin. De Meric is the type of champagne I enjoy. However, I'm only representative of a small segment of the market and because we have a large investment in the company and employees to support, we need to have a broader appeal. Having two very different and distinct product lines allows me to continue to focus on implementing the methods of René Collard for Champagne De Meric, use the standard methods for Champagne Baron Martin, and try to match our products to the different target markets.

Our marketing effort is really a work in progress. We will adjust to market conditions and our changing product line.

7. Use the Home Field Advantage

IN PREVIOUS CHAPTERS, I have alluded to the difficulties of the U.S. market for a small champagne producer. The United States is a challenging market for small companies in many fields due to the size of the nation and media costs. In the case of wine, however, the main problem is a legal one.

The Federal and state laws in the United States governing the distribution and sale of wine are antiquated, anticompetitive, and illogical — and that's in the more progressive states. These laws make it difficult and expensive to bring wine into the United States. They make it difficult to buy and sell wine across state lines, and they make it especially hard on small producers, foreign and domestic alike.

When I explain these laws to Europeans, for whom wine is an important part of both diet and culture, they often remark that these laws seem to belong to an earlier era whose time has passed. Sadly enough, they are correct. Before I describe the laws in effect today, let's look back at how and why they were developed.

The subject of regulating or restricting the sale of alcohol in the United States has been a contentious issue since the country was founded. However, the debate was primarily centered around hard liquor (distilled spirits) and beer rather than wine. Some people were against alcohol on religious grounds, especially in New England and in the Midwest, where Puritanism was strong. Often the activists were motivated by the perceived evils of saloons, establishments catering mainly to the working class. Saloons were blamed by many for most of the social ills in the country, including poverty.

Given that the working class in the nineteenth century had precious little income to spare for drinking in saloons, these establishments almost certainly did contribute to the suffering of many families.

The temperance movement — abstinence movement would have been a more accurate description — increased dramatically in popularity and power in the late nineteenth century. Organizations such as the Women's Christian Temperance Union and the Anti-Saloon League and the sermons of former major league baseball player Billy Sunday all played prominent roles in the movement's growth. Carry Nation became a legend, using "smashers" (stones wrapped in newspaper) and her famous hatchet to destroy saloons in her home state of Kansas.

These anti-alcohol forces gained an increasing amount of political power, and by 1913 a proposal was presented for the 18th Amendment to the U.S. Constitution to make alcohol illegal. By the end of 1917 this amendment had passed the Congress by the required two-thirds vote, and on January 16, 1919, Nebraska became the thirty-sixth state to ratify the 18th Amendment, giving the bill the two-thirds majority of states that it needed. The 18th Amendment was the law of the land, with the provision that prohibition was to take effect in one year.

It was now up to Congress to define the law and provide for its enforcement. The most controversial subject was to create a definition of "intoxicating beverages." Many who supported the concept of Prohibition assumed it would apply only to distilled spirits, but the definition put forth by Congress in what came to be known as the Volstead Act was that any liquid containing at least one-half of one percent of alcohol was deemed illegal.

As is well known, Prohibition was a disaster. People still wanted to drink, so organized criminals took over the distribution function. Gang leaders such as the notorious Al Capone used violence in their fight for turf, and after a relatively short time a large percentage of the population simply began to ignore the law. Prohibition became increasingly unpopular, and one of President Franklin Roosevelt's first actions when he took office was to fulfill a popular campaign promise by calling for the passage of the 21st Amendment to the Constitution to repeal Prohibition. On December 5, 1933, Utah ratified the 21st Amendment, thus ending Prohibition.

What the 21st Amendment did, however, was to make the regulation of alcoholic beverages the responsibility of each individual state. The net result is, in essence, 51 separate regulatory bodies — the Bureau of Alcohol, Tobacco, and Firearms (ATF) on the Federal level and an equivalent bureaucracy on each state level. Each state has different laws regarding the sale of alcohol, and in some cases the laws vary by county (in Kansas and Texas, for example, Prohibition laws still exist in a number of counties). Both Federal and state laws mandate the three-tier system, forcing U.S. producers to sell to wholesalers licensed in each state, who then sell to retailers (wine shops, restaurants, supermarkets, etc.), who finally sell to consumers. In the case of non–U.S. products such as champagne, the additional layer of an importer is added between the producer and the wholesaler, although many wholesalers also function as importers.

The original purpose of these laws was to prevent the sale of alcohol from being dominated and controlled by organized crime. By having a number of different levels, each separate, it was felt that the likelihood of mafia domination of the industry would be greatly reduced, and it worked — organized crime turned to other pursuits after 1933. However, Al Capone has been dead since 1947. The old-style saloons are gone. Deregulation of industry has become a major movement in the United States and around the world. Distribution and marketing systems have changed dramatically. Americans have become more interested in and knowledgeable about fine wine. The health benefits of wine have been proven, and clearly wine is consumed more responsibly than beer or hard liquor. The regulations designed for the United States coming out of 13 years of Prohibition in 1933 are not only still on the books, however, they are being vigorously enforced.

Let's look at the impact the U.S. system has on the market for champagne from small producers such as Champagne De Meric. First of all, each level in the distribution system adds its mark-up, which drives up the price to the consumer. The more levels one must go through, the higher the mark-up and the higher the price to the consumer. Because it is more efficient for wholesalers to deal with larger volume products, the mark-up is usually larger on products coming from small producers, which makes it difficult to sell these products. This discourages importers, wholesalers, or retailers from carrying the products of small producers, which limits consumer choice in the United States.

In addition, the existence of 50 state bureaucracies means that the United States is no longer one major market but a series of 50 separate smaller markets. Although many importers are able to work across state lines, states require that the wholesaler be a separate legal entity in each state (although some large wholesale groups own a number of these entities). The wine must usually be warehoused in the state, which is not a requirement for other industries. So unless one works with one of the largest wholesale groups, who are volume driven and therefore have little interest in products with limited production, one must find a wholesaler for each individual state. This doesn't include states like my native Pennsylvania, in which the state itself is the only licensed wholesaler or wine shop.

The grandes marques and cooperatives can function in this system because their huge production volume is attractive to the largest wholesale groups. For many smaller champagne producers, however, the complexities and cost of these regulations make marketing in the United States a low priority.

I have nothing against wine regulation such as the Appellation d'Origine Controlée (AOC) system when these regulations are designed to protect quality. Regulation of this sort, even if it is sometimes cumbersome, benefits the consumer by ensuring a certain minimum level of quality. The U.S. system of regulation and the three-tier system, however, have nothing to do with quality. They only serve to increase price and decrease product availability for consumers. Of course, they also result in a lot of tax revenues for states, something near and dear to the hearts of these regulators.

One loophole that has served to decrease complications for producers and increase choices for consumers exists in the system. This is the possibility of selling via direct marketing. Customers around the nation have been able to increase their choices by ordering from wine merchants throughout the country via mail, phone, fax, or Internet. This allows a champagne producer to focus his or her efforts on a small number of states and reach connoisseurs across the country through a few outlets. In the case of U.S. wineries, direct shipping to consumers allows producers too small to be of interest to wholesalers to bypass the three-tier system entirely.

The laws on direct shipping vary by state. Certain states, such as California, Illinois, Washington, and Oregon, allow direct shipments with some limitations on quantity. Other states allow direct shipping with permits and other limitations, and some have prohibited direct shipping completely.

Despite the fact that direct shipping is totally prohibited in many states, the law was largely ignored until fairly recently. Given the other issues facing the states, most had little interest in devoting their resources to policing from which sources consumers were buying their wine. However, as the direct marketing industry has grown and Internet access has made finding and buying fine wines on a national basis easier and more convenient than ever, some states have begun to take a very aggressive stance in enforcing the ban on direct shipping of wines. In fact, states such as Florida, Maryland, Tennessee, and Kentucky made shipping wine (or any other alcoholic beverage) to consumers in their state a felony. This opens the possibility of actually extraditing a wine merchant or consumer who commits the crime of shipping wine to stand trial in one of these states, ensuring that these dastardly deeds do not go unpunished just because the shipper is not a local resident. Although I'm not aware of anyone actually being hauled off to jail for this crime, the felony laws have made it virtually impossible for consumers in these states to purchase wines other than the ones sold through their local three-tier system.

The Moulin de Verzenay, one of the best vantage points to view the Montagne de Reims (photograph by Berengo Gardin/Collection CIVC).

Given the myriad of more important problems in today's world, why are these states so concerned about the interstate sale of wine? One reason sometimes put forth is that bypassing the three-tier system will promote underage drinking. In these days, when every teenager seems to have his or her own car, I concur that teenage alcohol abuse is a very serious issue. Somehow I find it hard to imagine teenagers scheming to purchase bottles of Champagne De Meric or the latest California cult wine via the Internet, to say nothing of the fact that transport services almost always require the signature of someone 21 or older when they deliver wine. In addition, at least when I was a teenager, there were plenty of easier ways to get a few six-packs of beer than shopping through mail order.

The real concern about interstate wine sales has nothing to do with teenage drinking and everything to do with money. The wholesalers have a legislated monopoly on the distribution of wine, and they are not about to give it up without a fight. The passage of felony laws in some states was the direct result of intensive lobbying by the Wine and Spirits Wholesalers Association (WSWA) and their members. The states, constantly searching for sources of revenue, have no interest in losing tax dollars from the sale of wine, which is what currently happens when the wine is shipped in from another state.

The issue of interstate shipping has become a hotly contested one during the last five years. On one side is the WSWA, supported by a number of anti-drinking groups who oppose any easing of restrictions on the sale of alcohol. On the other side are the U.S. wine producers, represented by groups such as the Wine Institute, Family Winemakers of California, the American Vintners Association, and the Coalition for Free Trade, who have joined together to form a group called Free the Grapes!, an organization headed by Napa Valley marketing consultant Jeremy Benson. This particular battle deals with direct shipments from U.S. wine producers to consumers, so producers of champagne and other imported wines are, at most, an afterthought.

For some time this was a state-by-state battle, and although progress was made, it was a slow process. In late 2004, however, the United States Supreme Court heard a case based on these laws, and in early 2005 the Court ruled that the many current restrictions on shipping wine between states was unconstitutional.

The basis for the decision, however, was not that consumers had an inherent right to have wines brought in across state lines. Rather, the laws were struck down because they allowed for shipping by in-state wineries, but prohibited the same by out-of-state wineries. Therefore, the law was discriminatory, and a violation of free trade.

In the wake of this decision, states are now reviewing their laws. Some, like New York, have opened up their markets. Others now allow direct shipping, but with fairly draconian restrictions, which may be the subject of future court cases. Others have yet to take action, perhaps waiting to follow the lead of other states.

Logically, states with significant in-state wineries have been, and are, more open about allowing direct shipping, since they want their wineries to have the right to ship into other states. Some of the more conservative states may continue to look for ways to limit access to their markets.

To me, the real issue is not simply a question of shipping wine between states but why these regulations that have long outlived their usefulness and contradict the American spirit of free enterprise are still in force. The entire concept of these laws is flawed because it rests on one of the many errors of the Volstead Act, that of failing to make a distinction between wine, beer, and distilled spirits. Numerous studies have shown that daily wine consumption has many health benefits that are not derived from the consumption of other alcoholic beverages. In addition, the problem of alcohol abuse, both among teenagers and adults, is not widely based on the consumption of wine. According to the University of California at Davis, only 2 percent of all drunk driving arrests involve wine.

This is not to say that wine is not sometimes used irresponsibly — it is. I believe, however, that these relatively rare cases are not prevented by the antiquated set of regulations in force and the irresponsible use of wine would not increase if these regulations were repealed.

I'm not trying to minimize one of the major concerns of anti-alcohol activists, the problem of underage drinking and driving. Drinking and driving is a serious problem, no matter what the age of the offender, and I have no problem with the licensing of retail establishments to help enforce the minimum drinking age. However, the three-tier system, which mandates the use of wholesalers in each state, does nothing to control this problem. I fail to see how an adult consumer who prefers to drink Champagne De Meric and orders it from an out-of-state retailer or directly from us in Aÿ is harming the public interest. After all, wine is legally and readily available in each state. What is gained by limiting a consumer's choice?

Putting aside the problem of drinking and driving, I find the concern over the health problems caused by alcohol abuse a bit hypocritical. All evidence shows that the typical Western diet based on the heavy consumption of animal products is geometrically more harmful to the health of Americans than the damage caused by alcohol abuse. However, there are no labeling requirements and virtually no regulations put on the meat and dairy industries — in fact, these industries are heavily subsidized by the government.

I understand that the states are concerned about the loss of tax revenue if the current system is eliminated, but interstate wine sales are a minute part of the overall direct marketing industry. If there is a problem with lost tax revenue due to interstate commerce associated with direct marketing, then regulators should look for a global solution instead of focusing on the wine industry. In addition, the wine industry has expressed its willingness to work with the states on this problem.

The only party who would seem to have a real vested interest in the current system are the licensed wholesalers, the group leading the battle to preserve the status quo. In reality, they have little to fear. Wholesalers serve a valuable function in the marketing and distribution system for wine, and they will continue to play a major role in the wine industry whether or not regulations are present. Wholesalers today are unable to provide a full range of choices for consumers as they did when the regulations were developed. The alcoholic beverage wholesale industry, like many other industries, has undergone a major consolidation during the past few years. In 1950 there were more than 5,000 wholesalers nationwide, while today there are less than 250, and the top 10 wholesalers control 51 percent of the U.S. market. At the same time, the number of wines on the market has grown dramatically as new producers and new wine regions have emerged.

There is no doubt that under the current system, wholesalers do an excellent job for large producers, but the wholesale business is volume driven and most large wholesalers are simply unable to profitably service small producers on a state-by-state basis. If small producers could work with a few wholesalers or retailers who would have the right to ship product on a nationwide basis, producers would have more market access, consumers would have more choices, and the most efficient and creative wholesalers would prosper.

It is worthwhile to compare the U.S. system to that of most European nations. In Europe, producers generally work through importers who also function as wholesalers. These importers are limited geographically only by the logistics of servicing their customers, not by legal constraints. Consumers and retailers can also order directly from the producer provided the appropriate taxes are paid. In short, the wine business is treated like any other business. It's worth noting, however, that distilled spirits are much more highly taxed and highly regulated than wine or beer.

An example of the absurdity of these laws is that when I moved from Champagne back to the United States, I had to work through an importer to bring in my personal wine collection. I had to put warning labels on the backs of bottles and obtain all label approvals. The fact that these bottles were for my private consumption did nothing to reduce the red tape.

I believe U.S. laws relating to alcoholic beverages need a major over-haul. Unfortunately, this does not appear to be on the horizon any time soon. So how can Champagne De Meric succeed in the U.S. market?

I strongly believe that the potential for us in the United States is sig-nificant. Aside from the size and wealth of the United States, the fact that, for the most part, only the grandes marques and a few cooperatives are widely available means that there is a real opportunity to appeal to United States wine connoisseurs looking for something different. In fact, a num-ber of champagnes from smaller producers are beginning to appear on the market, and some are selling quite well.

In addition, as an American with a marketing background I have a distinct advantage. Although I have only limited experience in the wine segment in the United States, my advertising career had given me broad experience in marketing a wide range of products and services in this coun-try. When I moved from Champagne to California in the second half of 2001, I began developing a strategy for the U.S. market.

I started by analyzing our strengths. Our most important asset is qual-ity; I believe there are very few brut nonvintage champagnes of the quality level of our Grande Réserve Sous Bois. Another asset is price — the De Meric line is less expensive than the typical Grande Marque, and the Baron Mar-tin line has an even lower price point. Another advantage is my presence in the United States to support the brands because I am the only champagne producer living in America.

At the same time, we are faced with some significant obstacles. For one thing, our brands are totally unknown in the United States, and we don't have the funds to undertake a major advertising or public relations effort to change this situation. In addition, our small size means that we are of no interest to a national wholesaler because the possibility of selling 25,000 bottles of our wines per year is not attractive to a volume-oriented com-pany. In spite of the increasing presence of some good-quality, small cham-pagne brands, only a small market niche has much interest in champagne as anything other than something to drink on New Year's Eve.

I felt that one of the first priorities was to develop appropriate, American-style sales tools for the brands. We created a Champagne De Meric website, complete with a short film on our company (www.Cham-pagneDeMeric.com). We already had a brochure for Champagne De Meric, and we created one for Champagne Baron Martin. We also created specific product pieces for Grande Réserve Sous Bois and Blanc de Blancs Sous Bois. These pieces have the key facts about the product (annual production, grapes used, etc.).

The key challenge, however, was how to most effectively reach the market, especially the niche market of champagne connoisseurs. We spoke with some large wholesalers, but our size and small volume were not of interest to them. In addition, because consumers aren't familiar with our brand, our wine needs to be "hand sold" — recommended by a knowledgeable wine shop or restaurant staff. These staff members must like the product and be familiar with its key selling features.

I also looked at our European experience. Our best customers are the ones with whom we have strong contact. For example, we work with an excellent importer in Belgium, and each year they bring some of their key clients to Ay to visit our cellars and spend time with us. This allows us to communicate directly with these clients and reinforce the key selling points of our products. If we worked with a large U.S. wholesaler, we'd have little contact with their restaurant and retail clients and almost none at all with the end consumer.

Therefore, I decided to concentrate on a small number of major wine retailers and a few wholesalers as our targets. These companies sell a significant amount of wine and have knowledgeable and professional staff members, but they are small enough to hand sell our products.

Our offerings to these partners are strong — very good quality/value, direct pricing, exclusivity in their market, and marketing support not available from other small champagne producers. Our first three partners, all for the De Meric brand, were K&L Wine in the San Francisco Bay Area; Zachy's in Scarsdale, New York; and Binny's in Chicago. The results have been extremely positive to date. We are now expanding to other key states such as Florida, Texas, Maryland, and Washington, DC.

It is hard for other small producers to duplicate this strategy. Of course, some small champagne producers have friends or relatives in the United States who can act as agents, but these agents will normally be far less passionate about the wines they sell and less committed to the sales process than I am. Because this is in essence a labor of love for me, I am willing to invest the time to work with our partners to make our brands successful. Although my investment of time and money in this sales process will not be profitable in the short term, I am content to take a longer view in my native land. I believe that we can build a solid base of loyal U.S. customers in key markets, which will be an important part of the company's success.

8. How to Make a Small Fortune in the Champagne Business

TO PARAPHRASE AN OLD JOKE, the best way to make a small fortune in the champagne business is to start out with a large fortune. You'll soon find yourself with only a small fortune left.

Of course, I'm exaggerating, because the picture is not nearly that bleak. In fact, according to a study conducted by Banque de France in October 2001, the négociant-manipulant (NM) class in Champagne has an overall profit margin of 12.4 percent, a very respectable performance. However, this figure is highly skewed by the profitability of the large producers. The median profit margin for an NM is only 6.4 percent, which is not the type of figure that excites investment bankers.

The major difficulty in the champagne business, however, is not the profit/loss account. It is the horrendous cash flow. Let's look at the *minimum* schedule for direct product costs (not including labels, corks, capsules, and other items applied after the bottle is disgorged) until there is a return on investment. Of course, I am also not including overhead, selling expense, financial costs, or capital investment.

Month 1 (harvest): Juice arrives at cuverie
Month 3: Payment for pressing and first quarter payment for grapes due
Month 4: Earliest possible date for bottling
Month 6: Second quarter payment for grapes due
Month 8: Payment date for bottles
Month 9: Third quarter payment for grapes due

Month 12: Final quarter payment for grapes due, including all bonuses

Month 19: Earliest possible date for disgorgement and sale

Month 21: Earliest date for payment (standard terms are 60 days)

Keep in mind that this is a minimum timeframe. In our case, we don't normally bottle until month seven or eight, disgorge before month 44, sell before month 48, or receive payment before month 50, and we often disgorge and sell later. We're looking at a four-year investment cycle for each harvest, and during these four years we have continued to pay salaries and other expenses, make capital investments, and purchase the grapes from three subsequent harvests.

This helps explain why most producers don't age their champagne much more than the minimum. Take the case of a large producer making 4 million bottles of nonvintage champagne per year. The grapes necessary to make these bottles, assuming average quality, will require an investment of at least 18 million dollars. The burden of waiting 48 months rather than 21 or 28 months for some return on this 18 million dollars is a very significant one.

One key to the champagne business is to have adequate working capital, either from shareholders or from a bank. In our case, the majority of our working capital has been supplied by shareholders, primarily me. However, we do have a line of credit at Société Générale, and we have been able to finance some of our capital expenditures. Cash flow is always an important issue for us, however, and trying to speed collections and delay the payment of invoices (other than for the grapes) is a way of life.

To deal with the cash flow burden, we have increased our capitalization three times. It is currently more than 1.5 million dollars. I own more than 80 percent of the company, and the rest is split between the Besserat family, my German friends Volker Schöne and Eike Wolff, U.S. Marketing Director Melissa Culmer, and Directeur Générale Kirsten Neubarth. Volker and Eike were my partners in the advertising business (they founded and ran our very successful agency in Stuttgart, Germany), and Kirsten is a former client who worked with their agency, so one could say that we are in some ways still a type of family business.

Let's turn to profit/loss items beginning with the direct costs, the cost of goods sold. The numbers that I will use are based on actual costs for Champagne De Meric.

The biggest expense item, of course, is the grapes. Our cost, including all bonuses and pressing, is approximately $6.00 per kilo of grapes. It takes 1.2 kilos to produce 75 cl of juice, the contents of a standard champagne bottle. However, because we are now using only the cuvée in Champagne

De Meric rather than both the cuvée and the taille, it takes 1.5 kilos of grapes for each of our bottles. However, we recoup some of our investment from the taille by selling it, so we will use a figure of 1.4 to calculate costs.

Therefore, the grapes necessary for each bottle of Champagne De Meric cost approximately $8.40. Although no statistics are available for what other houses pay for grapes, I'd estimate that the average is around $6.50 to $7.00 per bottle. Our cost is higher due to the quality of our grapes on the échelle des crus and our bonus system for quality.

One might ask, why not buy vineyard land in order to reduce the cost of grapes? Unfortunately, in Champagne this is both a difficult and expensive proposition. There are often preemptive rights on vineyard land, so a sale is never sure. More important, there isn't much land for sale. Vines get passed down from generation to generation, and land is the primary asset of most vignerons. It is rare to see sizeable amounts of vineyard for sale and when they are for sale, the price is high, on average more than $800,000 per hectare in today's market.

Because the appellation system strictly limits what land is vineyard land, one can't simply put vines in one's yard. In addition, being a vigneron in Champagne is extremely labor intensive if one is quality oriented, so most of the savings from not having to purchase grapes would be consumed by interest expense and the cost of quality viticultural help.

We do plan to buy vineyard land if and when it comes available at a reasonable price. In fact, once we reach profitability, this is one of the key things I would like to do with the surplus. This is as much for quality control as for improving our bottom line.

In addition to the grapes, there are other elements in the direct-cost category. The largest are the costs related to bottling, including the bottle itself, the labels, and the cork. We spend approximately $1.00 per bottle on these items. All together, this gives us a direct cost of goods sold of approximately $9.40 per bottle. There are also a few other minor costs (yeast, crown corks, etc.), but these are not significant.

The largest indirect cost is salaries. There are a number of basic tasks to be performed: overall management, sales and marketing, winemaking, and lots of paperwork. The Comité Interprofessionnel du Vin de Champagne (CIVC) and the French government impose massive paperwork requirements on producers (I consider this the full-employment act for bureaucrats), and much of this paperwork burden is not variable depending on size and volume. This is one reason why small producers have thinner profit margins than large producers.

We have a staff of three full-time employees in France (Directeur Générale Kirsten Neubarth, Cellarmaster Johann Golanski, and an administrative assistant), plus a part-time secretary and a part-time assistant in the cellars. I spend a significant amount of time as a noncompensated chairman of the board, and Christian Besserat still contributes in a nonsalaried capacity. This is a difficult overhead burden, but it is necessary to ensure product quality, strong marketing and communications efforts, proper financial reporting, and compliance with all of the government paperwork.

As you can see, there are many cost items. On the other side of the ledger, our primary source of revenue is selling our champagne. We do make some margin on vinifying the taille into vin clair and selling it to other NMs, and when cash flow needs have dictated we have sold undisgorged bottles to other NMs (this is known as the sur latte trade, or spéculation). However, most of our revenue and almost all of our margin come from selling our champagne to our clients.

Champagne De Meric cellar master Johann Golanski (courtesy Alexandre Verguet).

Including all of the sales for both brands, we expect to sell approximately 40,000 bottles in 2005. We need to sell approximately 60,000 bottles at our current price points to break even. While our sales have grown every year, we still have a ways to go to bridge the gap. While I am confident that we could increase sales by increasing our price, this would accomplish little since it would raise the level of sales necessary to break even.

Financially, the last few years have been difficult ones. Between 1997 and 2003, the company has had losses totalling more than $700,000. Of course, losses were expected because we had very little stock to sell during our first two years and we were re-creating two brands and their product lines. However, there were some things that we could have done better, and the losses exceeded our projections.

Because of the financial situation, I am now looking at ways to reduce costs and overhead. Since we now have a large stock, one option is to reduce production of De Meric, eliminate Baron Martin, and focus on the U.S. market. This will allow us to reduce our number of employees, and perhaps share office space and administrative functions with a fellow producer. Another option is to merge with another producer, and keep the existing inventory to service our existing clients, which will eliminate most of our costs. I plan to make a decision on our direction by the end of 2006.

Part II

THE WORLD
OF CHAMPAGNE

9. The History of Champagne

To understand the situation in Champagne today, it is important to understand the history of the wine and the marketplace. Tradition is very important in Champagne, and many aspects of today's champagne industry are the result of what has taken place in the past.

One of the longest lasting legacies of the Roman Empire is the wine culture in Europe. As the Romans conquered Europe more than 2000 years ago, they brought along their love of wine and planted grapes throughout the continent, especially in what is now France. However, there is some evidence based on fossils that wine grapes existed in Champagne long before the coming of the Romans.

Champagne has been known for its wine since the Middle Ages. However, until the seventeenth century, the wine from Champagne was still wine, in most cases red wine. There are many references to this red wine in historical texts, although the still wines of Champagne were often overshadowed by those of neighboring Burgundy. Many monarchs and other notables, including Henry IV of France, Catherine de Medici of Italy (known as Catherine de Medicis in France), Charles V of Spain, Henry VIII of England, and Pope Leo X enjoyed the wines of Champagne and owned vineyards in the region.

According to noted wine historian Cyrus Redding, the wines of Champagne really came into their own in the early 1600s, with the coronation of Louis XIII. By today's standards, it seems natural that the wines of Champagne were popular at the French court because the outer limit of Champagne is only 100 kilometers from Paris. Before the advent of modern transportation, however, 100 kilometers was a long way, and the heart of the

Champagne region is an additional 50 kilometers from Paris. Also, largely due to the northern location of Champagne, these still wines were (and are) often somewhat thinner and less expressive than the wines of southern regions. Therefore, these still wines, now known as coteaux champenois, are not for everyone.

In addition, the Champagne region has had more than its share of political upheaval. Known as the "crossroads of Europe," the region's central location attracted trade and commerce in good times, but the region was frequently a battleground for various European wars throughout history. In fact, one can still visit the site where the advance of Attila the Hun through Europe was finally halted near the city of Chalons-en-Champagne in the year 451.

The wines of Champagne were especially highly regarded by Louis XIV, the Sun King. Under the reign of Louis XIV, France grew into a major world power, a position it enjoyed until World War II. Louis XIV was a great statesman and must be considered on a par with Napoleon Bonaparte as the greatest French leader in history.

Louis XIV especially liked the still wines of two key villages in Champagne, Ay and Sillery. Both these villages are still rated grand cru and are dominated by the pinot noir grape. Champagne Bollinger, Champagne Goutorbe, Champagne Deutz, Champagne Gosset, and many other outstanding producers are still located in Ay (including Champagne De Meric, of course). Sadly, Sillery has lost its place as a leading wine town, although the vineyards that remain are still highly rated.

The great leap forward for the wines of Champagne came with the arrival of Dom Pérignon. Born in the town of St. Menehoud in 1638 or 1639 (records were less accurate in those times), Pierre Pérignon grew up in a somewhat well to do family. In 1657 he entered the monastery of St. Vanne, located in the World War I battleground of Verdun, just east of the Champagne region. The next year he was officially accepted into the Benedictine order, renounced all of his worldly possessions, and became a monk. In 1668, he was appointed procureur of the Abbey of Hautvillers in the heart of Champagne. As the procureur, Dom Pérignon was in charge of the business affairs of the abbey, the most important of which was winemaking.

It may seem strange in our day and age that a Benedictine monk spent most of his life making wine. However, one must remember that before the French Revolution, most of the land was owned by a small number of noble families (the first estate) or the Catholic Church (the second estate). In fact, this unequal distribution of land was a leading cause of the French Revolution, which resulted in much of the land owned by these two estates being redistributed to the third estate, the rest of the population of France.

The various churches and abbeys supported themselves primarily through taxes on the population but also through various forms of agriculture, including viticulture. Thus Dom Pérignon, as the procureur, was the vineyard manager and cellarmaster of the abbey.

By all contemporary accounts, Dom Pérignon was a master winemaker. His wines were held in very high repute and reportedly sold for premium prices. These wines were initially still reds, but he eventually began to work more with white wines and, eventually, he shifted his emphasis to sparkling wine.

Popular legend has it that Dom Pérignon invented sparkling wine. However, more recent evidence makes this claim unlikely. In his book *World Encyclopedia of Champagne and Sparkling Wine*, leading wine journalist Tom Stevenson presents evidence that sparkling wine existed in England before Pérignon's birth. Others have presented evidence that sparkling wine existed in China many centuries ago. The important fact, however, is that no one really invented sparkling wine — it was a naturally occurring phenomenon.

The fermentation of grape juice is always a somewhat tricky proposition, and this was even truer in the eighteenth century. The conversion of sugar to alcohol needs to be carefully controlled. In a cold climate like Champagne or England, the air temperature may drop during the fermentation. Without temperature control (in this case heating), this will lead to the premature end of fermentation, leaving unfermented residual sugar behind. In the spring, when temperatures begin to climb, the fermentation process may start again, leading to a second fermentation.

Initially wine was kept and sold in casks, so this second fermentation was at most a nuisance. However, during Dom Pérignon's day, glass technology had improved to the point where wine could be bottled rather than left indefinitely in barrels. Once the wine was bottled, the unwanted second fermentation became much more than a nuisance because the carbon dioxide that is a by-product of fermentation takes the form of bubbles, and the pressure in these bottles would result the loss of a significant portion of the bottles due to explosion.

Dom Pérignon's initial thrust was to eliminate this unwanted second fermentation. Over time, however, he shifted his efforts to controlling the second fermentation rather than eliminating it. In doing so, he pioneered the techniques still used today, justly earning the title the Father of Champagne.

Dom Pérignon died in 1715. By that time his methods, along with continued improvement in the quality of bottles and the introduction of cork tied with string to seal the bottles, led to a gradual increase in the amount of sparkling wine produced in Champagne. This conversion, however, was a long process. The still wines of Champagne continued to enjoy a strong market until the twentieth century, although coteaux champenois is now only a very minor part of the total wine produced in Champagne. We will use the term "champagne" the way it is used today — sparkling wine from the Champagne region.

The wine business in Champagne became better organized in the beginning of the eighteenth century. Many of the leading champagne houses were formed during this era, including Moët & Chandon, Ruinart, Veuve Clicquot, and Heidsieck, which is now divided into three separate brands (Heidsieck & Cie Monopole, Piper Heidsieck, and Charles Heidsieck). As early as the 1720s there is evidence of increasing demand for champagne from export markets. Germany was by far the biggest export market, followed by Flanders (Belgium), Holland, and England. The British market was particularly erratic, partly because sparkling champagne went in and out of style and partly because England and France were bitter enemies who were at war throughout the century.

Despite changing styles and political upheaval, the market for champagne continued to grow. By 1780, Moët had production of approximately 50,000 bottles, and other houses also showed impressive growth. By comparison, Moët's 1780 total is not much less than that of Champagne De Meric in a typical year!

The coming of the French Revolution in 1789 led to major changes in the wine business. Land was redistributed from the Church and the nobles to the third estate, and large landholdings were divided up into small plots. Wars raged and disrupted commerce as the European monarchies sought to restore the Bourbons to the throne. Worse yet, some key battles were fought in the Champagne region itself. Fortunately, these wars had pretty much ended by the late eighteenth century.

The entire nineteenth century was a time of political upheaval, but the production and sales of sparkling champagne grew steadily. However, for many years the majority of the wine from the region continued to be still wine. For example, Cyrus Redding reported that in 1832 the Marne Department produced 480,000 hectolitres of wine, of which only 50,000 hectolitres were made into champagne. This gradually changed throughout the nineteenth century as champagne became synonymous with sparkling rather than still wine.

One of the most interesting developments of the nineteenth century was the influx of Germans into the champagne business. This isn't totally surprising given the proximity of the German states to Champagne (the various German states were not united until the second half of the nineteenth century), but the number of successful German champagne houses is certainly more than one would expect. Famous names such as Bollinger, Mumm, Krug, and Deutz all established their houses during this period.

In addition to these German pioneers, most of the other major houses made their appearances in the nineteenth century. Two of the most famous, Champagne Clicquot and Champagne Pommery, were built by women who, after the sudden deaths of their husbands, found themselves in charge of a champagne house. Their success is truly remarkable when one remembers that women had virtually no rights in that era, and successful women in business were a true rarity.

The nineteenth century also heralded the arrival of some great promoters to the champagne business. Two of the most famous were Charles Heidsieck and Eugene Mercier. Heidsieck is best known for being one of the champagne pioneers in America, where he earned the nickname Champagne Charley. Mercier's focus was on the domestic market. His most famous promotional stunt occurred on the occasion of the 1889 World's Fair in Paris, when he built a special barrel weighing more than 20 tons, with a capacity of 215,000 bottles, and had it drawn by a team of horses from the firm's cellars in Epernay to the fair in Paris. Legend has it that in order to transverse several narrow streets in Paris, Mercier was obliged to purchase and subsequently destroy several homes along the way. This giant barrel is displayed today in the Mercier cellars in Epernay.

The last part of the nineteenth century was a great era for champagne. In his book *A History of Champagne*, André Simon refers to the period between 1889 and 1908 as the Golden Age of Champagne. According to Simon, "There has not been any [champagne] quite comparable in excellence to the best cuvées of 1889, 1892, 1899, 1900, 1904, and 1906." In addition to the quality of these vintages, the market for champagne, both in France and abroad, was increasing. According to official statistics, champagne sales rose from just over six million bottles per year in the 1840s to 28 million bottles in 1899.

By the end of the nineteenth century, champagne was being sold throughout the world. England had emerged as the largest market, larger even than the French domestic market. Germany and Belgium continued to be important markets, and Russia emerged as a major player. Champagne was the fashion at the Russian imperial court; in fact, Roederer Cristal was created for the Tsar of Russia.

Champagne in those days was, for the most part, a sweet wine. Large quantities of sugar were added to the wine so that it bore little resemblance to the champagne we know today. In general the British market leaned toward relatively dry champagne, while the Russians liked their champagne as sweet as possible. Interestingly enough, today we associate sweet wines with dessert, but in the nineteenth century this wasn't necessarily the case because sweet wines were often served as aperitifs and throughout the meal.

As the twentieth century dawned, the future looked bright for the champagne industry. However, there were three storm clouds gathering on the horizon: the spread of phylloxera, the threat of war in Europe, and tension between growers and champagne houses.

The arrival of phylloxera was inevitable. First introduced into southern France in the mid-nineteenth century on vines shipped from the United States, phylloxera is a tiny insect that attacks the roots of vines, enters the vines, and gradually destroys them. Once introduced into France, these insects gradually spread north, destroying vineyards in their wake. Every imaginable method was tried to combat this plague—flooding the vines, organic products, chemicals, burning and replanting, even introducing insect predators—but nothing worked, and growers lost the majority of their vines.

The solution was finally found in grafting European grape vines onto U.S. rootstocks. Without getting overly technical, it's important to point out that there are many different types of families of grape vines. For example, native U.S. varieties are ideal for table grapes, jams, and other food-related uses. The European varieties are ideal for wine. The roots of the U.S. varieties, whether naturally or through evolution, are harder, and therefore the phylloxera insects are unable to penetrate the roots and damage the vines. Today virtually all French vineyards consist of grafted vines, as do those in the United States and most other wine-producing nations.

Phylloxera first appeared in Champagne in 1890 in the village of Treloup. As was the case throughout France, every possible method of combating these insects was tried, but ultimately the vineyards had to be replanted using grafted vines. Fortunately, the vines suffered gradual deterioration rather than instant destruction, so the replanting could be accomplished in a somewhat orderly fashion. This process continued for more than 20 years.

Like phylloxera, World War I turned out to be inevitable. The roots of the conflict started with the Franco-Prussia War of 1870–71, in which France lost the provinces of Alsace and Lorraine to Germany. This was a blow to French pride that would need to be avenged at a future date. Understanding this, German prime minister Otto Von Bismark attempted to isolate France, and in 1879 Germany formed an alliance with Austria-Hungary. Italy joined this alliance in 1882, creating the Triple Alliance.

In response to this, longtime enemies France and Russia formed their own alliance, known as the Entente Cordiale, in 1891. Britain entered this pact in 1907, creating the Triple Entente.

In the background was an aggressive arms race among the European powers as each country sought to put itself in the best possible position for a coming war. There was also a rise in Balkan nationalism, long a smoldering fire in Europe. The "Young Turk" revolution in the Ottoman Empire in 1908 created an opening for Austria-Hungary, which annexed Bosnia and Herzegovina from the crumbling Ottoman entity.

Tension in the Balkans continued to increase, leading to a series of European crises in the next few years, all of which were eventually resolved through diplomacy. Two minor Balkan wars occurred in 1913, but the major powers resisted the temptation to get involved.

In the summer of 1914, Austria-Hungary scheduled a series of military maneuvers in Serbia. Austrian Archduke Franz Ferdinand, heir to the Austro-Hungarian throne, announced plans to attend with his wife. Warnings from the Serbian government that the royal couple would be in danger went unheeded, and on June 28 the Archduke and his wife were assassinated by a Serbian nationalist.

The tensions that had been building in Europe finally boiled over. With the support of Germany, the Austrian government presented a list of ten demands to Serbia, some of which were humiliating. After consultation with their Russian allies, the Serbians agreed to seven demands, suggested some modifications to the other three, and proposed arbitration to resolve their differences. This was rejected by Austria, and on July 26 the Tsar of Russia ordered a partial mobilization of troops.

Germany had long been fearful of the Franco-Russian alliance. Bismark had warned of the dangers of a two-front war, and in response to these dangers the Schlieffen plan was created by the German military in the 1890s. This plan stated that in the event of war, Germany would attack France first with full power, hopefully winning a quick victory before turning its attention to Russia.

As the crisis continued to brew, Russia ordered a full mobilization of its armed forces. Germany demanded that this mobilization be halted immediately, and when the demand was refused Germany proceeded to a full mobilization, followed by France.

At this point war was inevitable. A sea of nationalism swept over the populations of Europe, and the armies marched off joyously to war. It was expected to be a short war, as most European wars had been, and everyone expected the soldiers home for Christmas. However, advances in military technology made this war deadlier and longer than anyone expected.

The German army advanced through Belgium and into France. The Germans made strong initial progress, but their advance was checked in the heart of Champagne. From 1914 through 1918 Champagne became a battleground, and much of the region was damaged or destroyed. Most active men were called to military service, and the vines were generally not well maintained.

After more than four years of fighting, including the critical entry of the United States on the side of the French and British, the war finally ended as Germany and Austria surrendered.

The aftermath of the war was devastating for the champagne business. In addition to the necessity of rebuilding, the Russian Revolution led to the loss of a key export market. Due to ruinous demands for war reparations, the German economy was in disarray, severely limiting another key market. Prohibition in America closed another important market. In fact, the champagne business didn't fully recover until after World War II.

The third crisis was purely internal. This battle was part geographic and part commercial.

The geographic aspect dealt with which areas had the right to produce grapes to be used in the making of champagne. As will be discussed in a later chapter, the Champagne region covers parts of five different French departments, the most significant of which are the Marne and the Aube. The Marne is the heart of Champagne and is considered to produce the best quality grapes. However, more than 20 percent of the region's grapes come from the Aube, so that department is by no means insignificant.

The commercial part of the equation deals with the practices of some of the champagne houses in sourcing their grapes. Although there was no legislation in effect at the time, it was generally understood that the grapes used to make champagne must come from the region. However, grapes in Champagne were (and are) relatively scarce and expensive. Therefore, some unscrupulous champagne producers were using inexpensive grapes from other parts of France to make their "champagne." It is unclear exactly how widespread this practice was, but in his book *The History of Champagne* André Simon demonstrates that once this practice was outlawed, official counts of the inventory of champagne in producers' cellars dropped approximately 20 percent.

Poor harvests in 1908 and 1909 followed by a disastrous harvest in 1910 sent tensions skyrocketing. Certain growers refused to pay their taxes, and incidents of vandalism occurred. The growers demanded action from the French government to stop the fraud and protect the rights of the growers in Champagne.

After bureaucratic delays, a law was passed and published on February 11, 1911. This law called for separate cellars and declarations for champagne and other sparkling wines (vins mousseux). It also set forth that only grapes grown in Champagne could be used for champagne. However, in the territorial definition of the law, the Aube was excluded. This led to protests and violence in the Aube, and the government recommended that the Aube be included in the territorial definition. The legislature then proposed eliminating all territorial definitions because these caused disharmony between the regions.

On April 11, 1911, violence erupted in the Marne. Vignerons took to the streets in Epernay, Damery, Cumières, Dizy, Moussy, Pierry, and other villages. Soldiers were called out to keep the peace, but on April 12 the growers marched on Ay, causing major damage.

The crisis was finally resolved by a definitive "appellation" for champagne, the first of its kind. The Aube was given the designation of Champagne deuxième zone (second champagne zone), a designation that eventually disappeared, although some in the Marne still view the Aube in this manner. In the end, the result was good for growers because it protected their rights, good for consumers because it provided assurance that wine sold as champagne was indeed champagne, and good for champagne producers because it created a level playing field.

The period after these three crises—the years between the two great wars—was difficult. In addition to the problems previously mentioned, Britain dramatically raised the duties on champagne, which reduced demand from the key export market. The global depression of the 1930s was disastrous for a luxury product such as champagne.

On the positive side, a steady decrease in the value of the French franc reduced the price of champagne to export markets. More important, however, the inflation that was a by-product of this devaluation of the currency made the people of France less interested in saving money and more likely to follow the principle of "carpe diem" (seize the day). Champagne sales in France grew dramatically as the domestic market became the dominant one for champagne, a trend that has continued through the present time.

However, the increase in the French market by no means offset the negative global economic factors. Sales of champagne slumped, and the price of grapes dropped to the point where they were barely worth picking. This situation led to improved organization of the champagne industry in the mid–1930s under the leadership of Robert-Jean de Vogue, who as the head of Moët represented the champagne houses, and Maurice Doyard of Vertus, who represented the growers. Limits were put on yields, and quality standards were increased. These trends continued even during the German occupation of France. In fact, it was in 1941 that the governing body of the champagne industry, the Comité Interprofessionel du Vin de Champagne (CIVC), was formed.

Unlike during World War I, the Champagne region suffered little physical damage during World War II. However, the Jewish community of Champagne was largely wiped out in Nazi extermination camps, and many other residents of Champagne were deported to Germany for forced labor. Others were arrested or killed, especially in the closing days of the war. The Germans seized much of the production of champagne for their own use, and one still hears stories of false walls in the cellars and various other intrigues designed to keep as many bottles as possible from being appropriated.

Thanks largely to the Marshall Plan, relative prosperity returned to France a few years after the end of World War II. Sales steadily increased and passed the 100 million-bottle mark in 1970. The postwar prosperity in the developed countries has greatly increased the market for champagne, as has the collapse of the USSR in the 1990s.

As mentioned earlier, Champagne was a pioneer in the appellation system. Today, the key winemaking regions in France are governed by the Appellation d'Origine Controlée (AOC) system that serves to govern the better quality wines and ensure consumers a standard of quality that they can depend on. Yields, viticultural methods, winemaking methods, conservation, aging, and even some marketing methods are regulated by the CIVC. Although I don't agree with every one of their policies, on the whole I feel this organization does a tremendous job and provides strong benefits to both the champagne industry and consumers of champagne.

The total area delimited for champagne grapes has remained at 34,500 hectares since it was set in 1927. However, the fact that land is in the Champagne Appellation does not necessarily mean that the CIVC will give growers permission to plant vines on the land. Increased prosperity, good management, and effective marketing have led to an increased demand for champagne, and as this has occurred the CIVC has gradually increased the proportion of AOC land allowed to be planted. According to CIVC figures, in 1970 just under 20,000 hectares of AOC land in Champagne were planted. Today almost the entire AOC area is planted.

This increased supply and the increased demand have allowed champagne sales to grow from 49 million bottles in 1960 to 102 million bottles in 1970, 176 million bottles in 1980, and 232 million bottles in 1990, with sales peaking at 327 million bottles in 1999, as consumers around the globe prepared to welcome in the new millennium.

Today the champagne business faces a new set of challenges. I'm confident, however, that these challenges will be met.

10. Past Harvests in Champagne

WE DISCUSSED AGED CHAMPAGNE AND some of the older vintages in Part I. In this chapter, we will examine some of the past harvests and vintages in the Champagne region.

In the case of the vintages since 1969, I have either personal experience or have obtained much of my information from talking with my friends and fellow producers. In the case of most of the older vintages, however, I am relying on secondary sources for my information. These include *The Great Vintage Wine Book* by Michael Broadbent; *Champagne* by Tom Stevenson; *The History of Champagne* by André Simon; *Un Siècle de Millésimes* by Jean-François Bazin, Mathilde Hulot, and Hèléne Piot; and *Un Siècle de Vendanges en Champagne* by Dominique Fradet.

According to Michael Broadbent, 1743, 1753, 1783, and 1788 were among the best vintages in the eighteenth century. In the early nineteenth century, André Simon ranks 1802, 1803, 1804, 1806, 1810, 1811, 1818, 1819, 1822, 1825, 1828, 1831, 1832, 1834, 1839, 1840, 1842, 1846, 1848, 1856, 1857, 1858, 1862, and 1863 as meriting a rating of six or higher on a scale of one to seven. Broadbent rates 1815 as a top vintage (Simon gives it a ranking of two) and, like Simon, gives high marks to 1846 and 1857.

Beginning in 1865 and until the end of the nineteenth century, these two experts agree that 1865, 1868, 1870, 1874, 1892, 1893, 1899, and 1900 are classic vintages. Simon also rates 1875, 1880, 1884, 1889, 1895, 1897, and 1898 very highly; Broadbent only concurs on 1880, 1889, and 1898, and in all three cases he is less enthusiastic than Simon.

Much more information is available about the twentieth century. What follows is a brief overview of each harvest between 1900 and 2003.

1900: This year had a very cold winter and a very hot summer. Summer thunderstorms did little damage, and the crop was excellent. Although 1900 was generally an outstanding year in France, opinions differ a bit regarding the quality of the champagne vintage. However, all agree that it was a very good year, and Stevenson and Simon give it top marks.

1901: This year started out with great promise. Flowering progressed well, and the summer heat was described as "tropical." However, continuous rainstorms in the period leading up to the harvest brought widespread rot, leading to a large (for the time) crop of medium-quality grapes. Ratings range from mediocre to poor.

1902: A May frost damaged the crop, reducing the quantity. Torrential rainstorms again led to rot, this time accompanied by mildew. The net result was another crop of mediocre quality, and the quantity was less than half of that of 1901.

1903: One of my partners says bad things always happen in threes. The vintage of 1903 supports this theory. Another hard frost damaged the crop, although this time it came on April 18 and 19, which limited the destruction somewhat. There was much damage due to hail and pests, and heavy rains again led to rot. Again, quality was mediocre.

1904: After three years of poor weather, 1904 brought a welcome change. Conditions were described as "perfect" by all, with just enough rain and plenty of sun. There was very large crop for the period, but the ideal weather conditions led to top-quality vintage wines. All reviewers gave this vintage top marks.

1905: This was a year of difficult weather conditions. A number of frosts occurred in May, although none was major. June and July featured thunderstorms and hail, leading to mildew and rot. Quantity was similar to 1903. Broadbent describes the quality as poor, while Simon gives it a five out of seven. Everyone else rates 1905 as mediocre.

1906: There was a good recovery after a difficult 1905. Frosts in May caused some damage, but it was not overly serious. There was a hot summer; even a bit of a drought in August. This year produced a smaller quantity than 1904, and quality was almost up to the standards of 1904.

1907: This champagne vintage was made famous by the discovery in 1998 of 3,000 bottles of 1907 Heidsieck Monopole at the bottom of the sea aboard a World War I shipwreck. Weather conditions in 1907 were challenging, leading to poor flowering. Heavy rainfall in the period leading up to the harvest led to rot and other diseases on the vines, reducing the crop. Ratings on quality are mixed from mediocre to very good. Having sampled four bottles of the Heidsieck Monopole from the shipwreck, I can add that I found the quality to be very good.

The vines during the early spring (photograph by John Hodder/Collection CIVC).

1908: The year started out well, with only mild frosts in May. However, rains started in June and continued throughout the summer. Mildew, pests, and rot decimated the crop, leading to a very small harvest. Quality was generally rated as mediocre, although both Broadbent and Stevenson called it a disaster.

1909: This year was a slight improvement over 1908. A very cold winter was followed by a cold spring, and frosts continued into May. Insects further damaged the crop over the summer. Rain during the harvest affected quality, which was generally considered to be mediocre.

1910: Ah, for the good old days of mediocrity! Frost in April didn't do much damage, but the good news ends there. Thunderstorms and hail occurred throughout the year, and mildew was a huge problem. All of this led to one of the smallest harvests on record. In terms of quality, ratings range from "zero" to "without a doubt the worst year of the century." It doesn't get much worse than this.

1911: Ratings went from "zero" in 1910 to "excellent" in 1911. In many ways the weather was perfect, although a lack of rainfall reduced the size of the crop. There were virtually no insect or disease problems. The major problem was one of quantity—vines damaged by the mildew of 1910 were not very productive in 1911. The net result was a very small crop of extremely high quality, the best in the century until that date.

1912: This year was not a memorable vintage. Early May frosts didn't do much damage, but mildew in July had a significant impact. A dramatic drop in temperature just before the harvest stopped the maturation of the grapes prematurely, reducing the quality. Overall there was an average-size crop of mediocre grapes.

1913: This was another challenging year. Major frosts in April reduced the crop by up to 50 percent. This was followed by hailstorms that inflicted further damage. Mildew arrived in July, and, like in 1912, cold nights during early September limited maturation. Rain during the harvest further clouded the picture. The net result was a very small crop but one of pretty good quality. All sources other than Broadbent rated the quality as good, and Simon gave this vintage a six out of seven.

1914: This year was especially significant because it marked the beginning of World War I. Weather conditions were generally good. A mildew attack in early July caused some damage and limited the size of the crop. Excellent September weather led to a pleasant harvest, although war-related shortages of manpower and the fear of a renewed German advance made for less-than-ideal work conditions. In the end, the quantity was small, although it was much better than 1913, and the quality was rated excellent. I've tasted a bottle of Pol Roger 1914 with friends and although it had lost its bubbles, we found the quality to be excellent.

1915: As the war dragged on, manpower shortages in the vines led to problems, especially during the summer when insects arrived. Fortunately, weather conditions were good, and the harvest was able to be widely spread out to accommodate the labor shortage. Overall quantity and quality were good to very good.

1916: After two decent war vintages, 1916 was a disappointment. Variable weather conditions prevailed, and there were strong attacks of mildew and insects throughout the summer. Add the continuing labor shortage, and the result was a very small crop of mediocre grapes in poor condition. Quality was generally rated as mediocre to poor, although Simon was a bit more generous in his appraisal.

1917: This was an intense year for the war effort, and the Champagne region was a major battlefield. As one can imagine, there was significant damage to the vines as a result. In addition, a strong attack of mildew in July reduced the crop. Despite all these problems and an increasing shortage of labor, the harvest was of average quantity and above-average quality.

1918: Champagne was still a war zone in 1918. This led to a severe lack of attention in the vineyards because as those few available to work the vines had to contend with the risk of bodily harm due to war action. The weather was unremarkable other than some major frosts in the spring. Overall there was a small harvest of average quality.

1919: With the Great War finally over, the vignerons were able to return to their craft. Snow and frost in April caused some damage, as did the scorching temperatures in August. The weather conditions during the harvest were ideal, and the result was a fairly good size harvest of very good quality. Wines were described as refined.

1920: Things did not look good for the 1920 vintage. After a mild winter and spring came a wet summer capped by a cold August. Mildew and other diseases appeared in the beginning of July, followed by major hailstorms in the Vallée de la Marne. The vintage was saved by a superb September that resulted in a surprisingly large crop of good to very good quality. In fact Simon rated this vintage a seven out of seven.

1921: This was a classic vintage, one of the greatest of the century in terms of quality. Quantity, however, was another story. A powerful mid–April frost destroyed up to 80 percent of the crop. This was immediately followed by unseasonably hot weather. Great weather the rest of the year and a hot summer resulted in great quality from this small harvest. Because this is the birth year of René Collard, I've tasted several bottles of 1921, and they were universally outstanding, full of flavor and still bubbling. One of the bottles, a 1921 Moet, looked like it had been out of the producer's cellars for many years, which is usually a danger sign for champagne, but it was still excellent.

1922: After two years of excellent quality, 1922 was a disappointment. However, if measured by quantity, 1922 was indeed a classic vintage. There were no spring frosts, and a mediocre summer had just enough sunshine to avoid major disease problems. The rot finally appeared in September, and although it had a strong negative effect on quality, it had little effect on quantity. The average quantity of grapes per hectare was 12,400 kilos— large even by today's standards and 61 percent more than the record harvest of 1904. In fact, the exceptional size of the harvest led to shortages in manpower, harvesting equipment, and barrels. Quality was rated as average to mediocre.

1923: A series of frosts, beginning in April and lasting until mid–May, destroyed almost half of the crop. Problems with insects and fungus further damaged the crop during the summer months. The result was a small harvest of excellent quality and not a classic, but a quality vintage.

1924: This was another challenging year. Spring hailstorms were followed by mildew and almost every other known vine disease in the region. Continued rain slowed maturity and led to a slow, late harvest. Given all of the problems, the quantity of 6,400 kilos per hectare was a pleasant surprise.

Opinion was somewhat split on the quality of this vintage; opinions range from poor to acceptable.

1925: This vintage was a bit of a replay of 1924. Spring hailstorms caused a great deal of damage, especially in the Montagne de Reims and the Côte des Blancs. A cool summer included insect problems, mildew, and rot. The harvest was spread out over a month, and quality was similar to 1924, but quantity was down 40 percent.

1926: This looked like another case of bad years coming in threes. Insects, disease, and hail all served to reduce the crop well below the level of 1925. However, a superb September led to a late increase in sugar levels, resulting in a small but very good harvest. Opinions ranged a bit, with Simon the most enthusiastic and Broadbent the least, but there is a clear consensus that this was a fine vintage.

1927: By all standards, 1927 was a poor year. Rot began in July and was followed by insects. September saw intense rain, leading to a new attack of disease that destroyed much of the crop. The average quantity of grapes per hectare was only 1,700 kilos, and the quality was universally rated poor. This was a year to forget.

1928: This was an outstanding vintage in all of the major wine regions of France. The winter was very cold and was followed by a wet spring. Some May frosts and hailstorms served to reduce the crop, but not severely. A warm, sunny summer helped the grapes mature, and the perfect weather continued through the harvest. There were virtually no disease problems in 1928, which helped to make up for the frost and hail. All this produced a good-sized crop of outstanding grapes. The 1928 vintage was universally lauded and is considered one of the best of the century. I've tasted three different 1928 champagnes; all were quite good although, in my opinion, they were not up to the level of those of 1921.

1929: This was another great wine vintage in many areas. In Champagne, the weather was cooperative, although there were hail and windstorms in the summer. The harvest was conducted in rain, leading to rot at the end. The quantity of the harvest was almost 11,000 kilos per hectare, second only to 1922 in the first 70 years of the century. The quality was universally judged to be excellent but was overshadowed a bit by the 1928 harvest.

1930: As the world's economies headed into depression, times were difficult for the champagne economy and the weather wasn't any help. Frosts in late April and early May destroyed about half the potential crop. It rained almost continuously from the end of June until the harvest, and the vines

Opposite: The vines of Champagne in the summer (photograph by John Hodder/ Collection CIVC).

suffered from a variety of diseases. There were also hailstorms and a brief period of high heat, which is not good when the vines are wet. The harvest was average in quantity, and quality was rated mediocre to poor.

1931: This vintage was much like its predecessor. Lots of rain and a full deck of vine diseases set the tone again. Late September brought better weather, leading to a somewhat larger harvest than 1930. The consensus is that quality may have been marginally better than 1930, but not much.

1932: This year provided further proof of the "bad things come in threes" rule. After a May frost reduced the potential crop by more than 50 percent, rain brought mildew and other diseases. The harvest was similar in size to 1931, and quality was on a par with the preceding two years, which is to say not very good.

1933: The three-year string of mediocre quality ended in 1933. Like the previous three years, however, a spring frost reduced the potential crop, although this time the damage wasn't as severe as in some years. The bad weather continued during flowering, leading to a condition known as millerandage, where the grape clusters are not full and some grapes never fully mature. This reduces the size of the crop. The weather improved during the summer, and September was excellent. This helped deliver a crop of very good quality, although it was a bit on the small side.

1934: The 1930s were generally a bleak era in all respects, including the quality of wine. The vintage of 1934, however, was an exception. No major frosts or hailstorms developed, and the weather was good through the harvest. The crop was large (10,500 kilos per hectare), and the consensus was that the quality was quite good. Broadbent rated 1934 four stars out of five, and Simon gave it a seven out of seven.

1935: I guess good things also happen in threes sometimes, because 1935 qualifies as a good, but not exceptional, vintage. Weather was less than ideal but acceptable. Rain brought on mildew, but the damage was not major. The harvest was large, and the quality was good to very good. Because the two previous years were better, this vintage is often overlooked.

1936: The three rule held true, as 1936 was a disappointing vintage. A deep freeze on April 13 destroyed much of the potential crop, and hail soon followed. Because of a rainy summer, mildew was a major problem. The crop was relatively small (3,400 kilos per hectare), and the quality was no better than mediocre. This was not a year to remember.

1937: This vintage generally vies with 1934 for the title of "vintage of the decade." However, 1937 was certainly more challenging than 1934. Both rot and insects were a problem due to rain, but the end result was a relatively small crop of surprising quality. I've tried only one bottle and it was disappointing, but I suspect that was due to poor conservation.

The vines in autumn (photograph by Valérie Dubois/Collection CIVC).

1938: There is a wide divergence of opinion regarding the quality of the 1938 vintage. I should start by saying that it is fairly rare, because by the time it was ready to be released France had lost the war against Germany and was occupied by the Nazis. In general, 1938 started out with great promise; there were good weather and no major problems. However, September rains led to diluted grapes and rot, which greatly reduced the quality. A relatively large harvest, it is generally considered an average year in terms of quality, although Stevenson rates it quite high.

1939: This was a transition year as France mobilized for World War II. The weather started out well, but conditions turned difficult after midsummer. Rot was a major problem between late summer and the harvest, which was large for that era (7,400 kilos per hectare). Stevenson gives this vintage high marks, but everyone else considers this an average or below-average year.

1940: World War II began, and France quickly fell. The conditions led to severe manpower shortages, and mildew ravaged the vines. The net result was an extremely small harvest of forgettable quality.

1941: Champagne was under German occupation. The weather was fairly dry, which helped prevent diseases, which would have been catastrophic due to manpower shortages. The harvest was of average size and quality.

1942: Early May frosts reduced the potential crop, especially in the Vallée de la Marne. Mildew was a major problem throughout the summer. The end result was a harvest of slightly higher quantity and quality than the previous year, but nothing exceptional.

1943: This was by far the best of the wartime vintages in Champagne. In fact, the champagnes of 1943 may be the best wines produced in France during the war years. The crop was limited due to low temperatures during flowering, which led to millerandage. Weather was ideal for the mid–September harvest, and the crop of 5,000 kilos per hectare was the largest since 1939. Although 1943 was by no means a great year, quality was considered very good. This was René Collard's first vintage, and I have tasted it on a number of occasions. Of course, the wine was exceptional, but everything produced by René Collard is exceptional.

1944: The 1944 vintage was more typical of the war years. Roughly half the potential crop was destroyed by a deep frost in early May, and the vines suffered from various diseases in the summer. Heavy rain during the harvest period led to further disease, and the constant soaking diluted the grapes (increasing the quantity of the juice but decreasing its quality). The harvest was of average quantity and quality for this difficult period.

1945: The Nazis and their Vichy collaborators were defeated and the Allies liberated France. As perhaps a sign from the heavens, the wartime run of mediocrity ended, and the 1945 vintage became perhaps the vintage of the century in most French wine regions. In Champagne, severe April frosts greatly reduced the potential crop, especially in the Montagne de Reims. The same district experienced problems with disease during the summer months. Overall the weather was excellent, leading to an average-size harvest of outstanding quality. I have tasted this vintage on three occasions (René Collard, Salon, and Pol Roger), and each bottle was extremely memorable.

1946: Rain and cool weather in the spring led to intense millerandage, which reduced the crop. Conditions improved in the summer and fall, and the grapes were in good condition when they were harvested. The quantity was below average, and the quality was rated average. My own experience is limited to tasting the excellent Bouzy rouge produced by Champagne André Clouet.

1947: This was another classic vintage. A beautiful, sunny summer led to great maturation and an absence of disease. However, the atypical lack of rain reduced the crop. The harvest was quite early, beginning on September 5 in perfect conditions. Quality was universally rated as outstanding, and I concur.

1948: This was a good but not outstanding vintage. Hailstorms in May,

July, and August damaged the crop. Cool wet weather in July followed by alternating heat waves and thunderstorms led to many difficulties. A magnificent September helped avert disaster and produced a crop of slightly better than average quantity and quality.

1949: Cold weather during flowering produced severe millerandage, which reduced the crop. The summer was generally excellent — warm and dry — although scattered hailstorms caused some damage. The crop was of average quantity but excellent quality. Although the decade started out as a horrible time in every aspect, it ended by producing three classic vintages: 1945, 1947, and 1949.

1950: April frosts and May hail caused great anxiety in the vineyards. Conditions improved somewhat, but a rain-soaked September ruined any hopes of a good vintage. The crop was the largest since 1939 (6,800 kilos per hectare), but rot on the grapes was widespread and quality was rated as mediocre at best.

1951: The 1951 vintage was forgettable in all regards. A major freeze on April 30 reduced the potential crop by more than two-thirds, and things didn't get much better. A rainy summer led to disease and slow maturation of the grapes. A late harvest produced a small crop of mediocre to poor quality.

1952: The 1952 vintage was a mixed one in France. Perhaps the best success was achieved in Champagne. Good spring weather was followed by a stormy summer, but the damage was limited. The harvest was about average for the period in size, but the quality was rated very good to excellent. I have tried two different cuvées from this vintage, and both exceeded my expectations.

1953: This renowned vintage got off to a shaky start, as May frost and a cold period during flowering reduced the crop. However, the weather during the summer was sunny and dry, leading to full maturation of the grapes. Mid-September rain during the harvest served to soften the overly concentrated juice, producing an average crop of excellent quality. I've had champagne from 1953 on a number of occasions and from a number of producers, and it has proved to be a long-lived, excellent vintage.

1954: The run of two top-quality vintages did not extend to 1954. Insect damage occurred throughout the summer, and disease occurred in August. An extremely wet September made things worse, leading to a harvest of slightly above average quantity and below-average quality.

1955: A cold wet spring was followed by a warm and sunny summer. The excellent weather continued throughout September, allowing harvesting to be postponed until the beginning of October. The volume of 8,500 kilos per hectare was the greatest since 1935 in Champagne. The quality was

The vines in the dead of winter (photograph by Visuel Impact/Collection CIVC).

generally rated very good to excellent. I have tried champagnes from 1955 on many occasions, and I consider this vintage to be of classic quality.

1956: A frequent topic of conversation in Champagne is one's birth year and the quality of wine from that year. I missed the 1955 vintage by 13 days and thus became a product of 1956. The 1956 vintage was a total disaster in most parts of France, especially Bordeaux, where a month-long frost in February not only ruined the crop but also destroyed a large portion of the vineyards. Champagne also had severe weather, but the vines were more acclimated to the cold so the damage was not as severe. Spring was cold and wet, and the summer wasn't much better. A sunny September helped, but in the end the harvest was slightly below average in both quantity and quality. I have never tried a champagne from my birth year, although I've had many other wines from this vintage.

1957: Although Champagne suffered less from the cold weather in 1956 than most other regions, 1957 was a different story. Budding started early, and major frosts in April and May wiped out much of the potential crop. The summer gave some promise for the quality of the grapes, but rainstorms in September ruined these hopes. The crop was the smallest since 1940, and the quality was mediocre.

The year 1957 also marked the beginning of a four-year period during which grapes from part of the Vallée de la Marne were negatively influenced by pollution from a factory producing copper wire. The juice had a strange, bitter taste. After four years of vehement protests from vignerons, the factory was forced to move.

1958: This year provided further credence to the "bad things come in threes" theory. Although the year started off well with no major spring frosts, rain and hail dominated the period between June and August. The vines endured a succession of diseases and insect infestations. September was sunny, which prevented a complete disaster. Still, the harvest produced an average-size crop of below-average quality grapes.

1959: The string of three bad years was broken with a vengeance in 1959. Weather conditions were generally excellent, although there was a bit of millerandage. The late spring and summer were hot and dry, and the good weather lasted through the harvest. Quantity was above average (7,000 kilos per hectare), and quality was excellent. The only exception occurred in part of the Vallée de la Marne, where the grapes from this great vintage were ruined by the industrial pollution discussed earlier. I've tasted a number of champagnes from the 1959 vintage and certainly concur with the consensus that this was a great year.

1960: The new decade started out quite cold, with severe frost in January. A relatively cool, wet early spring led to a certain amount of millerandage. The summer, particularly July, was cold and rainy, leading to fairly widespread rot in certain areas. The harvest took place in mid–September, and the wet weather led to a crop of heavy, diluted grapes. The average yield was 10,100 kilos per hectare, the fourth highest in the century until that time. The quality was considered average.

1961: Storms in April and a cold May gave way to an excellent summer — warm and sunny with just the right amount of rain to refresh the vines. The good weather continued through the harvest, and the grapes arrived at the presses in excellent condition. The quantity was 7,800 kilos per hectare. Our experts rated the 1961 vintage excellent but not up to classic standards. I have had many champagnes from the 1961 vintage from many producers, and I must disagree. I believe this was a classic vintage, the best since 1945 in Champagne. Perhaps the discrepancy is due to the fact that the 1961 wines were high in acid and needed longer to mature.

1962: This was a rather strange year. The flowering stretched over a long period, and there was a great deal of millerandage, much more than in the previous three years. The summer was relatively dry, but a lack of sunshine led to a slow maturation. The sun finally arrived in September, and the harvest took place in early October. The quantity was 6,300 kilos per hectare, somewhat below average for the period. The quality was rated quite high; in fact, Michael Broadbent rated the 1962 vintage higher than

Champagne after a snowfall (photograph by Visuel Impact/Collection CIVC).

1961. I have had several champagnes from 1962, and although they were good they were in no way on the same level as 1961. Again, this may be a question of the speed at which the wine aged, with the 1961 champagnes still excellent, and the 1962s well past their peak.

1963: The 1963 vintage was a disappointing one throughout France, and Champagne was no exception. Despite a cool spring, there was little damage to the crop. June was warm, but August and September were cool and sunless. The harvest again took place in early October, yielding a large (9,100 kilos per hectare) crop of mediocre quality.

1964: Of all the champagnes that I've tasted, nothing quite measures up to those from the 1964 vintage. After a cold winter, the weather turned warm and dry throughout most of the spring and summer until late August, when showers arrived. September was a bit of a mixture — a heavy period of showers followed by sunshine. The harvest took place in mid–September, and the yield was identical to that of 1963, in part because the late rain swelled the grapes. The quality was rated excellent; in my opinion this is an understatement. The 1964 vintage may have been the greatest of the century for champagne.

1965: The 1964 vintage was a hard act to follow, and 1965 didn't even come close. A slow flowering period led to widespread millerandage, especially among the chardonnay grapes. The summer brought frequent rain and hailstorms, damaging certain crus and leading to rot. September brought better weather and prevented a total disaster, but the net result was an average yield of mediocre quality.

1966: Major winter frosts did some damage to the crop. A hot spell in the late spring led to early flowering, and the crop was then limited by a cold spell and a variety of diseases. August hail destroyed almost 200 hectares of production. September weather was excellent, however, leading to a vintage of average quantity and very good to excellent quality. I've tasted only a limited number of champagnes from 1966, and only the blanc de blancs were truly memorable (chardonnay tends to age more slowly than the other champagne grapes).

1967: One of the interesting facts about Champagne De Meric is that the majority of the partners were born in poor vintage years, including 1944, 1956, 1960, 1967, and 1968. Perhaps we are driven to erase this stigma by creating top-quality champagne. Anyway, 1967 started out well, but April/May frosts limited the crop. A good summer featuring a hot dry August gave promise, but a rainy September doomed this vintage to mediocrity. The yield was 8,500 kilos per hectare, which was above average, but the quality was only average at best.

1968: The 1968 vintage was a poor one throughout France. In Champagne, three frosts in May limited the crop by destroying the grapes in 2,000 hectares of vines. A slow flowering led to millerandage, and early summer rain and hailstorms were followed by rot in August. A late harvest produced an average-size crop of below-average to poor quality. Finding a vintage champagne from 1968 is quite difficult, and I've never tasted one.

1969: At this point we enter the period where I have more personal experience with the various vintages. Appropriately, the 1969 vintage is one about which my opinion differs widely from that of many experts. A rainy spring and rainy, hail-filled early summer gave way to a sunny, hot late summer and early fall. An early October harvest brought a below-average (6,100 kilos per hectare) crop of extremely ripe grapes. The quality was generally rated very good, but these wines were high in acidity and they didn't really reach their peak until the 1990s. I've tasted a number of different champagnes from this vintage and found them full bodied, flavorful, and generally excellent. I rank 1969 above 1962 or 1966 in Champagne.

1970: The year started out very poorly, as a cold spring led to late flowering. June was wet and cool, but the summer was much better. The harvest took place in late September and yielded a record crop of 13,800 kilos per hectare. Quality was widely praised at the time, but the wines didn't hold up over time. I've tasted 1970 champagnes from many producers and found them good but not excellent.

1971: To balance the bounty of 1970, 1971 was a very challenging vintage. A severe frost in late April destroyed part of the crop, and a major hailstorm in late May added to the toll. July brought ideal weather, but early August hailstorms brought great devastation. With a significant part of the crop destroyed, the harvest began on September 18 and the yield of 5,100 kilos per hectare paled in comparison to 1970. However, the quality of the grapes was rated quite high. Although champagnes from the 1971 vintage are a bit difficult to find, they are worth the effort. I prefer these to the wines from 1970.

1972: After three good years, it was inevitable that the string would end, and this was indeed the case in 1972. After a good beginning, April hailstorms followed by frost caused widespread damage, especially in the Aube. Rain and hail dominated June, which was followed by a decent summer. A lack of sunshine led to a slow maturation, delaying the harvest until October 12. Unfortunately, a freeze on October 5 did a great deal of damage in the Côte des Blancs. The overall yield was 9,000 kilos per hectare, and the quality was generally considered to be below average.

1973: After a good start, isolated hailstorms in early May caused damage in selected villages. Late spring and early summer saw good weather conditions, despite the occasional thunderstorm. A short heat wave in August and an infestation of spiders influenced the crop somewhat, and a tornado in the vines on September 20 caused further damage in isolated areas. All in all, 1973 was a large vintage (11,750 kilos per hectare) with very low acidity. I've had some very good wines from this vintage and found them similar to those of 1970 — good, but not great.

1974: A mild winter led to a good early fruit set, but April frosts caused a great deal of localized damage to the crop. In addition, variable weather during flowering led to millerandage and coulure, a similar condition in which the sap of the vines is diverted from the grape clusters, resulting in undeveloped grapes on some clusters. June hailstorms caused severe localized damage, but a sunny, somewhat cool summer bode well. A period of rain in late September, however, led to disease. The crop was relatively large (9,250 kilos per hectare) and of average quality.

1975: A long, cold winter led to a late bud break, which is generally a good omen in Champagne due to the threat of frost until mid–May each year. There was a significant amount of millerandage following the late June flowering. July, August, and September were hot and sunny. The late September/early October harvest yielded 9,082 kilos per hectare, which was somewhat above average for the period. The vintage was rated very good to excellent. I would lean toward excellent. I have tasted a wide variety of wines from this vintage and have found them to be soft and elegant with a great deal of life left.

1976: This is a classic vintage. A dry winter and a lack of heavy storms or frost in the spring led to a good crop that was affected only by a bit of coulure at flowering. An extremely hot, dry summer led to an early ripening. The harvest began on September 1 and was a large one. The grapes were noted for very high sugar levels and low acidity. According to science, this would indicate that these wines would be of excellent quality but would only have a short lifespan. Nature

The important step of pruning the vines in winter (photograph by John Hodder/Collection CIVC).

doesn't always follow science, and this classic vintage is still excellent today. This is one of my favorite vintages. I have tasted champagne from many producers, including Champagne De Meric, and have many bottles in my cellar.

1977: Cold and wet weather gave way to spring frosts, which were especially destructive in the Côte des Blancs. An extremely wet July and August led to widespread mildew, rot, and other diseases. The weather improved at the end of August, and a sunny September improved conditions for an early October harvest. The quantity was average, which was a positive surprise given the poor climate conditions. The wines were generally mediocre, although I've found that this was a good vintage in some parts of the Côte des Blancs, probably because the yields were lower due to the frosts.

1978: Good spring weather led to high hopes for this vintage, but a late flowering (end of June/beginning of July) led to widespread millerandage and coulure. Disease further reduced the crop, and localized hail caused extensive damage. A late harvest yielded a very small crop — 3,678 kilos per hectare — a disaster for the vignerons. This vintage was generally rated fairly high, but I agree with Tom Stevenson's assessment that this really wasn't a quality vintage year.

1979: A long, cold winter led to a late start for the growing season. Frosts in early May led to some damage, but the loss was not excessive. A good summer led to mostly healthy grapes, although there was a widespread occurrence of chlorose, a disease resulting from a mineral imbalance. Some other diseases also were noted, but the late harvest resulted in a large crop of very good to excellent quality. I have had a number of wines from this vintage and would classify it on a par with 1975, although it was not up to the standard of 1976.

1980: After a promising beginning of the season, a long flowering period that took place in poor weather conditions led to coulure throughout the vineyards. Rain and cold weather persisted until mid–July. August and September were dry, giving the grapes a chance to mature. A late harvest yielded only 5,289 kilos per hectare, and quality was average. Not a great deal of vintage champagne was made from the 1980 harvest, and those that were made were ordinary in quality.

1981: Spring frosts wiped out nearly a quarter of the potential crop in 1981. This was followed by an unseasonably cold flowering period, leading to widespread coulure and millerandage. A wet June brought on disease. The grapes were generally quite small, and the yield was only 4,353 kilos per hectare, an especially unwelcome development after the small harvest of 1980. The quality was generally rated good to very good, an assessment with which I concur.

1982: This was a renowned vintage throughout France. A late bud break under excellent conditions brought hope of a much-needed large crop. The late spring and summer were warm and sunny, with enough rain to nourish the vines. Some mildew occurred, but the damage was minimal. Excellent weather prevailed, which led to good maturation of the grapes. The harvest was the largest to date (14,054 kilos per hectare). Because of the ideal climate conditions, the quality was also excellent. I especially recommend the blanc de blancs champagnes from this vintage.

1983: Poor early spring weather did little to limit the size of the crop in 1983. A warm, sunny late spring and summer led to a record-size harvest of healthy grapes. Quality was by no means equal to the level of 1982, but I have enjoyed numerous wines of this vintage from throughout Champagne. Although only a few top-quality producers sell older vintages, one occasionally can find a 1983 champagne as part of a special reserve, and these are well worth acquiring.

1984: A good start to the season was more than offset by spring frosts and poor weather during flowering, the latter of which led to widespread coulure. Weather conditions throughout the summer were generally good but cooler than usual, leading to a slow maturation. A late harvest resulted in an average crop. The 1984 vintage is generally considered to be of mediocre quality, but I have had a few very good bottles from this difficult year.

1985: Despite a poor start, 1985 turned out to be a classic vintage. Severe frosts in January and a cold winter served to limit the crop significantly, and certain sectors lost much of their potential harvest. This was followed by another frost in late April, although this one was much less severe. Beginning in July, however, the weather was ideal, and a late harvest yielded a small (6,827 kilos per hectare) crop of excellent quality. Although this vintage was highly acclaimed, I don't feel that it has really received its due. I've tasted the 1985 vintage from scores of producers, from grandes marques to small récoltant-manipulants (RMs) to cooperatives, and I have never found one that wasn't at least very good to excellent. I unconditionally recommend champagnes from this vintage.

1986: A very cold winter led to a late bud break in 1986. A very sunny, warm spring produced excellent flowering, and July was hot and dry. August was cold and rainy, and the rain reappeared during the period leading up to the harvest in early October. The yield was at a normal level for the last 20 years. This is not a very highly rated vintage, but I have had some excellent 1986 champagnes, especially those from the Montagne de Reims.

1987: This vintage was dominated by rain, and the first six months of the year also featured below-normal temperatures. The crop was not extensively damaged, however, primarily due to late flowering. However, disease was prevalent, especially rot, which reduced the quality of the grapes. The

Pinot meunier vines after pruning (photograph by John Hodder/Collection CIVC).

harvest, which began in late September in the Aube and the second week in October in the Marne, was wet and unpleasant. The yields were approximately the same level as those of 1986, but the quality was a step or two below. Still, I've tasted several good bottles from this vintage.

1988: The 1988 vintage was, in my opinion, very underrated. A mild, wet winter was followed by good spring weather, with the exception of a late May hailstorm that did quite a bit of damage in the Aube. The summer was quite variable, and the harvest began in mid–September amid predictions of heavy rain. This forecast proved inaccurate, however, and the crop was slightly below average in quantity and very good to excellent in quality. Some have written that the 1988 champagnes were of marginal vintage quality, but I have found this to be a very good vintage overall and an outstanding one for champagnes dominated by grapes from the Montagne de Reims. In fact, two of my favorite champagnes are the Maurice Vesselle 1988 and our Catherine de Medicis based on the 1988 harvest.

1989: The year 1989 was a strange one for weather. A mild winter and early spring led to an early bud break. However, a major frost in late April did significant damage to the potential crop. May was sunny and warm, and June brought cold, rainy weather followed by a heat wave. All of this led to significant millerandage and coulure. June was followed by unusually hot, sunny, and dry weather in July and August, which led to an early harvest. Quantity was normal, and quality was excellent.

1990: The 1990 vintage was proclaimed by some to be the "vintage of the century." A wet mild winter again led to early bud break, and two April frosts caused damage throughout the region. Difficult weather during flowering caused some millerandage and coulure. July started out with rain, but the summer unfolded to be hot and sunny, although storms reoccurred at the end of August. All in all, the weather was very similar to 1989. The harvest took place in two stages because the frost damage necessitated a second harvest period to pick the grapes from the second growth of the vines. These grapes are only harvested in difficult years. The total yield was somewhat above average and the quality was excellent. Although I don't agree with the "vintage of the century" label, there is no doubt that 1990 was a classic vintage.

1991: For the third year in a row, a mild late winter/early spring gave way to April frosts—three different frosts in the case of 1991. As much as a third of the potential crop was destroyed by this severe weather. May was mild and June brought cold and rain, but things improved in July. August and the first three weeks of September were beautiful. Late September rains caused some problems and certainly had a negative impact on quality. The harvest took place in early October. Both the quantity and quality were average. After three vintages of excellent quality, the 1991 vintage tends to suffer by comparison. I must add, however, that I've tasted some very good 1991 champagnes from the Côte des Blancs and the Aube.

1992: The year 1992 was generally warm, with a mild winter and early spring. The warm trend continued, but the late spring and summer were also wet, leading to problems with disease and insects. September was dry and sunny, which helped a great deal. The harvest began in mid–September, and the results were slightly above average quantity and quality. Although by no means an outstanding year, vintage wines from 1992 are quite respectable.

1993: The year 1993 began with a mild, wet winter and an early flowering throughout the vines at the end of May. This was followed by a wet spring, leading to concerns over mildew. Fortunately, August was hot and dry. The harvest took place in mid–September. The yield was a bit below average, and quality was considered above average to good. However, I've found that wines from this vintage have aged quite well and feel that they are underrated.

1994: A mild winter was followed by a wet spring. Two mid–April frosts caused some damage and served to limit the potential crop. The late spring and early summer brought good weather, but after mid–August conditions deteriorated. The harvest began in mid–September under cool and wet conditions. The yield was somewhat below average (9,577 kilos per hectare). Quality was generally mediocre, although I've tasted some good offerings from the Vallée de la Marne.

1995: After a cold, wet winter, the weather became variable. Warm spells were followed by periods of cold, rainy weather. Mildew was a major problem; according to Dominique Fradet, 1995 had the worst occurrence of this disease since 1958. The harvest began in mid–September, and the quantity was about average for the period. This vintage enjoys a very strong reputation, and it certainly was a good one. Many good wines were produced in 1995. However, I must say that I feel that the vintage is overrated.

1996: A cool, dry winter was followed by a warm April, a cool but dry May, and a sunny June. Flowering was somewhat difficult, with widespread millerandage as a result. The summer was generally hot with brief periods of thunderstorms. The first part of September brought clouds and unseasonably cool nights. The harvest began in mid–September, and good weather returned for most of that period. The yield in 1996 was just a bit below average, and the quality was excellent. This vintage has received wide acclaim. I feel that many of the cuvées were released too early, however, before they had reached their full maturity.

1997: This was a memorable year for me because it was my first harvest

A good view of the harvest activity (photograph by John Hodder/Collection CIVC).

as part of the champagne business. A very cold period in early January was followed by a mild period from late January until March. Spring brought a series of frosts; none was catastrophic but they were significant in total. A cool and rainy June was followed by a hot and stormy summer. The harvest began in early September. The yield was below average, but the quality was very good.

1998: A mild winter was followed by April frosts, but the damage was not severe. May was warmer than usual and was followed by a variable June. July was unseasonably cool and rainy. August, however, was extremely hot and dry with virtually no rain. September brought heavy rains, making an unpleasant harvest beginning in the middle of that month. Overall, 1998 yielded a large crop of better than average quality.

1999: This was another significant year for me because we launched our new strategy in earnest in 1999. A relatively mild winter was followed by scattered hailstorms that limited the crop. The summer was variable with periods of warm weather and occasional rainstorms. Mildew was a problem, but overall the grapes arrived at the press in mid–September in good condition. In my opinion, 1999 was the best vintage since 1996, especially in Ay and the surrounding area. I think these wines will age well.

2000: The old millennium ended on a negative note, as a huge storm on December 26, 1999, brought winds of well over 100 miles per hour, wreaking massive destruction throughout France. The new millennium also had its share of challenges with a cold spring and a late, rainy summer. Early July brought stormy weather highlighted by a very destructive hailstorm on July 2. Much of the crop in parts of the Valée de la Marne and the Montagne de Reims was destroyed, including the area around Ay. The cool rainy summer continued, and I was afraid we were in for a very poor quality harvest. Suddenly, August turned to September, and warm sunny weather appeared. After three perfect weeks, the grapes matured quickly and the harvest began in mid to late September. Quantity was large because some areas not affected by the hail had far more grapes than the appellation limit allowed them to harvest. Although the overall quality of the 2000 vintage was probably above average to good, the quality in the areas with the most hail damage was excellent because the smaller crop yielded more concentrated juice.

2001: The 2001 vintage started off with great promise. A mild winter and wet spring were followed by a superb, sunny May. The good weather continued through June, and a variable July did little to dampen hopes of an excellent vintage. Conditions began to deteriorate in August, however, and September was a disaster — cold and rainy up to and through the harvest. The result was a huge crop of mediocre-quality grapes with very low sugar levels, certainly the poorest quality in many years. We made the decision to sell our vin clair from the 2001 harvest rather than use it in our Grande Réserve Sous Bois.

2002: This will turn out to be the first classic vintage of my champagne career. A cold winter was followed by good weather conditions, especially during the late summer and early fall. Warm, sunny weather in September led to a mid–September harvest under ideal conditions. The grapes were in perfect health, and it was impossible to resist repeated tastings at the presses. The crop was of slightly below average size, but the quality was superb. In my opinion, 2002 will end up being the best vintage since 1985 or perhaps since 1976, which was in many ways a similar year.

2003: This was quite an atypical vintage. A mild winter led to early bud break. This was followed, however, by disastrous spring frosts that wiped out well over half of the potential crop. The summer brought record heat with almost no rain, and the grapes suffered from the drought. These exceptional conditions led to a late August start date for the harvest, the earliest in more than a century. The crop was the smallest in more than two decades. I've heard very mixed commentaries regarding the quality, but based on tasting our vin clair, I can state that this is the second best vintage during my tenure, trailing only 2002.

Table VII
Historical Champagne Harvest Data

Year	Average Kilos Per Hectare	Harvest Start Dates	Year	Average Kilos Per Hectare	Harvest Start Dates
1752	n/a	October 12	1892	n/a	September 25
1757	n/a	October 8	1893	n/a	August 28/ September 3
1762	n/a	September 15/29			
1782	n/a	October 25/ November 5	1894	n/a	October 1
			1895	n/a	September 23
1788	n/a	September 15	1896	n/a	September 28
1793	n/a	October 10	1897	n/a	September 26
1806	n/a	September 20	1898	n/a	October 11
1822	n/a	August 20	1899	n/a	September 26/ October 1
1858	n/a	September 22			
1859	n/a	September 21	1900	n/a	September 19/28
1860	n/a	October 10	1901	6,700	September 27
1862	n/a	September 20	1902	3,200	n/a
1863	n/a	October 3	1903	4,300	October 3
1865	n/a	August 28/ September 10	1904	7,700	n/a
			1905	4,300	September 20
1866	n/a	September 28	1906	4,500	September 18
1867	n/a	October 8	1907	3,200	September 30
1868	n/a	September 10	1908	1,400	Mid-September
1869	n/a	September 18	1909	3,100	n/a
1871	n/a	October 10	1910	115	n/a
1872	n/a	October 6	1911	1,600	September 10
1873	n/a	October 6	1912	3,400	n/a
1874	n/a	September 20	1913	1,400	n/a
1875	n/a	September 25	1914	2,200	September 28
1876	n/a	October 7	1915	3,600	September 10
1877	n/a	October 8	1916	700	n/a
1878	n/a	September 25/ October 1	1917	2,500	September 10
			1918	2,000	n/a
1879	n/a	October 15	1919	5,500	n/a
1880	n/a	October 1	1920	7,300	n/a
1881	n/a	September 27	1921	2,000	n/a
1882	n/a	October 8	1922	12,400	n/a
1883	n/a	October 3	1923	3,400	n/a
1884	n/a	September 20	1924	6,400	September 26
1885	n/a	September 25	1925	4,500	n/a
1886	n/a	October 4	1926	2,400	n/a
1887	n/a	October 3	1927	1,700	September 22
1888	n/a	October 8	1928	6,800	September 28
1889	n/a	September 25/28	1929	10,800	September 26
1890	n/a	October 5/10	1930	4,000	September 24
1891	n/a	October 14	1931	5,500	Early October

Year	Average Kilos Per Hectare	Harvest Start Dates	Year	Average Kilos Per Hectare	Harvest Start Dates
1932	5,100	October 4	1971	5,100	September 18
1933	4,400	September 22	1972	9,000	October 12/14
1934	10,500	September 12	1973	11,750	September 28
1935	9,500	End of September	1974	9,250	September 28
1936	3,400	October 1	1975	9,082	September 29/
1937	4,700	September 21			October 10
1938	8,400	September 28	1976	10,359	September 1
1939	7,400	October 4	1977	8,757	October 6
1940	1,100	n/a	1978	3,678	October 9
1941	4,000	n/a	1979	11,061	October 3/5/8
1942	4,200	n/a	1980	5,289	October 9
1943	5,000	September 15	1981	4,353	September 28
1944	4,200	September 27	1982	14,054	September 17/20
1945	4,400	September 8	1983	15,012	September 26
1946	3,600	End of September	1984	9,048	October 10
1947	4,100	September 5	1985	6,827	September 30
1948	5,200	September 20	1986	11,582	October 2
1949	4,500	September 19	1987	11,647	October 8
1950	6,800	September 11	1988	9,650	September 18/26
1951	2,900	October 1	1989	11,619	September 4/18
1952	5,500	September 8	1990	11,963	September 11/24
1953	5,400	September 15	1991	11,228	September 26/
1954	5,900	September 27			October 8
1955	8,500	Beginning of Oct	1992	11,844	September 17/23
1956	4,600	October 8	1993	10,379	September 8/23
1957	2,600	September 20	1994	9,577	September 15/25
1958	4,800	October 1	1995	10,986	September 18/
1959	7,000	September 10			October 2
1960	10,100	September 12	1996	10,356	September 16/
1961	7,800	September 20			October 1
1962	6,300	October 4	1997	9,402	September 12/25
1963	9,100	October 5	1998	12,926	September 10/26
1964	9,100	September 16	1999	12,989	September 15/23
1965	6,900	October 9	2000	12,577	September 11/25
1966	7,000	September 22	2001	10,990	September 22/
1967	8,500	September 28			October 2
1968	7,200	October 3	2002	11,967	September 12/26
1969	6,100	October 1	2003	8,251	August 18
1970	13,800	September 27			

Source: CIVC

11. Key Village Profiles

IN THIS CHAPTER, WE'LL PROFILE some of the key grape-producing villages in the Champagne region. I'll include all of the grand cru villages, most of the premier cru villages, and a few other villages that I feel merit special comment.

Grand Cru Villages

Ambonnay

This charming village is located in the eastern part of the Montagne de Reims vineyards. Ambonnay has a total of 335 hectares of vineyards; 80 percent are planted in pinot noir and 20 percent are planted in chardonnay. I've tried many Ambonnay-dominated champagnes, and I find them a bit softer and less expressive than those of neighboring grand cru Bouzy.

This charming village is a nice place to walk through, and there are some good small producers here. Stop by the Cave de Baccus, an interesting champagne shop. Affiliated with Champagne Soutiran-Pelletier, the store sells various champagnes and a great selection of champagne paraphernalia such as ice buckets, glasses, etc.

Avize

Avize is located in the heart of the Côte des Blancs. Its 455 hectares of vineyard are planted in 100 percent chardonnay. This is one of my favorite crus in Champagne, and some of my favorite producers are located in Avize.

In addition to a charming town center and many excellent producers, Avize houses the best known school specializing in champagne, where many of the best young producers have learned their trade. Technically a cooperative, the school produces and markets champagne under the Champagne Sanger label.

Ay

Home of Champagne De Meric, Ay is perhaps the most famous vineyard town in Champagne. Of its 350 hectares, 86 percent are planted in pinot noir, 10 percent in chardonnay, and 4 percent in pinot meunier. Technically there is not supposed to be pinot meunier in a grand cru, so these are primarily older vines that are grandfathered.

It goes without saying that I very much enjoy Ay-based champagnes, and there are many top-quality producers here. This charming village is well worth a visit if you're in the region. If you have the opportunity to be there the first weekend of July during an even-numbered year, you'll have the chance to attend the Fêtes Henri IV, a fun festival based around life in the Middle Ages.

Beaumont-sur-Vesle

Because things are so regulated and defined in Champagne, one often assumes that everything is logical and easily explained. A few of the rankings in the échelle des crus, however, are somewhat hard to understand. One such oddity is the ranking of Beaumont-sur-Vesle as a grand cru.

This is not a reflection of the quality of the terroir, although I must say that I have not been overly impressed with my limited tasting of champagnes based on this cru. Rather, I am puzzled as to why a village with only 28 hectares of vines (84 percent pinot noir, 13 percent chardonnay, and 3 percent pinot meunier) deserves such a distinction. In addition, there are no négociant-manipulants (NMs) based in this village, and I am aware of only one récoltant-manipulant (RM) here, although I understand there are three other vignerons who deliver to a cooperative.

I suspect the answer lies in history, and perhaps at one time Beaumont played a bigger part in the champagne world. Today it is merely a crossroads along a secondary highway.

Bouzy

Located just west of Ambonnay, Bouzy is another of my favorite crus. Of the 380 hectares of vines, 88 percent are planted in pinot noir, 11 percent

The town of Ay, home of Champagne De Meric (photograph by Huyghens Danrigal/Collection CIVC).

in chardonnay, and 1 percent in pinot meunier. In addition to champagne, Bouzy is known for the quality of its Bouzy Rouge still red wine.

I find the champagnes of Bouzy are especially distinctive, with a vineous, rustic character that I really enjoy. It has always been a goal of mine to have some Bouzy pinot noir to use in Champagne De Meric, and in 2003 we were finally able to achieve this goal.

Chouilly

Located just southeast of Epernay at the top of the Côtes des Blancs, Chouilly is best known for housing the mega-cooperative Nicolas Feuillatte. Of the 498 hectares of vines in Couilly, 98 percent are planted in chardonnay and the remaining 2 percent are planted in pinot noir. Interestingly enough, only the chardonnay is given grand cru status because the black grapes are rated at 98 percent on the échelle des crus. There are some good, independent small growers in Chouilly in addition to the cooperative members.

Champagne Nicolas Feuillatte hosts a wine fair each year that is worth attending.

Cramant

Located just north of Avize, many consider Cramant the most outstanding cru of the Côtes des Blancs. All 345 hectares of vines in Cramant are planted in chardonnay.

A key landmark in Cramant is a huge statue of a champagne bottle that welcomes visitors to the community. There are a number of high-quality small producers in Cramant, but this village is best known for supplying the grapes for the famous cuvée Mumm de Cramant.

Louvois

This attractive village lies at the crossroads of two spokes of the Route Touristique du Champagne, a way to help visitors who wish to visit the key wine villages in the region negotiate the sometimes confusing series of winding roads through the vineyards. Louvois is also relatively small, with only 40 hectares of vines, 84 percent of which are planted in pinot noir and 16 percent of which are planted in chardonnay.

Unlike Beaumont-sur-Vesle, there are a number of producers in Louvois, and I have been generally impressed with the quality of their champagnes. There is also an impressive chateau owned by Champagne Laurent-Perrier.

Mailly-Champagne

Located in the heart of the Montagne de Reims, Mailly-Champagne is the first stop on one of the most picturesque driving routes in the Champagne region. Of the 284 hectares planted, 89 percent are in pinot noir, 7 percent in chardonnay, and 4 percent in pinot meunier.

Although Mailly is only two villages from where I lived in the region, I actually haven't tasted too many different types of champagne from this village. This is primarily because the majority of the vignerons in this village are members of the Mailly Grand Cru Cooperative, one of the oldest (founded in 1929) and best cooperatives in Champagne. This cooperative only uses grapes from Mailly-Champagne, and the total production is marketed under the Mailly Grand Cru label.

Mailly-Champagne is also known for its annual food and wine fair, which takes place each year in late May.

Le Mesnil-sur-Oger

Located in the southern part of the Côte des Blancs, Le Mesnil is both a picturesque and interesting village. There are a total of 432 hectares of vines, all of which are planted in chardonnay.

In addition to many fine producers discussed elsewhere in this book, Le Mesnil-sur-Oger has a very good restaurant (Restaurant Le Mesnil), and Champagne Bernard Launois has an outstanding museum of antique wine and vineyard tools. I also recommend his champagne, which I enjoy very much.

Oger

Located between Avize and Le Mesnil-sur-Oger, Oger is a small, charming village with a number of small producers. All of the 350 hectares of vines are planted in chardonnay.

The main tourist attraction in Oger is a small museum dedicated to weddings, created by one of the local vignerons. However, the most significant piece of land is a small walled vineyard owned by Champagne Claude Cazals (located in Le Mesnil-sur-Oger), which provides the grapes for their cuvée prestige.

Oiry

This village is located a bit east of Cramant. Oiry's 87 hectares of vines are, typical of the Côte des Blancs, all planted in chardonnay.

Although this village produces quality grapes, it doesn't really have a "vineyard" feel to it, so if you are visiting the Côte des Blancs you would be well advised to focus your time on villages such as Avize, Cramant, Oger, Le Mesnil, and Vertus.

Puisieulx

Located near Beaumont-sur-Vesle, this is another town with very few vines. The total planted surface is only 18 hectares, 60 percent of which are planted in pinot noir, 31 percent in chardonnay, and 9 percent in pinot meunier.

As was the case with Beaumont-sur-Vesle, this village doesn't seem significant enough to merit grand cru status.

Sillery

Sillery has been a famous vineyard village for centuries. In fact, in the era when Champagne was known for its still red wine, Sillery was second only to Ay in reknown in the region.

A total of 92 hectares of vineyards exist in Sillery, 47 percent of which are planted in chardonnay, 44 percent in pinot noir, and 9 percent in pinot meunier. This is a charming and historic village, although only a few producers are located here.

Tours-sur-Marne

The village of Tours-sur-Marne is best known as the home of Champagne Laurent-Perrier. There are 53 hectares of vines, 60 percent of which are planted in pinot noir and 40 percent in chardonnay.

Like Chouilly, Tours-sur-Marne has only a partial grand cru status. In this case, the black grapes are rated grand cru and the chardonnay is rated 90 percent on the échelle des cru, the minimum rating to qualify as a premier cru.

Verzenay

This charming village is located just next to Mailly-Champagne in the Montagne de Reims. Verzenay has 417 hectares of vines, 85 percent of which are planted in pinot noir, 14 percent in chardonnay, and 1 percent in pinot meunier.

There are a number of good, small producers in Verzenay. However, the town is probably best known for the Moulin de Verzenay, an impressive windmill that provides a great view of the Montagne de Reims.

Verzy

Our 17th and final grand cru is the village of Verzy, located just south of Verzenay. Of Verzy's 405 hectares, 80 percent are planted in pinot noir and the remaining 20 percent are planted in chardonnay.

In addition to a number of interesting small producers, Verzy is known for the famous Faux de Verzy, a unique forest featuring a type of beach tree that twists itself to resemble something from an Arthurian legend. These trees are rare and protected and are well worth a visit.

Premier Cru Villages

Bergères-les-Vertus

Located in the southern tip of the Côte des Blancs, Bergères-les-Vertus has 218 hectares of vines, 96 percent of which are planted in chardonnay, with the remaining 4 percent planted in pinot noir. This village is best known for its brocante, which is something between an antique fair and a flea market. This brocante is held on Mont-Aimé, a beautiful park with a great view of the region.

A view of the countryside in Champagne (photograph by Frédéric Hadengue/ Collection CIVC).

Champillon

Located about five miles north of Epernay, Champillon is a charming town with beautiful views of the vines. Of the 146 hectares of vines, 47 percent are planted in pinot meunier, 45 percent in pinot noir, and 8 percent in chardonnay.

Champillon is best known as the home of the Royal Champagne hotel and restaurant. They also have a very interesting annual wine fair, featuring small producers from throughout France.

Cormontreuil

Sometimes appearances can be deceiving. Cormontreuil is primarily an industrial zone filled with chain stores and other high-volume retailers. However, there are 462 hectares of vines attached to this village, 45 percent of which are planted in pinot noir, 39 percent in pinot meunier, and 16 percent in chardonnay.

Cormontreuil is only about a mile from Reims. However, unless you run out of something during your trip, it really isn't a great place to visit.

Chigny-les-Roses

This is my old hometown, where I owned a house for seven years. Located in the Montagne de Reims, Chigny is dominated by champagne growers, the majority of whom are récoltant-cooperatives (RCs).

Chigny-les-Roses has a total of 438 hectares of vines, of which 62 percent are pinot meunier, 25 percent pinot noir, and 13 percent chardonnay. The village used to have a champagne fair called the Fete de Gout (tasting festival), but it was discontinued.

Cuis

This charming village is located just north of Cramant in the Côte des Blancs. As one would expect, chardonnay is the dominant grape variety and 90 percent of the 169 hectares of vines are planted with this white grape. The remaining 10 percent of the vines are planted in pinot meunier (9 percent) and pinot noir (1 percent).

Cumières

Located northwest of Epernay, Cumières is known as one of the leading villages for red coteau champenois. It is also known for normally being the most precocious of the champagne crus and, therefore, the first village to begin the harvest.

Cumières has 199 hectares of vines, of which 49 percent are planted in pinot noir, 35 percent in pinot meunier, and 16 percent in chardonnay. I've had a number of pleasant visits with producers in Cumières, and overall I've been impressed with the quality of their champagnes.

Dizy

This village is located just west of Ay and south of Champillon. Of the 322 hectares of vines, 34 percent are planted in chardonnay, 34 percent in pinot meunier, and 32 percent in pinot noir, almost a perfect balance of the three major grape varieties.

Driving through Dizy is worthwhile, and I highly recommend a visit to the cellars of Jacquesson & Fils.

Eceuil

Eceuil is located in the heart of the Petite Montagne de Reims. Of the 125 hectares of vines, 85 percent are planted in pinot noir, 10 percent in chardonnay, and 5 percent in pinot meunier.

Although rated at 90 percent on the échelle des crus, the minimum for a premier cru, Eceuil houses many fine producers, including two of my 20 favorites (Michel Maillart and Desbordes-Amiaud). This village is worth visiting.

Grauves

Grauves is located at the edge of the Côte des Blancs. Of the 184 hectares of vines, 84 percent are planted in chardonnay, 14 percent in pinot meunier, and 2 percent in pinot noir.

Grauves is another village with a split rating on the échelle des crus. The white grapes receive a rating of 95 percent, while the black grapes are rated 90 percent.

Hautvillers

This charming village is located on the hillside overlooking Epernay. The vineyards encompass 27 hectares, 53 percent of which are planted in pinot meunier, 34 percent in pinot noir, and 13 percent in chardonnay.

This is a very scenic village, and there are a number of quality producers. However, Hautvillers will always be best known as the home of Dom Pérignon. Today, Moët & Chandon maintains the Abbey of Hautvillers and the Dom Pérignon museum.

Jouy-les-Reims

This small village is located in the Petite Montagne de Reims, just down the road from Ecueil. Jouy-les-Reims has 94 hectares of vines. Official statistics list the distribution as 61 percent pinot meunier, 27 percent pinot noir, and 12 percent chardonnay, but Champagne L. Aubry also has vineyards with the ancient champagne grape varieties, as discussed on page 158.

Ludes

This attractive village is located between Chigny-les-Roses and Mailly-Champagne. There are a total of 315 hectares of vines, of which 50 percent are planted in pinot meunier, 30 percent in pinot noir, and 20 percent in chardonnay.

Like Chigny-les-Roses, the majority of the growers in Ludes are RCs and work with cooperative Nicolas Feuillatte. However, like Chigny, there are some good small producers in Ludes.

Mareuil-sur-Ay

This charming village is located just east of Ay. There are a total of

The village of Hautvillers, home of Dom Pérignon (photograph by Visuel Impact).

280 hectares of vines in Mareuil-sur-Ay, of which 82 percent are planted in pinot noir, 10 percent in chardonnay, and 8 percent in pinot meunier.

Mareuil-sur-Ay is probably best known for the Clos des Goisses, a famous walled vineyard owned by Champagne Philipponnat.

Montbré

The village of Montbré is located just northwest of Chigny-les-Roses. There are only 42 hectares of vines, 48 percent of which are planted in pinot noir, 42 percent in pinot meunier, and 10 percent in chardonnay.

This village is best known for housing an old fort. I've seen pictures of it in the local paper, and I tried hard to find it one afternoon without success.

Mutigny

This small village is located just northeast of Ay. Of the 85 hectares of vines, 65 percent are planted in pinot noir, 30 percent in pinot meunier, and 5 percent in chardonnay.

We work with some vignerons from Mutigny, and I've been pleased with the quality of the Mutigny grapes. Based on this experience, it would seem

The village of Mareuil-sur-Ay, home of some of the grapes that go into Champagne De Meric (photograph by Huyghens Danrigal/Collection CIVC).

that Mutigny's rating of 93 percent on the échelle des crus is probably too low.

Pierry

Pierry is located just south of Epernay. There are a total of 107 hectares of vines, of which 58 percent are planted in pinot meunier, 23 percent in chardonnay, and 19 percent in pinot noir.

The cooperative of Pierry, which produces Champagne Vincent d'Astrée, has a very good wine shop that offers both a selection of wines and various champagne-related accessories.

Rilly-la-Montagne

Rilly-la-Montagne is located just west of Chigny-les-Roses. Of the 312 hectares of vines, 44 percent are planted in pinot meunier, 35 percent in pinot noir, and 21 percent in chardonnay.

It is often the case in the Champagne region that many vignerons have vines in two or three neighboring villages. Such is the case in Rilly-la-Montagne, Chigny-les-Roses, and Ludes.

The village of Mutigny, a neighbor of Ay and the source of a portion of our pinot noir grapes (photograph by Huyghens Danrigal/Collection CIVC).

Taissy

Taissy is located approximately three miles southeast of Reims. Although it was once an important vineyard town, there are only 120 hectares of vines today, of which 45 percent are planted in pinot meunier, 32 percent in chardonnay, and 23 percent in pinot noir.

Taissy is an interesting town in that it is a cross between a country village and a suburb of Reims.

Tauxières-Mutry

Located between Mutigny and Louvois, Tauxières-Mutry is an interesting small village. There are a total of 237 hectares of vines, of which 78 percent are planted in pinot noir, 17 percent in chardonnay, and 5 percent in pinot meunier.

Tauxières-Mutry has one of the better small cooperatives in the region as well as an interesting antique shop.

Trépail

This interesting village is located to the west of Bouzy and Ambonnay. There are 270 hectares of vines, of which 88 percent are planted in chardonnay, 11 percent in pinot noir, and 1 percent in pinot meunier.

Trépail is unusual because, along with Villers-Marmery, it is an island of chardonnay in the Montagne de Reims, an area dominated by the pinot grapes. There are some very good small producers in Trépail.

Vertus

Vertus is the largest village in the Côte des Blancs. Of the 564 hectares of vines, 88 percent are planted in chardonnay, 11 percent in pinot noir, and 1 percent in pinot meunier.

I've always enjoyed visiting Vertus. There are some good producers, and there often seems to be something going on during the weekends.

Villers-Marmery

Villers-Marmery is located west of Ambonnay and just north of Trépail. Of the total of 220 hectares of vines, 98 percent are chardonnay and the remaining 2 percent are pinot noir.

Along with Trépail, Villers-Marmery forms a small chardonnay enclave in the Montagne de Reims. The chardonnay from these villages has different characteristics than that of the Côte des Blancs. I find it to be a bit more rustic, probably owing to the different soil.

Other Villages

Finally, there are a number of villages rated below 90 percent on the échelle des crus that merit special mention.

Boursault

Located six miles west of Epernay, Boursault is best known for the magnificent Chateau de Boursault. Unfortunately this castle, built for the widow Clicquot, is not open to the public. There is a Champagne Chateau Boursault made partly from grapes grown on the property.

There are a total of 230 hectares of vines in Boursault, of which 67 percent are planted in pinot meunier, 26 percent in pinot noir, and 7 percent in chardonnay. The vines in Boursault and some of its neighboring villages suffer somewhat from the northern exposure of the vineyards, which can be a negative in a cool climate such as that of the Champagne region.

Buxeuil

This is the first village from the Aube department that I am singling out. I enjoy visiting the Aube, and there are some excellent producers in that department, but overall I prefer the wines of the Marne and Aisne departments.

Buxeuil is an attractive village, and Champagne Moutard is definitely worth visiting. There are a total of 101 hectares of vines, of which 93 percent are pinot noir, 6 percent chardonnay, and 1 percent pinot meunier.

Chateau-Thierry

Chateau Thierry is best known as a battle site in World War I and the home of a cemetery for U.S. soldiers killed in that bloody conflict. There are only 34 hectares of vines, of which 65 percent are planted in pinot meunier, 28 percent in pinot noir, and 7 percent in chardonnay.

As the name implies, Chateau-Thierry also houses an ancient chateau as well as a museum dedicated to its most famous citizen, fable writer Jean de La Fontaine.

Chézy-sur-Marne

This picturesque village is located in the Aisne department, six miles south of Chateau-Thierry. There are 130 hectares of vines, of which 90 percent are planted in pinot meunier, 8 percent in pinot noir, and 2 percent in chardonnay.

The Chateau de Boursault, one of the most imposing sights in the region (photograph by Tor Eigeland/Collection CIVC).

I found this an attractive area. I also liked the champagnes of some of the local producers.

Congy

This village is located south of the Côte des Blancs. Of the 70 hectares of vines, 61 percent are planted in pinot meunier, 21 percent in chardonnay, and 18 percent in pinot noir.

This area is a bit off the beaten track. I visited this village and found the wines not overly memorable but somewhat interesting.

Courteron

This village is located just south of Buxeuil in the Aube department.

Courteron has a total of 66 hectares of vines, of which 95 percent are planted in pinot noir, 4 percent in chardonnay, and 1 percent in pinot meunier. Of special interest, however, is that there are three vignerons in Courteron, including Champagne Fleury, using biodynamic methods of viticulture.

Crouttes-sur-Marne

This charming village is located in the Aisne department on the very western edge of the Champagne region. Of the 140 hectares of vines, 71 percent are planted in pinot meunier, 20 percent in chardonnay, and 9 percent in pinot noir.

Crouttes-sur-Marne is definitely off the beaten track. The village enjoys a good reputation, however, and Champagne Françoise Bedel is definitely worth visiting.

Damery

This charming, bustling village is located five miles northwest of Epernay. There are a total of 382 hectares of vines, of which 70 percent are planted in pinot meunier, 20 percent in pinot noir, and 10 percent in chardonnay.

There are a number of very good producers in Damery. I am very familiar with the Damery terroir because René Collard has 1.5 hectares here. Also, there is an excellent bakery in the town.

Dormans

Dormons is the largest town between Epernay and Chateau-Thierry. There are a total of 220 hectares of vines, of which 92 percent are planted in pinot meunier, 7 percent in pinot noir, and 1 percent in chardonnay.

The most interesting things about Dormans are the fourteenth-century chateau and a good World War I museum.

Etoges

Located 13 miles south of Epernay, Etoges is worth visiting. In addition to the champagne, the Chateau d'Etoges is an interesting tourist site. Now a hotel and restaurant (I've neither eaten nor stayed there, but I have heard good reports), it is an impressive-looking structure.

Etoges has a total of 80 hectares of vines, of which 55 percent are planted in pinot meunier, 30 percent in chardonnay, and 15 percent in pinot noir.

Epernay

No visit to the Champagne region is complete without stopping in Epernay. Famous producers such as Moët & Chandon, Mercier, Pol Roger, Vranken, Perrier Jouet, Marne & Champagne, and Alfred Gratien are all located here. There are many things to see in Epernay and a couple of up-and-coming restaurants.

There are also 227 hectares of vines around Epernay. The majority (52 percent) are planted in chardonnay, and 27 percent are planted in pinot noir and 21 percent in pinot meunier.

Fleury-la-Rivière

In my opinion, Fleury-la-Rivière is one of the most charming villages in the Champagne region. I know this village quite well because my good friends Daniel and Nadia Duval are RMs there.

There are a total of 205 hectares of vines in Fleury-la-Rivière. Of these, 76 percent are planted in pinot meunier, 15 percent in pinot noir, and 9 percent in chardonnay.

Germaine

This village is located in the forest approximately halfway between Reims and Epernay. There are only 26 hectares of vines, all of which are planted in pinot meunier.

Germaine is best known for La Musée du Bucheron, a museum dedicated to the forest and the nature in the region.

Mardeuil

Located just west of Epernay, Mardeuil has 165 hectares of vines. Of these, 60 percent are planted in pinot meunier, 30 percent in pinot noir, and 10 percent in chardonnay.

There are a number of quality producers in Mardeuil. In my opinion, this village deserves a much higher rating than the 84 percent it receives on the échelle des crus.

Montgueux

This attractive village is located six miles west of Troyes in the Aube department. Although most of the Aube is dominated by pinot noir, Montueux's 187 hectares of vines are primarily planted in chardonnay. In fact, 85 percent of the vines are planted in this white grape, and the remaining 15 percent are planted in pinot noir.

I visited Montgueux during a champagne festival and had the opportunity to taste a number of different blanc de blancs champagnes from this village. I was pleasantly surprised by the overall quality.

Monthelon

This charming village is located four miles south of Epernay. There are a total of 250 hectares of vines, of which 60 percent are planted in pinot meunier, 35 percent in chardonnay, and 5 percent in pinot meunier.

I have been very impressed with the champagnes from Monthelon I have tried. I believe that this village merits premier cru status.

Reims

Like Epernay, Reims (pronounced like "rance") is known for the champagne houses it contains, not its vines. Such famous houses as Krug, Charles Heidsieck, Piper-Heidsieck, Veuve Clicquot, Mumm, Pommery, Roederer, Ruinart, and Taittinger are among the most famous residents of Reims.

There are a total of 49 hectares of vines around Reims, of which 38 percent are planted in pinot meunier, with the balance equally split between pinot noir and chardonnay.

There are many things to do and see in Reims, including the famous Cathédrale Notre-Dame de Reims in the middle of the city. There are also some nice hotels, shops, and excellent restaurants in Reims.

Reuil

As discussed in previous chapters, Reuil is the home of Champagne René Collard, and as such the spiritual capital of Champagne. There are a total of 151 hectares of vines, of which 70 percent are planted in pinot meunier, 25 percent in pinot noir, and 5 percent in chardonnay.

Les Riceys

Located in the Aube department, Les Riceys is actually three villages: Ricey Haut, Haute-Rive, and Ricey Bas. The three villages contain 712 hectares of vines, of which 96 percent are planted in pinot noir, 3 percent in chardonnay, and 1 percent in pinot meunier.

Les Riceys is the only area in France with three distinct appellations: champagne, coteaux champenois, and Rosé des Riceys. The latter is a pinot noir-based rosé still wine made from only excellent-quality grapes from vines at least 25 years old. It is hard to find in the United States, but Rosé des Riceys is one of the best still rosé wines I've ever tried

Sézanne

Located approximately 20 miles south of Epernay, Sézanne is known for its chardonnay grapes. Of its 61 hectares of vines, 55 percent are planted in chardonnay, 27 percent in pinot meunier, and 18 percent in pinot noir.

Sézanne is a significant town in the region, and there are a number of historic buildings worth seeing there.

Venteuil

Venteuil is located just west of Damery. There are a total of 170 hectares of vines, of which 49 percent are planted in pinot meunier, 39 percent in pinot noir, and 12 percent in chardonnay.

Venteuil is another village I feel rates premier cru status.

Troyes

Troyes (pronounced twa) is located in the Aube department and is the ancient capital of the Champagne region. It was famous in the Middle Ages as a center of European commerce.

There are no vineyards in Troyes. However, the old city is extremely interesting and is well worth a visit. Troyes is also famous for its factory outlet stores.

Villers-sous-Chatillon

This modern village is located just north of Reuil. There are only 20 hectares of vines in Villers, but a number of vignerons with vines in neighboring villages live here. The vineyards are planted mainly in pinot meunier (94 percent), with the remainder split between pinot noir (5 percent) and chardonnay (1 percent).

Villers-sous-Chatillon has earned the nickname "little California" due to its large, modern homes. This village is also known for the Christmas decorations put up by residents, an unusual practice in the Champagne region.

12. *If You Run Out of Champagne De Meric*

ALTHOUGH I AM THE PROPRIETOR of a champagne house, I am first and foremost a lover of champagne. Of course I am a bit prejudiced when it comes to Champagne De Meric, but Catherine de Medicis is one of my favorite champagnes, and I consider our Grande Réserve Sous Bois to be one of the best brut nonvintage champagnes on the market. I also consider our current vintage champagne (1993) to be above average, and I have high hopes for the products we will be introducing over the next few years.

There are, however, many very good champagnes on the market today. What follows is a list of my favorite champagne producers. I profile my top 20 (not including Champagne De Meric) and indicate which ones are available in the United States. I then provide a brief overview of some other recommended champagne producers.

The Top 20

Champagne René Collard

By far my favorite champagne producer is Champagne René Collard. This will not be a surprise to those of you who have read this far, since René is my primary role model for champagne.

Everything starts in the vines, and this has always been the focus for René Collard. In terms of the vines themselves, he is opposed to clone selection and prefers a broad mix of the different subvarieties. He is a great believer

In Champagne, vines with southern exposure tend to produce better grapes (photograph by John Hodder/Collection CIVC).

in keeping older vines rather than early replanting, guarding his vines for 60 to 70 years. These older vines have lower yields and produce concentrated grapes of higher quality. The vines of René Collard have a strong southern exposure which ensures maximum access to nature's greatest gift, sunlight.

Regarding viticultural methods, René Collard has strictly observed the biologique (organic) methods of production. He has never used any chemical products on his vines, relying instead on hard work and natural products. For him, producing champagne was a seven-day-a-week job, with few vacations. From spring until the harvest, he was in the vines every day, trimming back leaves, plowing under the grass between the rows of vines, and checking to make sure the vines and the grapes were in good health.

The harvest was conducted by René, his family, friends, and a small team of workers who arrived each year for the harvest. He was almost always the last grower to harvest his grapes, generally starting as most growers were finishing. These extra days always carried the risk of bad weather but usually brought a reward of riper, higher quality grapes.

The respect for tradition continued in the vinification methods. Two-thirds of the wine was aged in oak barrels, and bottling usually took place in June or July after the harvest. His reserve wine and red wine for the production of rosé were aged in barrels at least two years. He also kept a small quantity of red wine for his own private enjoyment. For example, 1969 was a great year in Champagne for making both sparkling and still champagne wine (coteaux champenois), and he aged his 1969 red wine in barrels for 17 years. The result is a 100 percent pinot meunier still wine comparable to a great red Burgundy.

Unlike virtually all other producers, René Collard does not believe in filtering his wine. His reason for this is simple — although the filtration removes sediment, it also removes some of the richness and taste. He also did not put his wines through the "passage au froid," a process by which the wine is dropped to subfreezing temperatures to further clarify it by removing calcium tartrate and potassium bi-tartrate. These cold temperatures can damage the wine and remove some of the aromas and flavors. He has never used malo-lactic fermentation that, as discussed earlier, leads to premature aging of the wine.

Today Champagne René Collard offers a range of outstanding champagnes. On the official list of his products are vintage champagnes from 1975, 1976, 1979, 1985, and 1990; rosés from 1976 and 1985; and two nonvintage champagnes, Carte d'Or (currently 1992 with reserve wine added) and Carte Blanche (currently a mixture of 1994 and 1995, including the taille). Not on the official list but also available in limited quantities are three other champagnes: 1969, 1970, and 1973. He has also kept many bottles from earlier vintages, including 1943, 1949, 1955, 1961, and 1964, but these are not for sale.

Champagne René Collard is highly appreciated by connoisseurs who delight in a true champagne that is properly aged, without traces of pesticides or herbicides, and made using traditional methods. It is an authentic champagne and truly reflects the terroir of the Champagne region. I believe that if you want to experience the true taste of a great champagne that expresses what champagne really is, there is no better choice.

Champagne Bollinger

Champagne Bollinger is probably best known as the wine of choice of James Bond and, more recently, of the characters in the British comedy "Absolutely Fabulous." In real life, Bollinger is in many ways the prototype for what a champagne négociant-manipulant (NMs) should be. Located in Ay, it is De Meric's most famous neighbor and an outstanding role model.

Champagne Bollinger was founded in 1829 by Jacques Bollinger, a German native, and Comte Emanuel de Villermont. The families were combined when Bollinger married de Villermont's daughter, and over the next seven decades Bollinger grew to be a significant force in Champagne. The company was particularly successful in the British market and was named an official champagne supplier to the British court during the time of Queen Victoria. The company continued to be well managed by the family, most notably Elisabeth Bollinger, who took over responsibility upon the death of her husband in 1941. Known as "Tante Lily" (Aunt Lilly), she was famous for her zealous respect for quality and her choice of transportation — she traveled through Ay and the surrounding area for many years on a bicycle.

Bollinger has remained an independent company and is still controlled by the original family. Aside from making outstanding champagne, Bollinger's Charter of Ethics and Quality underscores the company's commitment to quality and its willingness to play a leadership role against industrialization and mass production in Champagne.

There are a number of factors that help make Bollinger so special. First of all, they own enough vines to supply about half of their needs (annual sales of around two million bottles), giving them the enviable benefit of being able to control the quality of the majority of their grapes. Also, Bollinger makes extensive use of their 4,000 oak barrels to ferment and age their vintage and reserve wine. Third, they market older vintages under the Bollinger RD (recently disgorged) label, providing champagne lovers the opportunity to enjoy outstanding mature champagnes from a top producer. Finally, Bollinger puts very strict standards on the grapes they use to make their champagne. I know of cases where Bollinger has rejected grapes from their growers.

In keeping with their Ay heritage, Bollinger champagnes are dominated by pinot noir. They have chosen not to make a blanc de blancs champagne and instead produce a nonvintage product (Spécial Cuvée), a vintage champagne (Grande Année), a vintage rosé (Grande Année Rosé), and various older vintages marketed under the RD umbrella. All these products are of extremely high quality, and the Spécial Cuvée is one of the best brut nonvintage products on the market. In addition, Bollinger has the good fortune to possess three parcels (two in Ay and one in a fellow grand cru village, Bouzy) of pre-phylloxera vines, to my knowledge the only such parcels that still exist in Champagne. The grapes from these vines are used to make the Bollinger blanc de noirs, Vieilles Vignes Françaises, which is only produced in outstanding years. The vines are grown "en foule" (in a crowd), as most European vines were before the coming of phylloxera, rather than in the neat rows of trellised vines used today.

For those unfamiliar with phylloxera, it is a small but extremely hearty insect that attacks the roots of vines and eventually leads to the destruction of the vines. Phylloxera came to Europe from the United States on vines transported for European planting in the second half of the nineteenth century. It started in the south and gradually worked its way north. Phylloxera reached Champagne in the late 1890s, and the problem continued into the twentieth century. Everything was tried to stop the spread of phylloxera—chemical and organic treatments, flooding, and burning, among other things—until the problem was finally resolved by grafting the European vines onto U.S. rootstocks, which are immune to phylloxera. This practice continues to this day.

Bollinger champagnes are not by any means inexpensive. However, with the exception of Vieilles Vignes Françaises, they are less expensive than either Krug or Salon. Bollinger Spécial Cuvée generally retails for around $40.00, and Grande Année between $80.00 and $90.00, although the RD is more than $100.00. All of these represent relatively good value for the price compared to Krug. The Vieilles Vignes Françaises is a rare product, so if you are lucky enough to find a bottle, expect to pay close to $300.00 for this outstanding champagne.

The family is truly dedicated to the pursuit of quality and because they are independently owned, there are no corporate owners to push for changes. I am confident that Bollinger will continue to produce champagne of outstanding quality. Champagne Bollinger is widely available in the United States.

Champagne Franck Bonville

Récoltant-manipulant (RM) Champagne Franck Bonville is located in Avize. The family traces its vigneron roots to Jules Bonville, who lived in neighboring Oger in the late nineteenth and early twentieth centuries. Jules Bonville worked in the vines for Champagne Werle, which later became part of Veuve Clicquot. Jules's son, Alfred, bought the family's first vines in 1931 in the middle of the global economic depression. In 1933 he was joined in the vines by his son Franck, who was born in 1921, the same year as René Collard.

Alfred and Franck slowly expanded their holdings, although at the time they sold all of their production (whether in the form of grapes, vin clair, or bottles) to NMs. In 1938 they bought their present headquarters in Avize, which includes the family house, cellars, and good space for vinifying and producing wine. During the ensuing years, they continued to acquire vines in Avize and Oger. After Alfred's death in 1954, Franck Bonville and his son Giles continued to expand the family's holdings and gradually shifted the focus from supplying NMs to producing and marketing their own champagne.

Today Giles Bonville works with his son, Olivier. They currently exploit almost 20 hectares in grands crus Avize, Oger, Le Mesnil-sur-Oger, and Cramant, and they use the majority of these grapes to make Champagne Franck Bonville. Like many growers, they also sell some of their grapes. Champagne Franck Bonville produces approximately 130,000 bottles per year, a significant quantity for a vigneron.

Although Champagne Franck Bonville makes a nice rosé, the company's focus and expertise is producing blanc de blancs champagne. The current product line includes a nonvintage blanc de blancs along with three vintage blanc de blancs. They also produce an excellent nonvintage cuvée prestige using grapes selected from their best parcels.

All of the blanc de blancs champagnes from Champagne Franck Bonville are of excellent to outstanding quality, and the older vintages are equal to or better than Salon (the 1976 is better, and the 1985 is roughly of equal quality) but at a far lower price. I've also had the privilege to taste some of their older vintages, including 1969, 1964, 1961, and 1959, and all were absolutely outstanding. Giles and Olivier Bonville understand that their key to success is to grow grapes of outstanding quality, and they also understand the importance of aging their champagne.

What I find extremely interesting and hopeful about Champagne Franck Bonville is the outlook of Olivier Bonville. As his father gradually turned over the responsibility for production to him, Olivier studied the methods the company uses and compared these to the methods of his grandfather. As a consequence, he has begun vinifying some of his cuvées in wood and, in fact, has produced a special cuvee that is 100-percent aged in barrels without malo-lactic fermentation. This champagne is great now and will only improve with age. It is especially hopeful to see a young producer (he is 34 years old) so focused on quality and tradition. Champagne Bonville is available in the United States through K & L Wine Merchants in California.

Champagne Maurice Vesselle

Although I'd heard of Champagne Maurice Vesselle quite often and had passed by their office a number of times, I actually did not try this outstanding champagne until 2000. Once one has tasted these great champagnes, however, they are impossible to forget.

Champagne Maurice Vesselle is located in the grand cru village of Bouzy. Bouzy is one of the truly outstanding crus in Champagne, as are Ay, Cramant, and Avize. In fact, if I had to pick a champagne based on no information other than which cru was used to make it, I might select one from Bouzy.

Aside from producing great champagne grapes, Bouzy is famous for being the best-known cru for red coteaux champenois, still red wine from Champagne. Because the region's still wines (red and white coteaux champenois and Rosé des Riceys, a still rosé from three villages in the Aube) are outside the scope of this book (we do not produce these at De Meric), I haven't focused on their merits. However, these wines are generally of good quality, although they tend to be a bit thin in all but outstanding years. Because they come from champagne grapes, they are also expensive and generally do not provide a very strong price/value relationship.

The Vesselle family has been growing grapes in Bouzy since the sixteenth century, and they have been major landowners in the village for many years. In fact, there are a number of members of this family still involved in champagne production, some of whom are very good producers.

Champagne Maurice Vesselle was founded in 1955, and the family (father, mother, and two sons—a third son is now a grower in Bordeaux) exploits more than eight hectares of vines. The vast majority of these vines are in Bouzy, and about one hectare is in neighboring Tours-sur-Marne, a fellow grand cru. Eighty-five percent of these vineyards are planted with pinot noir and the rest with chardonnay.

Other than René Collard, Maurice Vesselle is the most committed traditionalist I've met in Champagne. As is the case with Champagne René Collard, no herbicides are used on the vines of Maurice Vesselle, and the earth between the vines is regularly plowed under (labouré) to protect the authenticity of the terroir and to nourish the vines. Champagne Maurice Vesselle does not use malo-lactic fermentation, preferring to create wines that age naturally and are capable of being guarded for many years.

This RM currently markets an excellent brut réserve that has been aged five years; nonvintage rosé; and outstanding vintage wines from 1995, 1988, 1985, and 1976. They also offer red and white coteaux champenois, both of which are among the best I've tried in their categories. The 1988 vintage champagne is especially outstanding and is easily the best I have tasted from this vintage. These products also offer tremendous value; for example, the 1988 is available at the property for less than twenty dollars. Production is limited to about 30,000 bottles per year.

When one talks to the Vesselles about champagne, the focus is always on the vines. Maurice Vesselle believes outstanding grapes are the key to making an outstanding champagne, and his product proves he is right. These products are not currently available in the U.S. market.

Champagne Michel Maillart

While Champagne Bonville and Champagne Vesselle are located in and use only grapes from grand cru villages, Champagne Michel Maillart is located in Ecueil, a premier cru village in the Petite Montagne de Reims. Like Reuil, I believe that Ecueil is under appreciated and merits an increase over its current rating of 90 percent on the échelle des crus. There are a number of high-quality producers in Ecueil, and Michel Maillart stands above them all.

The Maillart family has been vignerons in the Petite Montagne since the early 1700s. In keeping with this family tradition, Michel Maillart began producing his champagne in 1972, initially working alongside his father. Although the majority of his 8.5 hectares of vines are in Ecueil, he also has vines in Villers-Allerand (premier cru) and Bouzy (grand cru).

Although top producers such as Salon (chardonnay), Bollinger (pinot noir), Franck Bonville (chardonnay), and Maurice Vesselle (pinot noir) are primarily focused on one grape variety, Michel Maillart prefers to produce a more balanced style of champagne (remember, the blend determines style, not quality). His vintage champagnes are generally two-thirds pinot noir and one-third chardonnay, and his nonvintage is a blend of all three of the principal champagne grape varieties.

The key to the success of Michel Maillart lies primarily in his methods of viticulture rather than his methods of vinification. However, he does believe in giving his wines proper aging. In fact, to truly appreciate the quality of Champagne Michel Maillart, it is necessary to taste one of his "millesime plus de 10 ans," his vintages more than ten years old that he considers his cuvée prestige products.

Currently, this RM offers a range of top-quality champagne, including a good quality nonvintage brut and rosé; a 1993 blanc de blancs; and vintage champagnes from 1986, 1987, 1988, 1989, and 1994. Perhaps the most impressive product is the 1986, a difficult year in which Michel Maillart was able to produce an excellent champagne.

Because I have been a client of Michel Maillart for some time I am familiar with some of his former vintages, including 1979, 1981, 1982, 1983, 1984, 1985, 1988 blanc de blancs, and 1990. All were outstanding, which was not an easy feat in 1981 and 1984. Unfortunately, Champagne Michel Maillart is not currently available in the U.S. market.

Champagne Krug

Perhaps the most prestigious of all champagne producers is Champagne Krug. Classifying Krug as one of the top champagne producers is not exactly a novel idea on my part — in fact, it would be hard to find anyone who would disagree with this ranking. Krug genuinely deserves the accolades.

This NM was founded in 1843 by Johann-Josef Krug, a German native who learned the champagne business while working for Champagne Jacquesson. He was succeeded by his son Paul, who played the major role in developing Krug into an internationally known and respected champagne producer. Quality has always been the main focus, and bottles of Krug from great vintages such as 1928 are treasured by collectors around the world.

After passing from father to son for four generations, Krug was sold to Compagnie Rémy-Martin, the famous cognac producer, in 1971. Fortunately, the management team of Rémy-Martin was smart enough to realize that they had purchased a jewel, and they left the Krug family in charge, providing assistance for investments but not interfering with the business of champagne production. The result was that the company continued to flourish, and the quality of the product and the financial results (35 percent profit) were both outstanding.

The company continues to practice many traditional methods and all of the wine is vinified and aged in oak barrels. The company owns 21 hectares of vines but buys the majority of their grapes from a carefully selected group of growers. The result is a range of outstanding products.

The key product, the nonvintage Grande Cuvée, makes up the vast majority of the company's sales. Although many producers age their brut nonvintage 15 months, Krug ages theirs at least five years. The result is a product that is often classified as a cuvée prestige rather than as just another nonvintage brut.

The company also produces a rosé, vintage champagnes, and a blanc de blancs produced exclusively from the Clos du Mesnil, an ancient walled vineyard in Le Mesnil-sur-Oger purchased by the company in 1971. At the time of the purchase, Le Mesnil-sur-Oger was classified as premier cru but has since been elevated to grand cru status. Krug also sells a limited quantity of older vintages under the title of the Krug Collection; its current offering is 1979.

All of the products offered by Krug are quite expensive. The Grande Cuvée has a retail price of more than $100.00, and the Clos du Mesnil and Krug Collection can cost two or three times that much. This is not the champagne for bargain hunters.

The key question, of course, is whether the quality justifies the price. Krug is generally more expensive than my other favorite producers, so from that perspective the answer is no. However, compared to the vast majority of champagnes available, Krug does deliver the quality to justify the price.

If one compares Krug's products to the disappointing cuvée prestige products marketed by some mass producers, Krug starts to look like a bargain in terms of price/quality performance.

In the late 1990s, Krug parent company Rémy-Martin became overextended due to acquisitions and sold Krug for the impressive price of more than one billion French francs. The buyer was the Moët-Hennessy-Louis-Vuitton Group (LVMH), by far the largest conglomerate in champagne. LVMH owns such champagne brands as Moët & Chandon, Veuve Clicquot, Ruinart, and Mercier. At the time of the sale there were assurances from all sides that nothing would change at Krug, and there seemed to be some logic behind these assurances. Krug is the jewel of Champagne and has unsurpassed profit margins, and changing the formula would appear to be risky. In addition, the Krug family remained at the helm, which was reassuring for Krug lovers everywhere.

However, in 2001 the company announced an investment program that included purchasing gyropallets to replace remuage by hand and the installation of new stainless steel tanks, reportedly for blending, although the skeptic must wonder whether blending is the only purpose of the tanks. Although neither of these changes is necessarily catastrophic in terms of quality, they do signal a move toward modernization and away from traditional quality methods.

More troubling is Krug's increase in its sales from 500,000 bottles per year to 650,000 bottles per year, a 30-percent increase. This is cause for concern on two fronts. First of all, finding additional grapes to make an extra 150,000 bottles is not easy, and finding that many top-quality grapes is a daunting challenge. (I speak from personal experience.) Of course, the LVMH group owns vines and has numerous contracts, which helps. Second, Krug has a very large stock of bottles because of their long aging, and the easiest and quickest way to increase sales will be simply to reduce the aging of the Grande Cuvée by a year or so. If Krug follows this course, they will lose an important qualitative advantage. However, I hope and believe Krug will continue producing excellent champagne. Champagne Krug is widely available in the U.S. market.

Champagne A. Salon

Champagne Salon is the most unique of all champagne producers because the product is only produced in excellent years and is always vintage dated. Only chardonnay grapes from grand cru Le Mesnil-sur-Oger are used to make Salon. There is no brut nonvintage, no reserve wine, and no rosé—just blanc de blancs from specific vintages. Sales are only 32,000 bottles per year, making it even smaller than De Meric!

The company was founded in 1911 by Aimé Salon, a French merchant. It was primarily a hobby, and Salon's goal was to make a great champagne for himself and his friends. In years he considered not up to his standards, he sold the grapes to other producers, choosing only to make a vintage product of the highest quality. He was so successful that A. Salon & Cie attracted many admirers among wine connoisseurs and became a champagne icon.

I've been fortunate to have tasted a number of different vintages of Salon, including 1945, 1964, 1966, 1976, 1982, 1983, and three more recent vintages, 1985, 1988, and 1990. Although of course each differed due to characteristics of the vintage (not to mention the age of the wine), all were at least excellent and some were superb. Like Krug, Salon is quite expensive (usually retailing for more than $100.00 in the United States), but given the quality and rarity, it is worth it if one has the means.

In 1989 Salon was bought by the Laurent-Perrier Group and linked with fellow Le Mesnil-sur-Oger négociant Delamotte, which Laurent-Perrier acquired at the same time. This actually makes a lot of sense given that Salon only produces in vintage years and Delamotte makes a range of champagnes. Most people feel that Laurent-Perrier has done a good job keeping the Salon tradition, which is supported by the quality of the 1990 vintage. Champagne Salon is available in the U.S. market.

Champagne L. Aubry Fils

Like many top vignerons, the Aubry family traces its roots back many generations, in this case back to 1790. Pierre and Philippe Aubry, the current proprietors, deserve the credit for having the vision and creativity to make dramatic changes in the way they work, thereby creating a range of excellent champagnes and one of the most unique product lines in Champagne.

L. Aubry Fils is located in Jouy-lès-Reims, a small village in the Petite Montagne de Reims just a few miles from Ecueil. Jouy-lès-Reims is a premier cru, with a rating of 90 percent on the échelle des crus. The majority of their 17 hectares of vines are located in Jouy-lès-Reims and neighboring premier cru Pargny-lès-Reims, but they also have vines in nearby Villedommange, Trigny, and Coulommes-la-Montagne. They produce approximately 130,000 bottles per year.

In 1986 the Aubry brothers decided to create a special cuvée to celebrate the bicentennial of their family's involvement in the champagne business. After rejecting the ideas usually put in place for events such as this (a different bottle, label, or packaging with the usual champagne), they decided to create a champagne similar to those produced in the late eighteenth century. As they researched the history of that era, they found that one of the fundamental differences was in the type of grapes grown. In addition to chardonnay, pinot meunier, and pinot noir, champagne was made using four other noble varieties— petit meslier, arbanne, enfumé (pinot gris), and fromenteau (meunier fumé)— as well as lesser varieties such as gamay. There are still small parcels planted with these ancient grape varieties in Champagne, but they are increasingly rare. The brothers decided that to make a true late eighteenth-century champagne it would be necessary to replant a part of their vineyards with these four ancient noble grapes, and this was accomplished in 1989 and 1990.

The result is a group of unique and outstanding products. Highlighting this list are the Sablé Blanc Des Blancs and Campanae Veteres Vites, both marketed under the umbrella Le Nombre d'Or. The blanc des blancs is a blend of the three white grapes: chardonnay, arbanne, and petit meslier. We have discussed other blanc *de* blancs champagnes (de is singular because chardonnay is the only grape used), but this is the only blanc *des* blancs (des is plural) of which I am aware. The Campanae Veteres Vites is made only from the four ancient grape varieties. Both are vintage dated, and both are unique and excellent. It is recommended that the Campanae Veteres Vites be opened a few hours before drinking.

The quality and originality of the Aubry line does not end with these two products. Their Sablé Rosé Nicolas François Aubry is, in essence, a light rosé made in the saignée method (a method of pressing that allows the juice to obtain its rosé color from the black grape skins). The current offering is a 1996, and after René Collard it is the best rosé product I have tasted. Champagne Aubry also produces a vintage brut tradition that truly merits the title (it is vinified in wood barrels), another high-quality vintage champagne titled Aubry de Humbert, a vintage blanc de blancs, a vintage rosé, and a brut nonvintage champagne. Although I am especially fond of the more unique products in the line, all Aubry products are highly recommended. Champagne Aubry is available in the U.S. market.

Champagne Fleury

This NM is the only producer in Champagne producing a certified biodynamic champagne. Located in the village of Courteron in the Aube department (rated 80 percent on the èchelle des crus), Champagne Fleury produces approximately 200,000 bottles per year. The majority of the grapes come from the 13 hectares of vineyards they own, and the remainder are purchased from two growers in Courteron who also utilize biodynamic methods. As discussed earlier, biodynamic methods are the most natural — and most effective — of all viticultural methods, and the results show in the quality of the champagne.

Champagne Fleury was established in 1895. Their vineyards have been cultivated using organic methods since 1970 and biodynamic methods since 1992. In keeping with the Aube terroir, 90 percent of their vineyards are planted with pinot noir, and the remaining 10 percent with chardonnay.

The product line includes an excellent brut nonvintage, another non-vintage product called Fleur de l'Europe, an excellent rosé, and a vintage champagne. Their 1992 vintage champagne is outstanding and is easily the best champagne I have tasted from that vintage. These excellent champagnes are available in the United States.

Champagne A. Loncle

Although most producers located in the Montagne de Reims are spe-cialists in pinot noir or pinot meunier, Villers-Marmery is an enclave of chardonnay due to a slightly different micro-climate. The best producer in this premier cru village (95 percent on the échelle des crus) is Champagne A. Loncle.

This RM exploits approximately six hectares of vines, five of which are located in Villers-Marmery and the balance in Verzy. The chardonnay of Villers-Marmery has different characteristics from the chardonnay found in the Côte des Blancs and other areas. Chardonnay always requires more aging than the black grapes of Champagne, and this is especially true for the cru of Villers-Marmery. Aging is just one of the reasons this producer stands above the crowd.

Champagne A. Loncle offers a high-quality range of chardonnay-domi-nated champagnes. His more basic products, brut tradition and rosé, are both quite good. He currently offers three excellent vintage blanc de blancs champagnes. The real star of his line, however, is his favorite product, the Veille Réserve. This is actually his brut nonvintage — 95 percent chardon-nay and 5 percent pinot noir — aged seven to eight years before disgorge-ment. Not only is this one of my favorite champagnes, it is the best way I know to show the increase in quality that can come from proper aging.

A. Loncle keeps all of his grapes to make his excellent champagne. The majority of his clients are in France, although he exports a small amount to neighboring countries such as Belguim. Champagne A. Loncle is not yet available in the United States.

Champagne Leclaire

Another excellent RM specializing in chardonnay-dominated champagnes is Champagne Leclaire. Located in grand cru Avize, Champagne Leclaire is only a few yards away from Champagne Bonville, which is quite convenient for the champagne connoisseur!

The current proprietors of Champagne Leclaire, Reynald and Virginie Leclaire, represent the third generation of RMs. Reynald Leclaire's grandfather, Earnest Alfred Leclaire, marketed his products under the Leclaire brand name (not to be confused with Leclerc, a rather depressing chain of French supermarkets). Other products have been produced under the labels Leclaire-Gaspard and Leclaire-Thiefaine. Therefore, the family presents their champagnes under the banner Domaine des Champagnes Leclaire, and each product sold uses the name under which it was originally produced.

Champagne Leclaire is a small producer with vines in Grauves, Avize, and Cramant. They have a relatively small product line that is a little difficult to decipher if you are not familiar with the house. As Reynald Leclaire explained to me, his grandfather did not like the paperwork associated with champagne (there is an incredible amount), and decided that it wasn't worth the extra trouble to declare a special vintage champagne at the time of bottling. (In order to use a specific vintage on the label, it must be declared at the time of bottling.) Therefore, they market a number of vintage products but are unable to actually say so. Instead, they use the "mise en bouteille" (put in the bottle) date, which is one year after the year of harvest.

Today, Champagne Leclaire offers champagnes bottled in 1994 (1993 vintage), 1990 (1989 vintage), and a small amount from 1974 (from the excellent 1973 vintage). A more "normal" nonvintage blanc de blancs is also offered, and the company now offers Cuvée R. Leclaire, a vintage champagne labeled as such. Champagne Leclaire is not yet available in the United States.

Champagne Henri Goutorbe

What is particularly interesting and impressive about the Goutorbe family is that they are able to produce an excellent line of champagne when this isn't even their primary activity. The family first made their mark in Champagne as pépiniéristes, specialists in growing and grafting vines in a nursery located in Ay for planting in the vineyards of Champagne. Although I doubt this activity is as important to them financially as their vineyards and champagne production businesses, I get the feeling that it is still their first love.

Henri Goutorbe first began producing champagne in the late 1940s, expanding his production by following his father's example of purchasing vines when prices were favorable and leasing vines when possible. Henri's son René, who with his wife Nicole manages the family business, continued this practice, and today the Goutorbes exploit 20 hectares, mainly in their hometown of Ay and the surrounding villages (Maureil-sur-Ay, Mutigny, etc.). Roughly 65 percent of the vineyards are planted with pinot noir, while 30 percent are planted with chardonnay and 5 percent with pinot meunier.

Today this RM markets a full line of excellent champagnes, including a very high quality brut nonvintage labeled Cuvée Traditionnelle and high-quality blanc de blancs and cuvée prestige champagnes. They also produce a very good rosé. However, I believe it is the vintage champagnes that truly reveal the excellence of Champagne Henri Goutorbe. I have tasted a number of their different vintages and have always been extremely impressed. The company also produced what I found to be the best quality cuvée l'an 2000 in all of Champagne, a 1986 vintage containing 50 percent Ay pinot noir and 50 percent Ay chardonnay, the same composition of De Meric's cuvée prestige, Catherine de Medicis. Although it pains me to admit it, I conducted a blind tasting of the Goutorbe Cuvée L'an 2000 against the current version of Catherine de Medicis (based on the 1988 and 1989 vintages) and found that although both were excellent, we preferred the one from Champagne Goutorbe.

The total production of Champagne Henri Goutorbe is 120,000 bottles per year. The majority (60 percent) is sold to private clients in France and the remaining 40 percent is sold to importers and private clients throughout Europe. One interesting fact about this company is that they bottle their Methuselahs (the equivalent of eight bottles) directly rather than creating a Methuselah by transferring the contents of four magnums at the time of disgorgement, as is the practice of the vast majority of producers (including De Meric). Methuselahs are both large and heavy and consequently difficult to manipulate, but the Goutorbe method of direct bottling leads to better quality.

Champagne Goutorbe is a member of a group called the Club de Viticulteurs Champenois. This group was formed 20 years ago and consists of selected good-quality RMs. Each member produces a Special Club champagne, a vintage champagne that is, in essence, their cuvée prestige. All of these Special Club champagnes use the same design for their labels and bottle shape, creating a recognizable brand family. I have found this concept to be a good one, and the members are all better than average producers.

I have had the extremely good fortune to get to know the Goutorbes both as champagne producers and as growers—today they are the largest supplier of grapes for Champagne De Meric. I have been consistently pleased with the quality of the grapes from the Goutorbes. As discussed earlier, the key to quality champagne is quality grapes, so it's no surprise that Champagne Henri Goutorbe produces excellent champagne. Unfortunately, these products are not yet available in the United States.

Champagne Severin-Doublet

Champagne Severin-Doublet is located in the premier cru village of Vertus (95 percent on the échelle des crus). Although the Doublet family has history in the vineyards of Vertus, the proprietor of Champagne Severin-Doublet, René Severin, was a newcomer to the champagne business. However, he has adopted the vocation of his family by marriage with a passion that is too often missing among winemakers, and he and his wife have succeeded in producing an excellent line of champagne.

René Severin is a man of strong beliefs and high standards. Like René Collard, René Severin produces champagne with himself in mind and applies his personal standards to Champagne Severin-Doublet. In fact, when I asked why Champagne Severin-Doublet does not produce a rosé, he explained to me that he doesn't like rosé champagne himself and therefore has no interest in making or marketing a rosé. When clients request rosé, he refers them to another producer.

Champagne Severin-Doublet has been made from six hectares of vines, all in Vertus. However, René Severin is now nearing retirement and plans to reduce his vineyards to four hectares. He currently owns four hectares and leases two hectares, and he plans to let his lease expire. Leasing vineyards is fairly common in Champagne because some people who inherit vines but have no interest in becoming growers prefer to lease rather than sell their land.

I first learned of Champagne Severin-Doublet while reading Tom Stevenson's excellent book *Champagne*. Stevenson talks of tasting a bottle of Severin-Doublet 1966 and calls it "probably the best grower champagne I have ever drunk." I made a point to visit Severin-Doublet on my next trip to Champagne, and I have been a client ever since.

The company's product line is small — a brut tradition, a Grande Réserve Blanc de Blancs, a cuvée 2000 (1995 vintage), an excellent 1992 vintage, and a recently released 1985 vintage. Although I haven't had a chance to taste the 1985 yet, the 1992 is excellent and the 1988 was outstanding. In fact, I was able to purchase one of the last magnums of 1988 and plan to drink it for a special occasion.

Like champagne from most RMs, the champagnes from Champagne Severin-Doublet are quite reasonably priced in regard to their quality. In addition, both René and his wife are very nice and interesting people, and a visit to see them in Vertus and buy some bottles is highly recommended. This champagne is not yet available in the United States.

Champagne Claude Cazals

Another excellent producer of blanc de blancs champagne is Champagne Claude Cazals of Le Mesnil-sur-Oger. This RM was founded in 1897 by Ernest Cazals.

Today, Champagne Claude Cazals exploits nine hectares in the Côte des Blancs. Included in this total is the 3.3-hectare Clos d'Oger, a rare and exceptional walled vineyard. Delphine Cazals, who manages the family business, has begun to use the grapes from this clos to make an outstanding cuvée. As an aside, Delphine is married to Olivier Bonville, which means that their household is responsible for some of the best blanc de blancs champagnes on the market.

All of the champagnes from Champagne Claude Cazals are blanc de blancs. In addition to the nonvintage Carte Blanche (premier cru) and Carte Or (grand cru), they offer vintage champagnes from multiple years. This RM also offers an extra brut (no dosage) called Cuvée Vive. Delphine has recently introduced a new champagne, Clos Cazals, a vintage wine produced exclusively from the family's walled vineyard in Oger. I highly recommend this excellent product. These products are not yet available in the U.S. market.

In addition to being excellent vignerons and champagne producers, the Cazals family has invented many labor-saving devices including the gyropalette, which was invented by Delphine's late father, Claude Cazals.

Champagne Collard-Chardelle

Champagne Collard-Chardelle is located in Villers-sous-Chatillon (86 percent on the échelle des crus). If their name sounds a bit familiar, it is because Daniel Collard, who with his wife Françoise is the proprietor of this company, is the son of René Collard, the greatest of all champagne producers in my opinion.

Today Daniel is joined by his son Olivier, who with his wife Caroline has created the label Collard-Picard. At least for the time being, champagnes marketed under these two brands are produced together, although the vineyards are divided. In all they exploit approximately 14 hectares in Villers-sous-Chatillon, Reuil, Damery, Le Mesnil-sur-Oger, and some new vines near Vitry-le-François.

The product line of this RM is fairly deep, including the ever-present brut nonvintage, a Cuvée Spéciale (réserve), a nonvintage rosé, an excellent cuvée prestige, another cuvée prestige known as Cuvée Perle Bleue that is based on the 1990 vintage, a 1996 vintage, and a 1986 vintage. The specialty of the house is its use of wood barrels, and Daniel's ambition in the next few years is to vinify 100 percent of his champagne in wood.

The result of the family's efforts is an excellent champagne and an outstanding value for the money. However, although Daniel has followed many of his father's production methods, especially the use of oak barrels, he does not have René Collard's respect for the land and uses chemicals to fertilize and treat the vines rather than following his father's example of organic viticulture. Champagne Collard-Chardelle is not available in the United States.

Champagne Debordes-Amiaud

Located just a few yards from Champagne Michel Maillart in Ecueil is Champagne Debordes-Amiaud. This producer is unique in that the family business has passed not from father to son, which is typical, but from mother to daughter. Women have played a major role in the champagne business since the days of Madame Clicquot and Madame Pommery, but this is the only case I know of in which a producer has had a female line of succession. At Champagne Debordes-Amiaud, this line of succession goes back to 1935, although the house has existed since the late 1800s.

Today this RM is managed by Marie-Christine Desbordes and her daughter Elodie. They exploit nine hectares of vines, all from premier crus in the Montagne de Reims. In keeping with their terroir, the champagnes tend to be dominated by pinot noir (80 percent in the case of their brut nonvintage). Wines from Champagne Debordes-Amiaud do not undergo malo-lactic fermentation and as a result tend to be long lived and improve with age.

The company's product line includes a brut nonvintage, a reserve champagne known as Grande Réserve 1er Cru, a rosé, and two vintage champagnes. The 1990 vintage is called Cuvée M'Elodie and features a photo of Elodie as a young girl in traditional Champagne costume during the harvest. Cuvée M'Elodie is positioned as a cuvée prestige and is the best product in their line, although the other products I have tasted are also quite good. I was particularly impressed by their 1985 vintage, which is no longer available.

This is an interesting producer to visit. The Petite Montagne is lovely, the family is very welcoming, and there is a small display of antique viticultural materials to see. Most important, Champagne Desbordes-Amiaud produces excellent champagne. These products are not available in the United States.

Champagne Duval-Prétrot

Champagne Duval-Prétrot is located in the charming town of Fleury-La-Rivière (rated 85 percent on the échelle des crus). Duval-Prétrot is an RM constantly striving to improve quality. Although small even by De Meric standards (sales under 30,000 bottles per year), they manage to produce a line of interesting and high-quality products and have more on the way. The key to their success, however, is their focus on the most important element — their grapes.

I should start by explaining that I know Daniel and Nadia Duval (Nadia's family name is Prétrot) quite well. They are friends of mine, and I even imported some of their products to the United States when I had an importing license. I've seen how they work and tasted their products at various stages. They have long been advocates and practitioners of culture raisonnée, and they are usually the last in their village to begin the harvest. In addition, they are always experimenting and striving to improve their product. For example, they recently started making their rosé by maceration, the saignée method, and have created a cuvée prestige using their best parcels of chardonnay in the best years.

Their current product line includes better than average brut nonvintage and rosé products, an excellent vintage champagne, and an excellent brut réserve which, unlike some réserve products, truly has been aged. These products are very reasonably priced and represent one of the better values in Champagne. Both the vintage and the réserve have received excellent scores in the tastings conducted by the Beverage Testing Institute in Chicago, one of the most reputable wine reviewers in the United States. These champagnes are not currently available in the United States.

Champagne Deutz

One of our neighbors in Ay, Champagne Deutz is owned by the Roederer group. This house, which was founded in 1838, has annual sales well over 1,000,000 bottles. About two-thirds of the volume is sold in France.

Champagne Deutz is best known for its excellent cuvée prestige, Cuvée William Deutz. However, this producer has a broad and interesting product line, including a brut nonvintage (Brut Classic) and three different vintage products (rosé, blanc de blancs, and a traditional vintage). All are quality products. I frequently order Champagne Deutz in restaurants in the United States because it is both widely available and reasonably priced.

Deutz has grown rapidly in the past few years, and the credit is due to the absolute commitment to quality made by Fabrice Rosset and his team. I highly recommend their wines.

Champagne Louis Roederer

Located in Reims, Champagne Roederer is one of the most highly regarded of all champagne producers. They own some excellent vineyards and have demonstrated a strong commitment to quality.

Champagne Roederer has many good attributes. They own 75 percent of their own land, giving them control over the majority of their grapes; they use wood barrels for aging a small part of their production; they give their wines much more aging than the typical producer; most of their grapes come from well-regarded crus; and they generally do not use malo-lactic fermentation for their vintage wines. Champagne Roederer enjoys a strong reputation around the world. They are especially famous for their cuvée prestige, Cristal, a symbol of luxury.

Champagne Pol Roger

This grande marque is best known for having been the favorite champagne of Sir Winston Churchill. In fact, the house's cuvée prestige is named Cuvée Sir Winston Churchill, and the Churchill heritage plays a major role in the company's marketing efforts. The company is also known for their collection of old vintages kept in their cellars, and these are occasionally sold through auctions or through a favorite restaurant. I was fortunate enough to purchase bottles of the 1914 vintage and the great 1921 vintage in an auction at Christie's.

What is most important is that the company produces a range of very good champagne. Although it has been quite some time since I tried the rosé or the blanc de blancs, the nonvintage (Brut Extra Cuvée de Réserve), the vintage, and the Cuvée Sir Winston Churchill are all consistently very good. This family-owned and-operated producer is to be congratulated on its commitment to quality. These champagnes are widely available in the United States.

Other Recommended Producers

You now have a list of my 21 (including Champagne De Meric) favorite producers. What follows are brief profiles of some other very good champagne producers. I have focused mainly on the lesser-known brands because information on the large grandes marques is widely available.

Champagne Daniel Adam

Located in the premier cru village of Rilly-la-Montagne, Champagne Adam is primarily a vigneron, selling grapes to NMs including Champagne

De Meric. However, they also produce their own champagne, a pinot noir-dominated cuvée that expresses the unique terroir of Rilly-la-Montagne.

Champagne Agrapart & Fils

This is a quality blanc de blancs producer located in Avize. Champagne Agrapart & Fils uses exclusively grand cru chardonnay grapes with the exception of their rosé, which includes 7 percent pinot noir. This producer has fared very well in taste tests in France and enjoys a good reputation for quality.

Champagne Ariston

This small producer located in the village of Brouillet does an excellent job in producing good champagne at very reasonable prices. In fact, it is one of the better price/values on the market. I have tasted their champagne at various trade shows and have always been impressed.

Champagne Paul Bara

Another very good RM from Bouzy is Champagne Paul Bara. This producer is another member of the Club de Viticulteurs Champenois.

Champagne Paul Bara has a heritage that goes back to 1833. I have had the pleasure of tasting several older vintages directly from the cellars (1953, 1959, 1961, and 1976), and all were excellent.

Although the current offering is not quite up to the same standard, Champagne Paul Bara produces a line of very good champagne today. Their range includes a brut réserve, a vintage champagne, a rosé (Grand Rosé de Bouzy), a Spécial Club, and cuvée Comtesse Marie de France. Champagne Paul Bara also offers an excellent and very reasonably priced Bouzy rouge (Coteaux Champenois).

Champagne Barbier-Louvet

This is a very small producer located in Tauxiéres (99 percent on the échelle des cus), with most of their vines in neighboring Louvois. Champagne Barbier-Louvet produces interesting champagnes that are a good value.

Champagne E. Barnaut

This is another quality producer from Bouzy. I enjoy their champagnes very much and they are available in the United States.

Champagne Andre Beaufort

Champagne André Beaufort of Ambonney, now run by Jacques Beaufort, is a small producer with vines in both Ambonnay and the village of Polisy in the Aube department. Champagne Andre Beaufort is a practitioner of organic viticultural methods and uses no chemical products on his vines. The result is grapes of excellent quality.

In addition to an excellent brut nonvintage, Champagne André Beaufort offers a wide range of vintage champagnes, separating those from Polisy (Réserves) from those of Ambonnay (Grandes Crus) going back to 1985.

The Beaufort name is a common one in Ambonnay, and a number of branches of the family produce champagne. The best of the Beauforts, and perhaps the best producer in Ambonnay, is Champagne André Beaufort.

Champagne Herbert Beaufort

Another branch of the Beaufort family, located in neighboring Bouzy, is Champagne Herbert Beaufort. Run by Henri and Hugues Beaufort, this producer has vines in Bouzy as well as some of the neighboring premier cru villages.

I haven't tried their champagne for some time, probably because there are so many other top producers in the Bouzy/Ambonnay area, but I have always been impressed with the champagnes from Herbert Beaufort. They offer a premier cru brut nonvintage and a grand cru (called Carte d'Or Tradition), both of which are well above average for the category. Their vintage champagnes are very good, as is their rosé. This producer also offers an ultra brut, but unlike some other better known producers, they recognize that a champagne without a dosage needs to be aged longer than other products. I have also found their coteaux champenois (Bouzy Rouge) to be very good.

Champagne Francoise Bedel

Françoise Bedel can be found in the village of Crouttes-sur-Marne, which is the outer limit of the Champagne region to the west. She and her son produce an excellent line of pinot meunier-based, biodynamic champagne. Using traditional methods such as vinifying in oak barrels and avoiding malo-lactic fermentation, Françoise is passionate about champagne. She has been using biodynamic methods exclusively since 1998.

Champagne Billecart-Salmon

Located in Mareuil-sur-Ay, which is just east of Ay, Champagne Billecart-Salmon enjoys an excellent reputation. This is partially the result of having their 1959 vintage champagne declared the "champagne of the century" in a very well organized and professionally run, but unfortunately incomplete (too much focus on grandes marques and extremely limited representation of small producers) tasting organized in Sweden by Richard Juhlin in 1999.

Billecart-Salmon is best known for their rosé. They also produce a Brut Réserve and a vintage champagne. All of these champagnes are well above the norm.

Champagne Marguet Bonnerave

This producer, located in grand cru Ambonnay, features fruit from grands crus Ambonnay, Bouzy, and Mailly-Champagne. Although I haven't tasted all of their line, I've been impressed with what I've tried so far.

Champagne Brice

One of the most creative producers in the Champagne region is Champagne Brice. Located in grand cru Bouzy, the house was created in 1994 by Jean-Paul Brice, a vigneron and former partner in Champagne Barancourt. The Brice family owns seven hectares in Bouzy. In addition, this NM buys grapes from other crus.

In addition to their more basic products (Brut Tradition, Brut Premier Cru, and Brut Rosé), Champagne Brice also produces a line of four "monocru" champagnes, each made using grapes exclusively from a single grand cru village. The grand cru villages selected are Ay, Bouzy, Cramant, and Verzenay. In addition to being very high quality champagnes, this gives connoisseurs the opportunity to taste the variations by terroir from four of Champagne's most renowned villages. Champagne Brice also produces a very good Bouzy Rouge.

Champagne Edouard Brun

Another of our Ay neighbors, Champagne Edouard Brun produces a line of quality champagne. In fact, the family's roots are not in Ay but in Chigny-les-Roses, where I lived. The Delescot family are serious winemakers, and I always enjoy their champagne.

Champagne Guy Cadel

This is a good producer located in Mardeuil, which is just west of Epernay. His pinot meunier-dominated champagnes are quite enjoyable. Champagne Guy Cadel is one of a number of good producers in Mardeuil.

Champagne Claude Carre

This is a small producer located in Trepail, which is, along with neighboring Villers-Marmery, an outpost of chardonnay in the black grape-dominated Montagne de Reims. I've only tasted the nonvintage blanc de blancs, which was above average. Champagne Claude Carre is a producer worth further study.

Champagne Cattier

This NM, located in my former hometown of Chigny-les-Roses, is a family-owned and-operated business. Growers since the eighteenth century, the family started producing their own champagne just after World War I. Originally an RM exploiting 18 hectares, they later changed their status to NM and today buy approximately 60 percent of their grapes. Annual sales are around 300,000 bottles per year.

For a small house, Champagne Cattier is extremely dynamic, and they have enjoyed good success in growing markets such as Japan, Singapore, Columbia, Thailand, and Slovakia. More important, however, they produce a line of very good champagne.

My favorite champagne from this producer is their Clos du Moulin, which is made using grapes from their 2.2-hectare walled vineyard. I have enjoyed this cuvée on numerous occasions and recommend it highly. I also very much like their blanc de blancs, and all of their products are above average. All of the champagnes from Champagne Cattier are premier cru.

Champagne Charlier & Fils

Champagne Charlier & Fils is a member of the Club de Viticulteurs Champenois and one of the better known vignerons in Champagne. This producer, located in Montigny-sous-Chatillon in the Valée de la Marne, is extremely hospitable and is known for giving excellent tours.

Champagne Chartogne-Taillet

Another producer located in a lesser known cru is Champagne Chartogne-Taillet of Merfy. Located just northwest of Reims in the Massif de St. Thierry, Merfy is rated 84 percent on the échelle des crus.

Champagne Chartogne-Taillet produces a line of quality champagnes and does well in competitions in France. I was especially impressed with the Cuvée Ste. Anne. I have not found many quality producers in the Massif de St. Thierry, which makes Champagne Chartogne-Taillet even more impressive.

Champagne Gaston Chiquet

Another very good producer belonging to the Club de Viticulteurs Champenois is Champagne Gaston Chiquet. Located in Dizy, the family also has some excellent vineyards in Ay. In addition to the Special Club, Champagne Gaston Chiquet produces an excellent blanc de blancs using chardonnay grapes exclusively from Ay. These chardonnay grapes grown in this pinot noir capital of Champagne give the blanc de blancs a distinctive flavor, and it is highly recommended. The other products in the line (vintage, rosé, two different nonvintage champagnes) are all above average and represent an excellent value.

Champagne Andre Clouet

As I've said earlier, I very much appreciate champagnes from the grand cru village of Bouzy. One of the better Bouzy RMs is Champagne André Clouet. I've tasted their entire line on two occasions and was quite impressed each time.

In addition, Champagne Clouet is one of the better producers of coteaux champenois, in this case Bouzy rouge. In fact, I was fortunate enough to purchase a lot of six bottles of 1946 Clouet Bouzy rouge in a charity wine auction several years ago. So far I've had three bottles and the wine was outstanding.

Champagne Louis de Sacy

This NM, located in grand cru Verzy, produces a line of above-average champagne. They exploit 25 hectares of vines that provide 80 percent of their needs.

Champagne De Sousa & Fils

Another very good producer from the Côte des Blancs is Champagne De Sousa & Fils of Avize. Erik de Sousa is the third generation of a Portuguese family, and he took over the family business from his father in 1986. The family's vines are in Avize, Cramant, and Oger. Champagne De Sousa produces 50,000 bottles per year.

The most distinctive feature of Champagne De Sousa is their ownership of several parcels of 50-year-old vines. Each year these vines produce grapes with among the highest degrees of sugar in the Champagne region. The juice from these grapes is vinified and aged in oak barrels.

In addition to Brut Tradition, the product line includes a rosé, a very good blanc de blancs réserve, and two cuvée prestige products, Cuvée du

Millénaire and Cuvée des Caudalies. The later is especially noteworthy because it is made exclusively from the older vines and vinified in oak.

Champagne J. De Telmont

Another very good producer is Champagne J. De Telmont, located in Damery (89 percent on the échelle des crus). This family-owned NM has sales of more than one million bottles per year, much of it through supermarkets and other mass distributors in France. Normally this is an indication of low quality, but Champagne J. De Telmont has succeeded in producing a champagne of surprisingly good quality at a very affordable price.

The product line of Champagne J. De Telmont consists of a brut nonvintage (Grande Réserve Brut); a vintage; a vintage blanc de blancs; a nonvintage rosé; and two different vintage cuvées prestiges, Grand Couronnement, and Consecration. The most impressive product is actually the Grande Réserve, which is one of the better brut nonvintage products on the market. It is also one of the best values available in the United States.

Champagne Paul Dethune

The Déthune family are proprietors of seven hectares in grand cru Ambonnay. The focus of this RM is on the vines, the key to quality. They have recently announced that they no longer use chemical insecticides, a strong step forward in improving the quality of both the grapes and the environment. Because of this, I expect even better results from Champagne Déthune in the future.

The product line includes a brut nonvintage, a rosé, a recently introduced blanc de noirs, a vintage champagne, and their cuvée prestige, Princesse Des Thunes. I haven't tasted the current vintage, but all the other products are of very good quality. The Princesse des Thunes is my personal favorite from Champagne Déthune, using 60 percent reserve wine aged in large wood foudres. This wine has a richness in taste, and I have found that it ages quite well.

Champagne Diebolt-Vallois

This is a fairly well known blanc de blancs specialist located in Cramant. It is better than average quality, and it is available in the United States.

Champagne J. Dumangin

Another of my former neighbors in Chigny-les-Roses, Jacky Dumangin is extremely personable, hospitable, and dynamic. He is a member of the Club de Viticulteurs Champenois and an above-average producer.

Champagne Jean Dumangin & Champagne Guy Dumangin

Also located in Chigny-les-Roses, Jean and Guy Dumangin are brothers and next door neighbors. They work together to produce very good champagne, which each markets under his own label. The majority of their vines are in Chigny-les-Roses and neighboring Rilly-la-Montagne, although they also have acquired vines near Vitry-le-François. I prefer their nonvintage Carte d'Or, which is pinot meunier dominated, to their vintage wines, which contain a majority of pinor noir, but both are quite good. The blanc de blanc is less interesting because black grapes are the specialty of these producers.

Champagne Dzieciuck

Located in grand cru Oger just south of Avize, Champagne Dzieciuck has vines both in the Côte des Blancs and in other regions of champagne. The quality is definitely better than average and arguably very good. De Meric had subcontracted our rosé production to Champagne Dzieciuck, and some of the grandes marques buy part of their blanc de blancs ready-made from this producer.

Champagne Egly-Ouriet

Another producer on our list from the excellent village of Ambonnay is Champagne Egly-Ouriet. I generally like many of the champagnes from the Bouzy/Ambonnay area, as you can tell from this list. Champagne Egly-Ouriet has vines in both Ambonnay and Bouzy, so all their products are grand cru.

Egly-Ouriet produces an above-average brut nonvintage and rosé and a vintage champagne. The star of the line, however, is their blanc de noirs Veilles Vignes, produced using the grapes from their older pinot noir vines. As discussed earlier, older vines produce lower yields and higher quality, and the Veille Vignes champagne is excellent. Like all champagnes from Egly-Ouriet, the dates of bottling and disgorgement are marked on a back label. The nonvintage products from Egly-Ouriet are currently aged 39 months, more than twice as long as typical industrial products.

Champagne Michel Fallet

This is another quality Avize producer. I've tried this champagne only at the home of a friend, and I was very impressed. Champagne Michel Fallet is a serious, professional producer.

Champagne Michel Furdyna

Located in the village of Celles-sur-Ource, this is one of the better producers in the Aube. I was especially impressed with his 1991 vintage. This is a producer worth looking for if you visit the Aube department.

Champagne R. Geoffroy

This is a well-regarded producer from Cumiéres. Cumiéres is notable because it is generally the first village to begin harvesting each year. Champagne R. Geoffroy is a quality producer with a broad line of fine wines, including a very good rosé.

Champagne Henri Giraud

This is a small, family operated NM from Ay. They produce champagne of above-average quality. Their best product is their Cuvée Fût de Chêne, a grand cru champagne vinified in oak.

Champagne Pierre Gimonnet

Champagne Pierre Gimonnet, a member of the Club de Viticulteurs Champenois, is located in Cuis. They also have vines in grands crus Cramant and Chouilly in the Côte des Blancs.

This producer presents an interesting contrast in that they were among the first to introduce the 1997 vintage barely three years after it was bottled (the legal minimum), while at the same time they still offer mature vintages such as 1989 and 1990 and, in very limited quantity, 1979 and 1983. Overall, I've been quite impressed with their vintage blanc de blancs champagne. I haven't tried the 1997 yet, but the 1983 and the 1990 are especially good. This grower has a very strong reputation in France, and it is well deserved.

Champagne Gimonnet-Gonet

This producer is the result of a marriage, and both husband and wife come from highly regarded families in the Côte des Blancs. It's been a while since I tasted their product, but I found their quality to be above average. This producer can be found both in Cramant (where I visited them) and at their principal location in Le Mesnil-sur-Oger.

Champagne J. M. Gobillard Et Fils

Champagne J. M. Gobillard is a small NM located in Hautvillers. They are a good producer, although I find their champagne a bit young. Still, I was delighted to find this champagne served on United Airlines in business class rather than the typical grande marque or cooperative brut nonvintage.

Champagne Paul Gobillard

Continuing in the Gobillard family, Champagne Paul Gobillard is also a small NM. This producer is located in Pierry and is most noted for being housed in the Chateau Pierry. Champagne Paul Gobillard produces better than average quality and has a broad product line.

Champagne Paul Goerg

Another very good cooperative is Champagne Paul Goerg of Vertus. The members of this cooperative come primarily from the Côte des Blancs. Although sales under the brand name Paul Goerg are smaller than those of Mailly Grand Cru (90,000 bottles per year), the vast majority of the production is sold by récoltant-cooperatives (RCs) under their own labels.

Champagne Paul Goerg sells a full line of champagne, but the best products are the nonvintage blanc de blancs and a vintage blanc de blancs. These are generally quite reasonably priced and represent a good value.

Champagne Gosset

Located in Ay, Champagne Gosset is best known for being the oldest producer of wine in the Champagne region. Pierre Gosset began producing still wine in 1584, and the house traces its heritage back to that event.

The product line of Champagne Gosset includes a brut nonvintage, Brut Excellence; their Grande Réserve; a nonvintage rosé; a vintage champagne; and their cuvée prestige, Celebris. Despite being located in the most famous pinot noir village in Champagne, the wines of Champagne Gosset include a very significant percentage of chardonnay.

Champagne Alfred Gratien

Champagne Alfred Gratien is a relatively small NM. If one were to rate champagne producers only in terms of their winemaking skills—the ability to maximize the quality of their product given the grapes that they work with—Champagne Alfred Gratien of Epernay would appear near the top of the list. Much of the credit for this must go to the Jaegar family, who have been the chefs de caves but not the owners of Champagne Alfred Gratien for three generations with a fourth in training.

At Champagne Alfred Gratien, 100 percent of the wine is vinified and aged in oak barrels. In addition, they avoid malo-lactic fermentation, enabling the champagne to age superbly. The absence of malo-lactic fermentation means they must age their champagnes longer, which contributes to their quality. The company currently produces approximately 150,000 bottles per year.

The company's specialty is producing outstanding vintage champagnes. There are also two above-average cuvée prestige products, Cuvée Paradis brut and Cuvée Paradis rosé, both of which are chardonnay dominated (more than 60 percent chardonnay). I have also had the good fortune to try some of their other vintages including 1991, 1990, 1985, and 1983. The 1983 was exceptional and was perhaps the best wine I've tasted from that vintage. Champagne Alfred Gratien is available in the United States.

Champagne Grongnet

In the far less celebrated village of Etoges one finds Champagne Grongnet. Etoges is a bit off the beaten track, about halfway between Epernay and Sézanne, and is rated 85 percent on the échelle des crus.

The entire product line from Champagne Grongnet is above average, but their best product by far is their Champagne Carpe Diem, marketed under its own label. This is a nonvintage wine made using all three of the champagne grapes. The wine is vinified in 40-hectolitre wood foudres without malo-lactic fermentation. The result is a rich wine that gives great pleasure, hence the name Carpe Diem, Latin for "seize the day."

Champagne Bernard Hatté

Champagne Bernard Hatté is a small producer located in grand cru Verzenay and a member of the Club de Viticulteurs Champenois. They produce above-average champagne.

Champagne Marc Hébrart

Champagne Marc Hébrart, located in Mareuil-sur-Ay, produces a line of above-average champagne. Mareuil-sur-Ay is the village next to Ay and is rated 99 percent on the échelle des crus. This producer is another member of the Club de Viticulteurs Champenois.

Champagne Charles Heidsieck

Champagne Charles Heidsieck of Reims has a colorful history and was one of the pioneers in developing the champagne market in the United States. Now part of the Rémy-Martin group, this NM is one of the few producers to put a mis en bouteille (bottled) date on their nonvintage brut, which allows the customer to know how long the bottle has been aged. This also has the benefit of allowing for "vertical tastings" of the bottlings from different years, each with the same style but different characteristics in taste.

Champagne Charles Heidsieck also markets a vintage champagne, a vintage rosé, and a demi-sec. The company suffered a major loss when Daniel Thibault, their talented cellarmaster, died of cancer in early 2002.

Champagne Henriot

This is a well-regarded, mid-sized NM located in Reims. Formerly a part of the LVMH Group, this house regained its independence in 1994 when it was purchased by Joseph Henriot, a descendant of the founding family. They have worked hard to improve quality and have done a very good job.

Champagne M. Hostomme

This producer, located in grand cru Chouilly, is technically an NM because the proprietor buys grapes from his brother's vineyard. The specialty is blanc de blancs (Chouilly is a grand cru for chardonnay and a premier cru for black grapes). The nonvintage blanc de blancs, the blanc de blancs réserve, and the vintage banc de blancs are all very good. The family is also very welcoming, making this an excellent stop during a visit to Champagne.

Champagne Bernard Hubschwerlin

Champagne Bernard Hubschwerlin is a small producer, exploiting four hectares of vines located in the village of Courteron in the Aube Department, home of Champagne Fleury. I very much liked his blanc de blancs, which is especially impressive coming from a cru totally dominated by pinot noir (95 percent of the vines in Courteron are pinot noir). This wine is made using old vines that produce low yields and higher quality grapes. All in all, Bernard Hubschwerlin has succeeded in producing a line of very good champagne.

Champagne Jacquesson & Fils

Champagne Jacquesson & Fils is in some ways responsible for my becoming a champagne producer. Jacquesson was the first small champagne producer I encountered during my first visit to the region, and their hospitality and quality played a major role in fueling my interest in champagne. Champagne Jacquesson was available in the United States, although not in our then home state of Florida, so with the help of an out-of-state wine merchant we were able to enjoy champagnes from Jacquesson at home. Their product line includes a brut nonvintage, a rosé, a vintage blanc de blancs, and their cuvée prestige, Signiture.

Located in Dizy, a neighboring town of Ay, Champagne Jacquesson & Fils has a rich history. This NM was founded in Chalons in 1798 by Memmie Jacquesson. Adolphe Jacquesson took over the company on the death of his father in 1835, and in 1844 he made a major contribution to the industry with the invention of the wire muselet, which is still used today to hold the cork securely in place. Before this, string was used to hold the bottle in place, a method that was quite attractive but less effective to ensure conservation. One of the major features of the company is their use of wood barrels to vinify a percentage of their wine. Champagne Jacquesson & Fils is available in the United States.

Champagne Jeeper

This is a small NM located in Damery. The founder, the late Armand Goutorbe, was injured in a German POW camp during World War II and returned unable to fully use his legs to perform the necessary tasks in the vineyards. The French government made it possible for him to buy a Jeep to help him in the vines, hence the name Champagne Jeeper. Today the company produces above-average champagne and offers excellent tours through the vines in, of course, a Jeep.

Champagne Lancelot-Pienne

This is a small blanc de blancs producer from Cramant. Champagne Lancelot-Pienne is of decent quality and good value and is available in the United States.

Champagne Lancelot-Wanner

Another very good producer from Cramant is Champagne Lancelot-Wanner. Yves Lancelot and his wife exploit a little more than three hectares in Cramant and Avize, all planted in chardonnay. Their vintage and nonvintage blanc de blancs are of very good quality and are properly vinified and aged. I've been especially impressed with some of their older vintages, which I've had the good fortune to try.

Both the Lancelot and Wanner families are well known in Cramant. We will discuss some other family members in this chapter.

Champagne Larmandier-Bernier

Located in Vertus, Champagne Larmandier-Bernier is another member of the Club de Viticulteurs Champenois. Specializing in blanc de blancs champagne, this producer is worth seeking out.

Champagne J. Lassalle

Another member of the Club de Viticulteurs Champenois is Champagne J. Lassalle of Chigny-les-Roses. I lived in Chigny-les-Roses for three years and know the wines there very well. Champagne J. Lassalle produces a line of above-average products including a very good rosé and their Special Club, but my favorite wine from this producer is their Cuvée Angeline, named after the granddaughter of the proprietor.

Although I did not visit Madame Lassalle and her daughter until after I moved to the region, I've known the champagne for quite some time and have always enjoyed it. In fact, I recall finding it on the wine list of a restaurant in Florida where we occasionally dined. Once I approached the sommelier of this restaurant to ask him to add De Meric to his list, but he explained to me that he had a very difficult time selling champagne from small producers to his clients. "In fact," he told me, "I have one on the list now, J. Lassalle, and I've only sold three bottles of it during the past year." I didn't have the heart to tell him that we had purchased all three bottles.

Champagne George Laval

This is a small organic producer located in Cumiéres. Their cuvée prestige is very good, and the brut nonvintage and brut réserve are above average.

Champagne Le Mesnil

Another good cooperative is the Union des Propriétaires-Récoltants, which markets under the brand name of Champagne Le Mesnil. As one might guess, this cooperative is located in Le Mesnil-sur-Oger.

Champagne Le Mesnil has primarily local members and markets a limited product line of blanc de blancs champagne. It has been some time since I conducted a full tasting, but overall I found the quality to be very good.

Champagne Leclerc Briant

This small NM located in Epernay is extremely interesting and innovative. Formerly an RM, they exploit 30 hectares, enough for approximately 80 percent of their needs. Included in these holdings are excellent parcels in Cumières, Hautvillers, and Damery. They have practiced organic and biodynamic principles in some of their vineyards for some time, which has made an important contribution to enhancing their quality. They also are very innovative marketers, doing a excellent job of developing relationships with their clients.

The product line of Champagne Leclerc-Briant is extremely well rounded. Included are a brut reserve; a blanc de blancs; a vintage rosé; two vintage champagnes; and three cuvée prestige products, each from single vineyards (Les Crayères, Le Clos des Champions, and Les Chèvres Pierreuses). They also produced one of the best and most creative special cuvées for the year 2000, Cuvée Du Solstice 2000. This product, from the excellent 1990 vintage, was perhaps the only cuvée l'an 2000 that combined excellent quality, innovative packaging (including a specially designed watch as the capsule, designed to sound at midnight December 31, 1999), and a reasonable price (less than $100.00).

Champagne Leclerc-Briant is a very good producer. My understanding is that they have had some financial problems, but hopefully these are now behind them.

Champagne David Leclapart

Located in Trépail, a chardonnay enclave in the pinot noir-dominated Montagne de Reims, David Léclapart produces an excellent line of biodynamic champagnes. I met David for the first time in early 2004, and I was impressed with his wine, his methods, and his passion. His production is quite small and very little is exported, but if you are in the Champagne region it will be well worth the effort to search out this young producer.

Champagne Mailly Grand Cru

Our next very good producer, Champagne Mailly Grand Cru, is a cooperative, the best cooperative manipulant (CM) on this list. Established in 1929, it is one of the oldest cooperatives in Champagne and one of the very few that have remained true to their traditional role of creating a quality champagne typical of the terroir of a single cru. All of the bottles produced by this CM are sold under their own label.

Champagne Mailly Grand Cru produces an interesting line of quality champagne, including a brut réserve, an extra brut, a rosé, and a vintage, all of which are better than the typical grande marque. The stars of the line, however, are their blanc de noirs (100-percent pinot noir), and their Cuvée Des Echansons. Mailly is a nice town, making this a good producer to visit if you are in Champagne.

Champagne Serge Mathieu

Champagne Serge Mathieu is another better-than-average Aube producer. They are in the process of converting their 10 hectares to organic viticulture, which bodes well for the future.

Champagne Jose Michel et Fils

There are a number of producers from the Michel family in Moussy and neighboring Pierry, but the best is Champagne José Michel. Another member of the Club de Viticulteurs Champenois, José Michel exploits 21 hectares of vines, primarily in the villages south of Epernay (Coteaux Sud d'Epernay). Moussy is rated 89 percent on the échelle des crus.

This producer has a surprisingly large product line, including a brut, an extra brut, a rosé, and multiple vintages of blanc de blancs and traditional blends. I especially like the Special Club and the Cuvée du Père Houdart 1983. However, don't overlook the standard brut nonvintage (Carte Blanche Brut), a pinot meunier-dominated champagne that is far above the average in its category.

Champagne Jean Milan

This small NM located in Oger offers a selection of better-than-average grand cru blanc de blancs champagnes. Like some other small producers, they will create very nice personalized labels for specialized occasions.

Champagne Robert Moncuit

This producer, located in Le Mesnil-sur-Oger, produces blanc de blancs champagnes of above-average quality. I especially enjoyed their older vintages.

Champagne Moutard

This midsized NM (600,000 bottles per year) is located in the village of Buxeuil and has succeeded in making a champagne far superior to the majority of those produced in more highly rated crus (like almost all of the Aube, Buxeuil is rated 80 percent on the échelle des crus). They succeed due to the quality of their grapes (their own vineyards supply 40 percent of their needs) as well as creativity and patience in making their wines.

Champagne Moutard presents a full line of products, all of which are better than the norm. The two best, however, are their high-quality vintage blanc de blancs and their Vieilles Vignes champagne, made 100 percent from the Arbane grape variety, one of the lost varieties discussed earlier under our profile of Champagne L. Aubry. I highly recommend both these products, especially the Vieilles Vignes.

Champagne Jean Moutardier

This is a rarity in Champagne because, like De Meric, the company is run by a foreigner. Jonathan Saxby, who with his wife Elisabeth (of the Moutardier family) manages Champagne Jean Moutardier, is English. I never met the Saxbys, probably because Le Breuil, where they are located, is a bit off the beaten path (southeast of Chateau-Thierry).

Despite the fact that their terroir is not highly regarded (Le Breuil is rated 83 percent on the échelle des crus), they manage to produce a range of very good champagne. I especially liked the Carte D'Or, a 100-percent pinot meunier champagne aged in wood, the Cuvée Centenaire, and a vintage champagne.

Champagne A. Soutiran Pelletier

At the other end of the échelle des cru, in grand cru Ambonnay, we find Champagne Soutiran Pelletier. This producer is probably best known in the Champagne region for their excellent boutique on the main street of Ambonnay, but they make a very good range of champagnes. I especially liked the Grand Cru Rosé, which is one of the few rosés made using the saignée method (maceration), and the Grand Cru Blanc de Blancs, which uses grapes from Ambonnay and Avize and has been aged more than four years sur latte. This producer is worth a visit if you are in the area.

Champagne Delamotte Père & Fils

Champagne Delamotte is located in Le Mesnil-sur-Oger. Owned by Laurent-Perrier, this NM is closely linked with Champagne Salon. The Delamotte brand, however, has its own history that dates back to 1760 and is a quality product in its own right.

As one would expect, the specialty of Champagne Delamotte is blanc de blancs champagne. The house offers both a nonvintage and a vintage blanc de blancs, and both are very good. In addition, Delamotte markets a classic brut nonvintage and a rosé.

Champagne Launois Père & Fils

In general, the producers offering the most entertaining visits in Champagne are not the best producers—they focus on the bells and whistles of the visit rather than the quality of their champagne to impress customers. An exception to this rule is Champagne Launois Père & Fils of Le Mesnil-sur-Oger, who manage to combine a great visit with a top-quality champagne. The visit is outstanding because of the hospitality of Bernard Launois and his family and the fact that they have created an incredible museum of ancient presses, tools, and machines for all aspects of viticulture and champagne production. This is an essential tour for any visitor to the region.

More important, Bernard Launois is a very fine champagne producer. This is a fairly large RM with 21 hectares in the Côte des Blancs. They are another member of the Club de Viticulteurs Champenois, and their Special Club champagne is consistently top quality, as is their Cuvée de Réserve.

Champagne Pierre Peters

This is another quality producer from Le Mesnil-sur-Oger. Champagne Pierre Peters exploits 17.5 hectares and produces 130,000 bottles per year.

Champagne Maurice Philippart

This is another of my former Chigny-les-Roses neighbors. Champagne Maurice Philippart is overall a better-than-average producer, and their nonvintage Carte D'Or is very good for its class.

Champagne Ployez-Jacquemart

Located in the town of Ludes (94 percent on the échelle des crus), Champagne Ployez-Jacquemart is a small, quality-oriented NM. The family owns 1.8 hectares of pinot noir vines in Ludes and neighboring Mailly (grand cru), which are supplemented by grapes purchased from a number of different crus. Total production is approximately 50,000 bottles per year.

Champagne Ployez-Jacquemart offers a very good brut nonvintage (Extra Quality), a rosé, and a vintage. The cuvée prestige, Liesse d'Harbonville 1990, is vinified in oak barrels and produced only in excellent years.

One final note: All of the champagnes from this producer are made from a single vintage with no reserve wine, although the bottles are not necessarily vintage dated.

Champagne Pointallart-Grand

This is a better-than-average producer located in Ecueil. Their Cuvée Reflet is especially good.

Champagne Ch. & A. Prieur

Located in the premier cru village of Vertus in the Côte des Blancs, Champagne Prieur has a history going back to 1825. Still owned and operated by the Prieur family, this house produces and markets their products under the Napoléon brand name in honor, of course, of the great Napoléon Bonaparte.

The product line includes two brut nonvintage champagnes (Carte d'Or Premier Cru and Réserve Carte Verte), a rosé, and a vintage champagne. The one thing that is a bit odd about this producer is that despite the fact that they are located in the Côte des Blancs, their champagnes are not chardonnay dominated and they do not even produce a blanc de blancs. Part of this can be explained by the fact that they buy 100 percent of their grapes, but it always seemed odd to me that they did not have more contracts in their home area. However, their formula seems to be successful for Champagne Prieur.

Champagne Quenardel & Fils

Another member of the Club de Viticulteurs Champenois, Champagne Quenardel & Fils is located in grand cru Verzenay but has vines in a number of locations. All their products are above average, but I especially liked their blanc de blancs. Their champagne often can be found at La Maison Du Vigneron, an excellent restaurant.

Champagne Bertrand Rafflin

Another very good producer in Chigny-les-Roses is Champagne Bertrand Rafflin. There are a number of Rafflins in the village and in neighboring Ludes, but most work with the local cooperative, a part of Nicolas Feuillatte. Bertrand Rafflin, however, is an RM, and quite a good one.

His best product is the vintage wine Cuvée Saint Vincent (St. Vincent is the patron saint of the vignerons). The 1989 was the best champagne from Chigny that I've tasted and was very reasonably priced. This producer also offers an above-average brut along with a rosé.

Champagne Ricciuti-Révolte

This company is remarkable primarily because of its unique story. During World War II, the late Al Ricciuti, a young soldier from Baltimore, met and fell in love with Paulette Révolte, daughter of a vigneron in Avenay-Val-d'Or (rated 93 percent o the échelle des crus). After the war Al returned to the United States, but he and Paulette stayed in touch. Finally, in 1963 they were married, making Al the first American vigneron in Champagne. This small company is now run by their son, John Charles (named after John F. Kennedy and Charles de Gaulle). The specialty of the house is called Cuvée Franco Américaine.

Champagne J. M. Rigot

This small producer located in Binson-Orquigny (rated 86 percent on the échelle des crus) makes a nice line of reasonably priced, pinot meunier-dominated champagnes for everyday drinking.

Champagne Alain Robert

Champagne Alain Robert is another very good producer specializing in blanc de blancs. I first tried this champagne a decade ago and was very impressed.

Located in Le Mesnil-sur-Oger, Alain Robert exploits 12 hectares in the Côte des Blancs. He is a strong believer in aging his champagnes (usually seven years or more), which allows these blanc de blancs to fully mature. These champagnes are by no means inexpensive, but I've found that they are worth the price.

Champagne François Secondé

Our next very good RM, Champagne François Secondé, is located in grand cru Sillery. In the eighteenth century, the wines of Sillery had a reputation rivaling those of Ay, but in modern Champagne, it is more a residential community than a major vineyard town. Champagne François Secondé, however, has kept up the Sillery tradition of producing quality champagne.

François Secondé and his family exploit a little more than four and one-half hectares of vines, all in Sillery. Sillery is primarily known for pinot noir, so it is no surprise that the majority of the grapes used to make their champagne are pinot noir, especially in the vintage champagnes. I found the brut nonvintage better than average and was extremely impressed with their vintage champagnes. Champagne François Secondé often appears among the winners in competitions held in France.

Champagne Jacques Selosse

Champagne Jacques Selosse, located in Avize, is a champagne that I have known and enjoyed for more than a decade. Operated today by Anselme and Corinne Selosse, this RM produces a line of creative, well-packaged, very good champagnes. However, the reputation of this producer has grown dramatically during the past decade to the point where Champagne Jacques Selosse is now one of the very few overrated RMs in Champagne.

Anselme Selosse does a number of things right in his champagne production. He minimizes chapitalisation and does not filter his wines. He vinifies and ages his wines in wood, although he uses a great deal of new wood, which I find gives the wines an artificial taste that is similar to a new world chardonnay rather than the subtle richness of a René Collard or a Krug. In addition, all of his vines are classified grand cru (chardonnay from Avize, Cramant, and Oger; pinot noir from Ay). The result is an interesting product line that includes a blanc de blancs (Tradition), an extra brut blanc de blancs, a vintage blanc de blancs, a rosé, a blanc de noir (Contraste), a sweet champagne (Cuvée Exquise), and a cuvée prestige (Substance) that is aged and fermented entirely in new oak barrels.

Champagne Gonet Sulcova

This chardonnay specialist has their offices in Epernay, but their roots are in the Côte des Blancs. Many of their vines are there as well, although they also have holdings elsewhere, especially in Montgeux in the Aube department. A total of 80 percent of this RM's vines are planted in chardonnay and 20 percent in pinot noir.

Champagne Gonet Sulcova is a member of the Club de Viticulteurs Champenois. This highly respected RM produces a fine range of champagnes, including two vintage wines.

I've gotten to know the family, especially Carla and her husband Cedric (the next generation) over the last few years. Cedric and Carla are also good friends of René Collard and are very knowledgeable and serious wine lovers. In fact, Cedric teaches classes on wine in the region. This dedication to wine shows in the quality offered by Champagne Gonet Sulcova.

Champagne Tarlant

Few producers do more with less than Champagne Tarlant. Located in Oeuilly, a northern-facing cru that generally produces good but unexceptional wines, Champagne Tarlant manages to produce a very good champagne from their terroir. They make extensive use of traditional methods such as wood barrels, which I believe is the secret of their success.

Champagne G. Tribaut

Located in Hautvillers, this extremely hospitable vigneron is worth visiting if you are in the area. The champagne is of above-average quality.

Champagne Alfred Tritant

This producer, located in Bouzy, produces grand cru champagnes of above-average, but not remarkable, quality. They offer a good value for the price.

Champagne J. L. Vergnon

Another very good producer from the Côte des Blancs is Champagne J. L. Vergnon of Le Mesnil-sur-Oger. This grower exploits a little more than five hectares of chardonnay in and around Le Mesnil-sur-Oger. All their champagnes are grand cru blanc de blancs, and the dedication to quality is equally evident in talking to M. Vergnon or in tasting the product line. I especially enjoyed the vintage 1987, generally not a great year in Champagne but a vintage of high quality from producers such as Franck Bonville and J. L. Vergnon.

Champagne Alain Vesselle & Champagne Jean Vesselle

These are two more growers from the Vesselle family of Bouzy. Both are very good, but they are not in the same league as their cousin Maurice Vesselle.

Champagne George Vesselle

George Vesselle is the best known of the Bouzy Vesselles, primarily because he was the mayor of Bouzy for 25 years. Champagne George Vesselle is an NM, purchasing 10 percent of their grapes from outside sources. Their champagnes are of above-average quality.

Champagne Vilmart

The Vilmarts first established their vineyard in Rilly-la-Montagne in 1872. Today, Laurent Champs is the fifth generation to manage the family business, as he has done since 1990.

Champagne Vilmart produces just under 100,000 bottles of top-quality champagne. All of the products are premier cru, and the grapes are grown primarily in Rilly-la-Montagne. Their vineyards are primarily planted in chardonnay, which is the dominant grape in all of their cuvées other than their rosé and their Vielle Réserve. All of their wines are vinified and aged in oak, including some in new oak.

I had an opportunity recently to taste the entire Villmart line with Laurent Champs, and I was very impressed with the overall quality. I was also impressed with the breadth of the line, which includes seven different cuvées. I have had their wines since then in restaurants and always enjoyed them very much.

Champagne Voirin-Jumel

We have discussed a number of Côte des Blancs producers located in Avize and Le Mesnil-sur-Oger, but many feel that the grand cru village of Cramant, located just north of Avize, produces the best chardonnay found in Champagne. In Cramant one finds Champagne Voirin-Jumel, another very good producer specializing in blanc de blancs champagne.

Like most growers, Champagne Voirin-Jumel is a family affair, exploiting a total of ten hectares. Unlike some of our other blanc de blancs specialists, they also have vines outside of the Côte des Blancs, and they use the black grapes from these vines to make their Brut Tradition, one of the better brut nonvintage champagnes on the market. They also produce a good nonvintage blanc de blancs, a reserve blanc de blancs (Réserve Brut Gilles Voirin), and a vintage. I often recommend that American and English friends visit this producer because they are very welcoming and speak English.

Champagne Wanner-Bouge

This is an above-average producer located in Cramant. Like most Côte des Blancs producers, they specialize in blanc de blancs. However, they also have vines planted in pinot noir and pinot meunier outside the Côte des Blancs.

13. A Visitor's Guide to the Champagne Region

A S A TOURIST DESTINATION, the Champagne region is fantastic ... if you are a champagne lover. Although there are a number of other things to do and see in the region, the major options of interest revolve around the wine. Because you are interested enough in champagne to have read this far, I'm pretty confident that you'd find a visit to the Champagne region a highly enjoyable and rewarding experience.

Practicalities

Planning

Let's start with planning the trip. The normal tourist season runs from mid–April to the end of July and again from the beginning of September until the end of October. Most of the people from the region take the month of August as vacation, so many of the things you'll want to do will be closed during that month. Many visitors come for the harvest in late September, but I don't think this is the best time to visit because most champagne producers are too busy to spend time with visitors. Instead, I'd recommend the period from mid–May to mid–July, after the weather improves (at least relatively) and before the vacation season begins.

Getting There

Assuming that Champagne is the first destination on your trip, you'll fly into Paris, preferably Charles de Gaulle airport because it is closer to the region than Orly airport. If you live near a major city, direct flights to Paris are often available. If you plan to start your trip in Paris, there is excellent train service to Epernay and Reims from the Gare de l'Est. If you are coming from another city in Europe, train service is available to Epernay and Reims, although you usually have to change trains in a major city such as Paris or Strasbourg.

Getting Around

You will need to rent a car to get around the region. The best option is Avis because they are located at all of the airports and train stations. As is true throughout Europe, almost all cars will have standard transmission rather than automatic transmission.

If your budget permits, an alternative to renting a car is to hire a car service/tour guide. Your hotel will be able to help set this up.

Where to Stay

There are good hotel options to fit almost every budget. The top of the line is Les Crayères in Reims. Formerly a mansion belonging to Madame Pommery of champagne fame, Les Crayères matches an elegant setting with impeccable service. Another outstanding option is Royal Champagne, located near Epernay in the village of Champillon. The rooms are beautiful, and the high elevation of Champillon gives visitors gorgeous views of the region. In 2005, one expected to pay $300 to $400 per night at either of those hotels.

Two other excellent hotels, both a bit less expensive than Les Crayères and Royal Champagne, are the Grand Hôtel des Templiers in Reims and the Hostellerie La Briqueterie in Vinay, which is about four miles southwest of Epernay. Both have very nice rooms and good service. I find the setting of La Briqueterie, in a vineyard village, to be more charming than that of the Grand Hôtel des Templiers, but both are recommended. Prices for both these hotels were, in 2005, in the $200 range.

The newest hotel in Champagne is the Hôtel Castel Jeanson in Ay, operated by the Goutorbe family. This is a small hotel with ten rooms and two suites. It is beautifully decorated, has a very nice lounge, and the whole atmosphere is geared toward making guests feel at home.

Also highly recommended are a few establishments a bit off the beaten track, the Auberge Le Relais in Reuilly-Sauvigny and the Chateau de Fére in Fére-en-Tardenois. Both are located in the Aisne department. These are very different types of establishments—Chateau de Fére is a converted sixteenth-century mansion located on the ruins of an ancient castle ($150–$275), while Le Relais is more of a country inn located in the vines ($60–$100). Actually, I prefer Le Relais due to the quality of its restaurant, which will be our next topic.

For those looking for a very nice, moderately priced American-style hotel, there are a number of good options available in Reims. The best is probably the Garden Court Holiday Inn, although the New Hôtel Europe and the Best Western Hôtel de la Paix are also nice. There is also a Best Western in Epernay. All of these hotels charged approximately $60 to $75 per night in 2005.

For the person on a more limited budget, I recommend the Hôtel Campanile in Dizy, which is two or three miles from Epernay. All rooms were in 2005 in the $40 per night range and are quite a good value. Dizy is the village next to Ay, so this is quite a convenient location for visiting Champagne De Meric!

There are a number of other options available in the cities (Reims, Epernay, and Chalons) and in the vineyards. Check the Internet for good deals.

Where to Eat

Aside from visiting champagne producers, the best reason to visit the Champagne region is its restaurants. Unlike Lyon or areas such as Burgundy or Brittany, there is not a distinctive style of cuisine in Champagne. Much of this is due to the fact that Champagne has always been a European crossroads and, thus, subject to many outside cultural influences. One can eat very well in Champagne because restaurants offer both traditional and modern French styles of cuisine.

The top restaurant in the region, and one of the top restaurants in the world, is Les Crayères. In terms of a total package—food, service, ambiance, welcome, wine list, and comfort—this is one of the finest restaurants I have ever experienced. The cuisine is excellent and well presented, and the service is always perfect.

Of special interest to the champagne lover is the wine list, which includes probably the largest selection of champagnes of any restaurant in the world. Dining at Les Crayères is expensive (with wine $100 per person and up), but compared to the more expensive restaurants in cities such as Paris, London, and New York, one receives a great value at Les Crayères.

My second-favorite restaurant in the region is Auberge Le Relais in Reuilly-Sauvigny. This is a great restaurant and an outstanding value. One receives a warm welcome, excellent service, and magnificent cuisine. The wine list is also quite good.

A third excellent restaurant is La Maison du Vigneron, located on the main route (RN51) between Epernay and Reims. This restaurant is surrounded by woods and decorated in the style of a forest inn. La Maison du Vigneron offers a great combination of excellent service, excellent cuisine, and moderate prices ($30 to $50 per person, including wine). Of special interest is the wine list, dominated by an ever-changing selection of champagnes from récoltant-manipulants (RMs).

I also recommend the Restaurant Continental in Place d'Erlon in Reims. The food is quite good, and the service and wine are excellent.

Two other restaurants I highly recommend are Les Cépages in Epernay and Le Mesnil in Le Mesnil-sur-Oger. Les Cépages has slightly better cuisine, while Le Mesnil has a better wine list, featuring champagnes from Le Mesnil-sur-Oger. Each is in an attractive setting and provides very good service. Both are reasonably priced and well worth a visit.

Although these are my favorites, there are a number of other good restaurants in the region. Other notable restaurants include Les Berceaux in Epernay, Le Foche and Le Chardonnay in Reims, Royal Champagne in Champillon, La Briqueterie in Vinay, Hostellerie du Chateau in Fére-en-Tardenois, Hôtel de La Poste in Vitry-le-François, Le Grand Cerf in Montchenot, and Jacky Michel in the Hôtel d'Angleterre in Chalons-en-Champagne. Also, I can recommend two very inexpensive options—Le Latin in Reims and Lys du Roi in Sermiers (near Ecueil).

All these restaurants are quite welcoming and will cater to special diets (vegetarian, vegan, etc.) if you let them know in advance. Although English is not a strong suit in some of these restaurants (exceptions are Les Crayères and Royal Champagne), most speak enough "food English" to help everyone through the menu. I recommend making reservations a day or two in advance if possible.

What to Do, Part One: Champagne Visits

Although nice hotels and fine restaurants are great, they can be found in a number of other areas. What can't be found elsewhere are champagne producers. In fact, I believe the only way to really learn about champagne is to visit the region at least once to see the terrain, visit different types of producers, and taste some of the champagnes that are rarely available outside of France.

I've visited hundreds of producers and played host to scores of visitors to the region. In my experience, I've found that the best program is to strive for variety. Visit at least one grande marque, one smaller négociant-manipulant (NM), and one cooperative. Visit at least one RM in each region of the Marne (Côte des Blancs, Vallée de La Marne, and Montagne de Reims). You should also spend a day in the Aube and visit at least one producer in that region. This program will allow you to get a feel for the region and see some of the differences in the wine for yourself.

Which producers to visit comes down to a question of what you are looking for as well as your French language skills (or those of your guide). What I will do is to provide you with some options in each category.

Let's start with the grandes marques. A visit to at least one of these producers is essential, since (a) they generally give entertaining tours, (b) they almost all offer tours in English, and (c) because their products are generally available in the United States, one does not need to feel obligated to buy anything. In fact, your very first champagne visit should be to a grande marque because this will give you a good overview of the champagne process.

The best options for this first visit are Piper-Heidsieck in Reims and Mercier in Epernay. Both provide high-tech, multi-media tours through the cellars in open trains followed by a tasting, and reservations are not necessary. Of the two I prefer the Mercier tour, which is guided, although the advantage of the Piper-Heidsieck tour is that the commentary is on a cassette tape, so a tour in English is always available. Mercier usually has a few tours a day in English.

Beyond this first visit, I'd recommend visiting one of the grandes marques of outstanding quality: Bollinger, Krug, Deutz, or Roederer. All offer tours in English. These visits are more serious and informative than the typical bells and whistles grande marque tour, and I highly recommend scheduling at least one of these producers.

There are a number of options for small and mid-sized NMs. You are, of course, welcome to visit De Meric, and a visit in English is available by appointment. Other quality NMs offering tours in English include Jacquesson in Dizy, Jean Moutardier in Le Breuil, Soutiran-Pelletier in Ambonnay, M. Hostomme in Chouilly, Cattier in Chigny-les-Roses, Leclerc-Briant in Epernay, Ch. & A. Prieur in Vertus, and Henriot in Reims.

There are a few interesting choices among the cooperatives. The best quality cooperative manipulant (CM) is Mailly Grand Cru, and they offer excellent visits and tastings in English. More typical cooperatives, however, are Nicolas Feuillatte in Chouilly and Jacquart in Reims, both of which offer tours in English.

By far the most interesting producers to visit are the RMs. The language, however, can be a difficulty. I feel these are the most important visits you will make, so it is worth some extra effort. For example, plan a day or two of visits to these growers and book the services of a guide for this period (this has the added benefit of leaving your group free to drink without having to choose a designated driver). In this way, you can arrange visits with any of the producers discussed in this book or anyone else you choose.

If having a guide is not of interest to you, there are a number of quality RMs who sometimes offer tours in English. In the Côte des Blancs, options include Voirin-Jumel and Lancelot-Pienne in Cramant, Launois Père & Fils in Le Mesnil-sur-Oger, Leclaire and Agrapart & Fils in Avize, and Larmandier-Bernier in Vertus. In the Montagne de Reims, choose from Maurice Vesselle, Herbert Beaufort, and Edward Barnaut in Bouzy; Paul Dethune in Ambonnay; Gaston Chiquet in Dizy; Champagne Goutorbe in Ay; and Ricciuti-Révolte in Avenay-Val-d'Or. In the Vallée de La Marne, quality options include Guy Cadel in Mardeuil, René Geoffroy in Cumiers, Champagne Bliard in Hautvillers, P. Guerre in Ventuil, and Charlier & Fils in Montigny-sous-Chatillon.

The etiquette when visiting a producer varies according to the producer's size. As mentioned earlier, appointments are absolutely essential, especially because many of the smaller companies must make special arrangements to provide a tour in English. Some producers, most notably the larger ones, charge for the tours. However, many smaller producers do not charge for visits, so when visiting a small producer, especially one that does not market in your home country, it is important to purchase a few bottles. You can enjoy these in the region and even take some home (you may have to pay duty if you live in the United States, but this is not very expensive and is often waived). For those producers who are especially welcoming it is good to follow-up with a thank you letter or even a small gift after you return home.

Finally, let me know how you enjoyed your visits, especially if you found certain producers especially welcoming, or if you had any problems. I can be reached by e-mail at *danielginsburg@ChampagneDeMeric.com.*

What to Do, Part Two:
Beyond Visiting Champagne Producers

I have no doubt that the various tours of champagne producers will be the highlight of your trip to the region. If you are going to be in Champagne for more than a few days, however, you'll definitely want to do some other things, if for no other reason than to give your palate (and liver) a rest.

The church is often the most imposing building in the villages of Champagne (photograph by John Hodder/Collection CIVC).

One obligatory destination is the Cathédrale Notre-Dame in Reims. Although it is not quite up to the standards of Notre-Dame of Paris, this is a magnificent building, parts of which date back to the thirteenth century. More important, this is the traditional site for the coronation of French kings and where Jeanne d'Arc brought Charles VII to be crowned. This building (along with much of the region) was almost totally destroyed during World War I and was rebuilt due in large part to financial aid from the United States.

There are also a number of other interesting sites in Reims, including the Salle de Reddition, where the Germans surrendered on May 8, 1945, to end World War II in Europe. There is also a fairly good art museum (Musée des Beaux-Arts), the remains of a third-century Roman gate (Porte Mars), and various religious sites (Palais du Tau, Basilique St-Remi).

Beyond Reims, there are a wide variety of interesting sites. I recommend a visit to the chateau at Condé-en-Brie, parts of which date back to the sixteenth century. English tours are available by appointment. When you pass through the Vallée de La Marne, you'll be able to see the Chateau Boursault, one of the most stunning pieces of the landscape in Champagne. This chateau, however, is not open for tours.

Keeping with the chateau theme, there are some interesting things to see in the town of Chateau-Thierry, birthplace of famed fable writer Jean de La Fontaine. In addition to a museum dedicated to this author, there are the ruins of a medieval chateau. The town of Chateau-Thierry and the surrounding area was a major battlefield during World War I, and the town contains many monuments as well as a cemetery for Americans killed in that bloody conflict.

Also of interest are a giant windmill in the town of Verzenay, an ancient wine press in Ay, and the Faux de Verzy, a forest containing beech trees that have grown in a fashion that makes this look like an enchanted forest. Champagne De Castellane in Epernay has a butterfly garden and a wine museum, and Champagne Launois Père & Fils has a fabulous wine museum.

Aside from these tours, I have always enjoyed simply driving around the region. There are a lot of beautiful forests, old buildings, and interesting architecture.

The Aube is an extremely scenic area with a great deal of natural beauty. The architecture is also worth mentioning. There are many old "half-timber" style buildings, which is very different from what one generally sees in the Marne department. Ancient stone cabins, called cadoles, are also worth seeing.

My favorite place to visit in the Aube, however, is the town of Bayel, known as the city of crystal. Bayel has been a glassmaking center since the fourteenth century, as generations of craftsmen have practiced their art there.

There are two artisan glassmaking concerns in Bayel, the Cristalleries Royales de Champagne and Aube Cristal. Both manufacture all of their products (hand-blown crystal) by hand and offer a variety of fine products. Although Aube Cristal offers glassware of excellent quality, Cristalleries Royales is by far the superior of the two (and, of course, the more expensive). Both offer tours, and tours in English are available at the Cristalleries Royales with advance reservations. Each of these glassmakers has a shop with an extensive and ever-changing inventory. In addition to glassware for the table, one can find vases and various high-quality glass ornaments.

A nice bonus when visiting the Champagne region is its central location. Epernay is only an hour and a half train ride from central Paris, and good train connections are available to a number of French and other European cities and regions. The French government is in the process of building a bullet train line (TGV) from Paris east, which will make the region only 45 minutes from downtown Paris and a short ride to Strasbourg and Germany.

All in all, the Champagne region has a lot to offer to visitors. I've always enjoyed my trips and hope you will have the opportunity to explore this unique area.

14. Life in Champagne

I'M OFTEN ASKED WHAT IT WAS LIKE to live in the Champagne region. Most people seem to either have a romantic vision of a dream life among the vines (I've also lived in the Napa Valley, and found people looked at it the same way) or they wonder how I could survive in a primitive land and ask such questions as: Do they have doctors in Champagne? What does one eat there? Do they hate Americans?

Actually, I enjoyed my time in Champagne very much. Of course, I still spend a lot of time there because of Champagne De Meric, but visiting — even for three or four weeks at a time — isn't the same as living there.

Probably the overriding daily issue and the most difficult factor to deal with is the language. Although there is usually someone in most major stores, hotels, and restaurants who speaks English well, most people living in Champagne speak little or no English. Many have taken it in school and know a few words, but for all practical purposes it is almost impossible to communicate if one doesn't speak and understand French reasonably well.

This is not meant to discourage those who wish to visit the region. As a tourist, your experience will be different than that of someone who lives in the region. Tourists don't need to chat with the neighbors, visit the small village bakery, go grocery shopping, explain a problem to the plumber, or speak French on the phone. As a resident, however, one must do all of these things and much more.

Speaking a foreign language is one of those things that sounds easy until one actually has to do it. I remember before I moved and was working hard to learn French, I was amazed by the number of American friends who told me they spoke French, or their spouse was fluent in French, or they had been to France on vacation and did just fine. However, when some of those same people came to visit me, they were totally lost. Knowing how to conjugate the verb être (to be) isn't too useful when someone is speaking quickly to you, using slang, and asking what part of England you come from. And the "fluent" spouse usually spoke about 50 words—they could express very basic thoughts but could neither understand nor respond in a conversation. And "getting by" when visiting Paris, the Côte d'Azur, or another tourist region where many people speak English and most are used to dealing with tourists is different than trying to communicate in a 500-person village in the countryside.

I enjoy learning French. I'm still learning, but it's not easy by any means.

I also met a number of French people who claimed to speak English quite well, with no evidence to support this claim. Probably the best example was a dentist in a small village who began the visit by asking us in French whether we preferred to communicate with him in French or in English, since he had taken English in school. It turned out that his command of English seemed to be limited to the word "good."

Another difficult factor is the lack of a service culture. As Americans, we're spoiled—we're used to near instant gratification. We want one-stop shopping, fast service, and overnight delivery. We want to eat when we want, shop when we want, and avoid wasting time.

In Champagne, things are different. Although there are a couple of Wal-Mart-like stores and department stores, one does a great deal of shopping in small, highly specialized stores. Even the big stores have limitations. One must go to a pharmacy to buy aspirin, for example. In addition, sales tend to be a coordinated event; all stores have their sales at the same time.

One learns to live with these minor inconveniences, which are offset by many positive factors. In some venues, however, there is a genuine lack of a service mentality or desire, and this can be downright frustrating. For example, about six months after my arrival, my new electric dryer suddenly stopped working. The store the machine was purchased from had ceased to exist, but another company was handling warranty work.

I called the company on a Monday and was told that a service technician would be there on Wednesday afternoon. Although this may not seem all that exceptional to you, I was very pleased they could come so quickly.

It turned out that the dryer needed a new part, which would take about a week—unacceptable by U.S. standards but not bad for France. A week passed, however, with no news. I called the service company and was assured that the part would be in on Monday.

Monday came and went with no news. On Thursday, I called again and was told that the part would be there any day.

Two calls the following week got the same response. After a few heated phone conversations and another week of hanging the wash on a rack, I finally went out and bought another dryer. I then waited to see how long it would take for the part to arrive.

Eight weeks after the original service call I received the exciting news that the part had finally arrived. The dryer was manufactured by a German company and I explained to the head of the service company (who was not affiliated with the manufacturer, I must add), that I literally could have walked from the Champagne region to the factory in Germany, picked up the part, and walked back in far less than eight weeks. My sarcasm fell on deaf ears, so I had the old dryer fixed and donated it to a local charity.

Although there is not a service culture in Champagne, there is outstanding service in some venues. Restaurants, hotels, and many small merchants in the region will work hard to make you a happy customer. The more one visits an establishment, the more one is valued, becoming almost a member of the family. This is not necessarily fast service, but it is caring, quality service.

On the subject of restaurants, one of the best things about living in Champagne is the whole area of "wining and dining." Food is an important part of French culture, not simply something one must consume to satisfy one's appetite. This is especially true in the countryside, and Champagne is mainly countryside.

Restaurants play a large role in life in Champagne. In the United States, restaurants are often either a convenience (fast food, take-out, etc.) or a fashion industry — everyone flocks to the new, "hot" restaurant, until another new entry comes along. In Champagne, restaurants tend to have been around for a long time. The restaurants are usually run by the owners, and the staff doesn't change much over time, so one develops relationships. Regular customers are treated in a special manner, almost as part of the family. I travel a great deal and often eat in restaurants alone, but even after all this time I'm a bit uncomfortable in this situation everywhere but in Champagne. Because I have a relationship with the staff in my favorite restaurants in Champagne, I know that if I'm by myself, a special effort will be made to stop by the table more often to talk and to make me feel welcome.

The amount of time devoted to eating is another major difference of life in Champagne. Virtually everything except restaurants is closed from noon until two. The only exceptions that come to mind are gas stations and supermarkets. It usually takes one and a half to two hours for lunch and longer for dinner. One doesn't go out for dinner and a movie; it is one or the other. I personally like this very much because one talks as well as eats during a more leisurely meal. I've developed more friendships and good business relationships at restaurants than I have anywhere else in Champagne.

The attitude toward wine, of course, is also quite different. Wine in general plays a much larger role in French culture than it does in U.S. culture, and this is especially true in a wine region such as Champagne. Furthermore, people in Champagne drink a lot of champagne. People drink champagne as an aperitif, with meals, at social gatherings, or as a symbol of welcome when friends stop by. Although most of the residents of Champagne are by no means connoisseurs, there are more than 4,000 champagne producers, and the majority of the residents of the region have a friend or relative involved in the business, giving them a bit of inside access. Of course, anything impacting the champagne business is big news in the region.

Another important aspect of life in Champagne is social integration, or fitting in. Living in a small village with a population of 550 was a much different experience than what I was used to. One of the biggest differences, however, wasn't the size of the village but the fact that most residents had deep roots. It was not uncommon to find that families had been in the village for eight to ten generations. In fact, the wife of the current mayor of my village was a twelfth-generation resident.

These deep roots mean that everyone knows everyone else and that they have done so since they were children. Therefore, it is difficult for an outsider to fit into village life. Some neighbors were friendly and welcoming, especially some of the champagne producers, yet I never felt part of the community.

Fortunately, I had no lack of friends in the region outside of the village. I made many of these friends before I arrived in Champagne, but I also made many new friends while I lived there. In fact, I would have to say that the majority of my close friends today are from the Champagne region.

I certainly never felt that my being an American was an issue. The more closed-minded people were suspicious of any foreigners, but foreigners were anyone coming from outside of their village or region. Most of the people that I encountered, however, had a positive view of Americans, even if they didn't appreciate some aspects of our culture (especially fast food).

No portrait of life in Champagne would be complete without mentioning the weather. Frankly, this is one of the major negatives of life in the region, especially the lack of sun. As mentioned in an earlier chapter, the Champagne region receives rain 200 days a year on average, and even when it doesn't rain it is often overcast. Winter isn't so bad because temperatures are normally a bit above freezing. Cold, rainy days in June and July, however, can be quite depressing.

There are also some curious weather phenomena. The Marne River runs through the Vallée de la Marne, and changing temperatures often lead to intense morning fog coming off the river. When driving from the Reims area toward Epernay or Ay one often runs into thick patches of fog, and these can be hazardous if the temperatures are in the freezing range.

This is not to say that the weather is always bad in the Champagne region. I have experienced beautiful, sunny days that were warm and pleasant without being too hot. I've also seen some very hot days, especially in August. In general, however, the weather is not great, and it is the thing that I miss least about not living in Champagne.

On the other hand, one of the nicest parts of living in Champagne was that there always seemed to be something fun to do when I wasn't working. Of course, I love champagne and food, so I was very content dining with friends or visiting a champagne producer to broaden my tasting experience. There are also many other things to do, from local festivals to brocantes (a cross between a flea market and an antique show). Visiting friends and acquaintances, especially other champagne producers, was always fun. Champagne people are, in general, very generous with their product, and I had the chance to taste many older vintages and unusual cuvees that are not available to the general public.

Driving in the region also takes some getting used to. Other than the auto routes, most roads are one lane in each direction, and people pass by moving into the oncoming traffic lanes. Of course, this must be done both carefully and quickly. There are numerous traffic circles or roundabouts, as they are known in England, on the main roads. The driver never has priority when entering the circle, so one must enter carefully. On the other hand people drive aggressively, and if one is too careful and not aggressive at these circles, it can take forever to get anywhere.

As is the case in much of Europe, most cars are small. Gas is very expensive in France and parking spaces are small, so large cars are not very desirable. The vast majority of all vehicles are standard shift, although automatic transmission is more popular than it once was. One seldom is able to buy a car off the lot. Dealers don't keep a great deal of inventory, so it is usually necessary to order a car, a process that takes about a month.

Getting a driver's license is also different because the test is more difficult and comprehensive in France, and of course it is in French. I was dreading the prospect of taking this test when my French accountant told me about a loophole. France has reciprocal agreements with five states. Unfortunately Florida, where I lived at the time, was not one of these states, but Illinois was one. So we used a friend's address to establish residence in Chicago, took the written test there, and were able to exchange these licenses

The vines in the morning fog (photograph by John Hodder/Collection CIVC).

for our French licenses, which never expire. I usually play by the rules, so it was fun to get away with something for once.

There are a number of things one must get used to when living in Champagne. However, much of the daily life in Champagne is the same as it is in the United States—working, running errands, cooking, and the like. These chores are not glamorous, but they are an essential part of life.

Living in Champagne has its pluses and its minuses. It's not for everyone, but it was a great experience for me, and my life is much fuller for having lived there.

15. The Future

I'VE LEARNED MANY LESSONS during my study of champagne. All these lessons have come through experience, either my own experience or that of my teachers. Experience is the best of all teaching tools.

Looking to the future, however, is a much different matter. Although we learn from experience, it doesn't necessarily tell us how to forecast future events in a company or an industry. I've seen far too many cases of businesses in a rapid growth cycle that have projected these growth rates into the future with disastrous results. Internet companies in the late 1990s are just one of many examples.

However, I do see certain trends that are having a profound effect on the world of champagne. Therefore, I will conclude this narrative with a discussion of some of these key trends affecting the art and business of champagne.

Let's start with the trends affecting the business of champagne. The past 15 years have been a period of consolidation for champagne. The large conglomerates, including LVMH, Vranken, Paillard, and wine and spirits giants such as Allied Domecq, have used acquisitions to fuel their growth, and large groups now dominate the industry. Midsize producers are being swallowed up by these groups, and with a few notable exceptions such as Bollinger, Roederer, Deutz, and Pol Roger, the remaining midsize independents face a very uncertain future. These producers need volume, and they are forced to compete with the grandes marques and large groups on their own turf. Lacking financial resources, distribution strength, and marketing power, only those that can carve out a real niche, such as Bollinger's niche of outstanding quality, can hope to thrive.

Many small producers will also be threatened. In the French market, which represents more than 60 percent of global champagne sales, small producers do not usually compete with the mass producers and midsize producers because there is a clientele that prefers to seek out values from lesser-known brands. In the international market, however, the champagne category is less well defined. Smaller producers without a clear market niche, such as Champagne De Meric was when I first became involved, are definitely on the endangered list. Unlike the midsize producers who have recognizable brand names and valuable customer lists, most small producers are not attractive acquisition targets, and many of those without a well-defined market niche will simply fade away.

During 2003 and 2004, the champagne industry had two very tense developments. The first was the failure of the Groupe Martin, owners of Champagne Bricout and Champagne Delbeck. In financial trouble, this group sold off most of its assets and was unable to make the payments on their grape contracts or meet other financial obligations in 2003. A solution was ultimately found by breaking up the company, but this was a shock to the region and the industry.

In June 2004 a potentially much more serious development occurred when troubled giant Marne et Champagne was unable to make their June 5 payment on their grape contracts. As I write this a short-term solution has been found, but the #2 champagne group's future is in doubt.

A second growing trend is the emphasis on product packaging. This is not really a new trend because many cuvée prestige products have long had attractive labels and nice gift boxes, but the trend gained tremendous momentum during the premillennium period. As the end of the twentieth century drew near, champagne producers large and small looked for ways to create special products by designing attractive labels, creating special bottles, and surrounding products with everything from leather sacks to silver cages. The vast majority of the champagne in these bottles was a recent vintage or the standard brut nonvintage product, so the producers were relying on creative packaging to sell unexceptional champagne.

Since the millennium, many producers, especially the larger ones, have continued this trend. Today one can purchase bottles in packaging of all shapes and sizes. One can even buy champagne in a special picnic sack, with a designer leather bag, with an attractive ice bucket, or even with a cigar humidor.

Another element related to packaging is bottle size. Champagne is bottled in ten different sizes. These range from a quarter-bottle (18.75 cl), half-bottle (37.5 cl), bottle (75 cl), magnum (two bottles), and Jeroboam (four bottles) up to a Nebuchadnezzar (20 bottles). Half-bottles, bottles, magnums, and Jeroboams are required to be fermented in their original bottle, while the others are generally transferred from magnums using a process known as transvasage, which is not conducive to quality. In addition, the surface/volume ratio is a factor in determining quality, making quarter-bottles of very marginal quality at best and, in my opinion, arguably not meriting the Champagne appellation.

However, a big trend today is the marketing of attractively packaged quarter-bottles. Leading this trend are Pommery (labeled POP), Piper-Heidsieck (labeled Baby Piper), Vranken (labeled Little Blue Top), Moët, and Veuve Clicquot. This new packaging, according to a leading wine magazine, "is being pushed in nightclubs and discos, where it is hoped that the trendy, young clientele will find it a viable alternative to beer, still wine, or mixed drinks." In the case of Pommery and Piper-Heidsieck, the champagne is extra dry (i.e., semi-sweet) rather than brut. These bottles retail for approximately $10.00 each.

According to a spokesman for Pommery, "We wanted to do something a bit different, you know, offbeat, to make younger adults think about champagne in a new way." I support this sentiment because far too many people view champagne as something to be drunk only on New Year's Eve. However, when these young adults drink lower quality champagne, they will be learning that champagne is a sugary, low-quality wine sold at a high price. This new way of thinking about champagne could be very damaging in the long run.

A third trend in the champagne business is an increasing difference in pricing between France and the export markets. Lower sales due to difficult global economic conditions and unsold inventory in the distribution system from the premillennium years have put many producers in a cash crunch, and they must now do whatever is necessary to raise revenue to pay their bills. In early 2003 one could purchase champagne in French supermarkets for less than $10.00 per bottle, which included a 19.6-percent value-added tax. Although prices have firmed up a bit, price is a major issue in the French market.

A fourth important trend is a general increase in costs for champagne producers. In 1998, France passed a law decreasing the workweek from 39 hours to 35 hours, without a corresponding decrease in salary. The idea was to force companies to hire more people to create jobs, but it has led to a number of multinational companies simply closing their operations in France and moving them elsewhere. Of course, champagne producers do not have that luxury.

Competition for grapes has also resulted in price increases in recent years. Although official prices have remained fairly stable, bonuses unrelated to quality have been increasing. These cost increases serve either to increase the price to consumers, which reduces demand, or to reduce margins for producers. Neither of these possibilities is a pleasant prospect.

A fifth trend that may affect export sales of all French wine, including champagne, is a growth in adverse publicity for the entire Appellation d'Origine Controlée (AOC) system. Today this system is coming under increasing attack from the international wine press, especially in the "new world." The AOC system is called unwieldy, limiting, and obscure. These journalists claim the system, which controls yields, production methods, and grape varieties, stifles creativity and argue that the winemaker should be free to make these choices. I disagree with these arguments because I believe the AOC system provides at least some guarantee of quality, but I'm in the minority.

In addition, casual wine drinkers and even many in the wine trade don't understand the complexities of the AOC system and the different quality designations such as the designations grand cru and premier cru and the échelle des crus. They prefer simpler labels with varietal designations such as merlot or chardonnay. Although varietal labeling is not really an issue in the champagne category, a decrease in appreciation for the AOC system and its benefit to consumers hurts all French wines, including champagne.

There are also a few trends on the artistic side. One is the increasing standardization of champagne. Much of this is a result of consolidation. As parts of large, short-term oriented corporations, producers are under pressure to increase efficiency, which has led to abandoning labor-intensive traditional methods in favor of lower cost industrial methods.

A second trend is the lack of openness in the champagne industry. I mentioned in an earlier chapter that many producers give little real information regarding their grapes and production methods. In addition, much of the marketing for champagne has little to do with the actual product. For example, *Decanter Magazine* recently featured the following as their quote of the month in a section entitled "The Good, The Bad, & The Ugly," taken from publicity material for 1995 Dom Pérignon:

> As the essence of a year, marrying respect for the constant pursuit of a distinctive style with the quest for perfection measured by the yardstick of degrees of refinement and strength, Dom Pérignon is the photograph of a grape harvest taken through the filter of style.

If you can figure out what this means, let me know.

In the interest of fairness, however, I must admit that my own company has been guilty of the same type of thing. For example, this is how the former version of the brochure for Champagne De Meric described our blanc de blancs:

> Reminiscent of a pretty woman, this is a delicious wine, both light and fresh and with a pleasant bouquet.

Not particularly enlightening. Compare this to how our new brochure describes Grande Réserve Sous Bois:

> The name Grande Réserve Sous Bois is derived from the fact that 50% of the wine used to make our champagne is vinified and aged in oak barrels, the traditional method. We believe that vinifying our wine in the 50/50 combination of oak barrels and stainless steel containers helps create a rich champagne, but one that is easy to drink.
>
> Our Grande Réserve Sous Bois is a multi-vintage champagne, a blend of recent harvests. The blend consists of approximately 80% pinot noir from Ay (grand cru), Mareuil-sur-Ay (premier cru), and Mutigny (premier cru), 15% chardonnay from Cramant (grand cru), Avize (grand cru), and Oger (grand cru), and 5% pinot meunier from Cumières (premier cru). The overall rating on the "échelle des crus" for the grapes used in our Grande Réserve Sous Bois is 97%.

This may not exactly be Tolstoy, but it does give the consumer some real information about our grapes and vinification methods, which is a bit more useful than "a filter of style" or "like a pretty woman."

Unfortunately, this lack of openness in Champagne sometimes goes beyond marketing. For example, although I support culture raisonnée in Champagne as a very positive step, as discussed in an earlier chapter this effort is still in its early stages. However, some industry sources have begun trumpeting this movement as being close to an accomplished fact, which is far from the case.

In the same vein, a few producers have promoted their supposed use of some "biodynamique methods." By the time the message gets to a market such as the United States it is distorted to imply that these are organic champagnes. In the case of one specific producer who fits in this category, he may well use a few of these methods, but he also treats some of his vines via helicopter, and I can assure you that what these helicopters spray is far from being organic. Yet I've seen this champagne referred to as organic on a highly regarded restaurant wine list in California.

A third trend is the increasing popularity of champagnes from récoltant-manipulants (RMs) and other small producers. These products tend to be more distinctive, and this increase in popularity allows champagne drinkers to experience more variety in quality and style. These are the equivalent of estate-bottled wines and tend to be an expression of their particular terrior, which accounts for the diverse taste of these champagnes. Top quality RM champagnes are never "standard."

Today, the champagne industry faces many challenges—adverse economic conditions, increasing competition from sparkling wines around the world, rising costs, and a general decrease in interest in French wine. However, we have many positive assets. Champagne is blessed with a unique terroir, and I have never found a sparkling wine that can measure up to a very good champagne, to say nothing of matching the quality of great producers such as René Collard, Bollinger, and Krug. In addition, champagne goes with most types of food, and food and wine pairing is a growing trend. Very few consumers really understand champagne, so there is potential to grow our category's popularity if we can better educate the public. We can only succeed, however, if we as an industry rededicate ourselves to quality in all aspects—viticulture, vinification, aging, and of course marketing.

There are many quality champagne producers, including a number of younger producers. There are also many younger connoisseurs of champagne who are searching for quality. This gives me hope that there will always be a thriving niche for quality champagne.

I am optimistic regarding the future of both the art and business of champagne. But as one says in France, "on verra"—time will tell.

Appendix I:
Champagne Surface Planted
by Department by Grape Variety

(Based on 1998)

	Pinot Noir	Chardonnay	Pinot Meunier	Others	Total
Aisne	431.80 ha	243.20 ha	2,129.10 ha	0.10 ha	2,804.20 ha
Aube	5,634.10 ha	606.90 ha	325.90 ha	82.10 ha	6,649.00 ha
Marne	5,695.20 ha	7,590.40 ha	8,353.40 ha	12.70 ha	21,651.70 ha
Haute-Marne	57.80 ha	5.10 ha	5.30 ha	0.00 ha	68.20 ha
Seine & Marne	8.30 ha	15.50 ha	23.20 ha	0.10 ha	47.10 ha
Total	11,827.20 ha	8,461.10 ha	10,836.90 ha	95.00 ha	31,220.20 ha
	38%	27%	35%		

Source: CIVC

Appendix II:
Eight Ways to Maximize
Your Enjoyment of Champagne

THE IMAGE OF CHAMPAGNE SUFFERS because it is often not treated as a wine that is worth serious study. This keeps many wine critics, and consequently many consumers, from learning about the majority of the best champagnes available today. The best champagne producers often lack the means or the motivation to mount advertising and publicity programs, and journalists rarely seek out these producers.

At the same time, the slightly lower profile of champagne has its advantages. One can enjoy champagne without most of the pretension often associated with wine — sniffing the cork, making sure to use the correct swirling technique, or hotly debating whether the bouquet of the wine has hints of blackberry or black cherry. There are fewer rules for the drinking of champagne.

However, there are some ways to maximize your enjoyment of champagne. Therefore what follows are eight tips to double your pleasure.

1. Look for quality and value. The key to enjoying champagne is to insist on a quality product. Everything else we will discuss is secondary to the quality of the wine.

However, one must be pragmatic, so in addition to searching for quality it is important to take value into account. This is especially true in the United States due to the limited selection of top-quality producers. Krug and

Bollinger are the most universally available champagnes of outstanding quality, but most regular champagne drinkers need a more affordable alternative. This is where the price/value equation becomes important.

This is not a major issue in my household. I have unlimited access to De Meric, and I arranged to import quantities of our other favorite champagnes before I left France. My advice is to find a few different champagnes that you like at various price points. For a special occasion, choose one of your favorite champagnes. For normal dining and entertaining, choose a champagne of very good quality but with a more modest price point. For a large function such as a wedding, look for a champagne providing excellent value (less than twenty-five dollars).

Another part of enjoying champagne is to learn more about the wine. Don't be afraid to experiment — try different champagnes. Don't worry about impressing people with a prestigious label. I've found that most wine lovers will enjoy discovering a new champagne.

2. Plan for proper storage. Champagne is perhaps the most fragile of all fine wines. Exposure to high heat or severe temperature changes can ruin a bottle of champagne. As mentioned earlier, once a bottle is disgorged, even bottles stored under good conditions have a limited life span.

Complicating the problem is that it is impossible to know what the bottle has gone through between the time it left the producer and the time you purchased it. Champagne is generally exported from France via boat, and although many importers use temperature- controlled containers, some economize by using standard containers. Although wholesalers generally have good storage facilities, your bottle may have sat for a long time in a wine shop under questionable conditions.

This is not to say that the champagne will be ruined before you buy it; bottles will generally arrive in fairly good shape. Even minor problems during shipping or in storage, however, make an already delicate wine even more fragile.

The best home storage solution is to have a deep cellar or professionally built, climate-controlled storage facility capable of keeping your champagne at a constant temperature. The ideal storage temperature is between 50 and 55 degrees Fahrenheit (although up to 60 degrees will be fine if the temperature is relatively constant). Because most homes do not have the terrain for a deep cellar or the space for a professional wine room, special wine storage units such as those available from Eurocave and Vinotemp are good options. The size of the unit you buy will, of course, depend on your needs, space, and budget, but there is generally something available for everyone. For example, an under-counter Vinotemp unit capable of holding around twenty bottles of champagne (or 24 bottles of still wine) is available for less than three hundred dollars. Although a unit of this size will not allow one to build a wine collection, it will provide safe storage and give you access to an excellent supply for current drinking, and champagne is a wine to drink rather than collect.

Despite all this, wine storage facilities are not essential to enjoy champagne. In the absence of any type of storage unit or cellar, my suggestion is to store your bottles in an area away from direct sunlight with a relatively constant temperature (an air-conditioned closet, for example). I'd also suggest drinking the bottle within one year after your purchase. Those with good storage facilities, however, should be able to keep the bottles for at least two to three years.

3. Serve champagne chilled but not too cold. Everyone knows that champagne should be served chilled, but there seems to be little agreement on the proper temperature. I've seen opinions ranging from around forty degrees Fahrenheit to approximately fifty degrees Fahrenheit, which is a pretty wide range.

In my opinion, there is no single correct temperature for serving champagne. Much depends on the age and the quality of the wine. When I serve better quality champagnes, I generally target a temperature of around 48 to 50 degrees. I've found this to be a good temperature to maximize the taste and bouquet of the champagne, allowing one to form an educated opinion on the merits of the wine. However, when drinking younger, lesser quality champagnes, it is best to chill the bottle to around 43 degrees. This lower temperature will help mask the overly acidic taste of these champagnes. For this reason I prefer to conduct serious tastings at home, where I can control all elements of the tasting, rather than in the cellars of the producer, where the champagne may be served too cold.

Champagne in the ice bucket and ready to drink (courtesy Champagne De Meric).

The easiest way to chill champagne is simply to put the bottle in the refrigerator for approximately two hours. However, many people whose opinions I respect insist that chilling champagne in an ice bucket will yield superior results. Although some use a mix of 50 percent water and 50 percent ice, I prefer to place the bottle in the ice bucket, fill the bucket with ice (to the neck of the bottle if possible), and let it chill for twenty minutes. I find the ice-only method neater than ice and water, although most people would disagree with me.

Like many things, serving temperature is a matter of personal taste. Many people prefer champagne to be served colder than I recommend. Try for yourself and see what best suits your needs and taste.

4. Champagne is not pop. With apologies for the pun, many people feel that opening a bottle with a loud popping noise is part of the theatre in serving champagne. However, this is really not good for the wine. The sudden pop is caused by a large quantity of gas escaping from the bottle and, as a result, your champagne may become a bit flat before the bottle has been finished.

In my opinion, the key to opening a bottle of champagne correctly is control. Once you have removed the foil covering the cork (called the capsule), carefully unwind the wire cage around the cork (the muselet), using the palm of one hand to hold the cork in place. This precaution is usually not necessary, but occasionally a bottle will have become agitated during transport (or perhaps the remuage was not properly conducted), and the cork will shoot out as soon as the muselet is loosened.

Once you have ensured that the cork is secure, it is best to remove the metal disk on top of the cork (the plaque de muselet) if this did not come off with the muselet. Then securely grip the cork with one hand and the bottle with the other. Professional wine waiters will generally hold the bottom of the bottle, but I find that I have better control if I hold the shoulder. While holding the cork firmly in place, twist the bottle to loosen the cork. Once you have made this first twist, which is the hard part, continue the process slowly and gently remove the cork, always covering the cork with the palm of your hand to maintain control. When the cork is removed, there should be a gentle sigh as a small amount of air escapes.

Sometimes bottles can be quite difficult to open. This often occurs when the bottle has been disgorged relatively recently and the cork hasn't fully assumed its shape, although sometimes difficulty removing the cork indicates an imperfection in the cork or the process used to insert the cork. In any case, if you encounter difficulty, start by twisting the cork rather than the bottle while holding the bottle firmly in place. If this doesn't work, pliers specially made for opening champagne bottles is a useful tool for the champagne lover. The downside is that using these pliers gives one less control, and as a result the cork tends to shoot out of the bottle. I suggest using this tool only when the cork won't budge, and even then only to loosen the cork rather than to remove it.

An even more important tool for the champagne lover is a recorker (bouchon hermétique). These devices, generally made of metal or plastic, will reseal the bottle once it is open, which removes the necessity of drinking the entire bottle in one sitting. In theory this tool will allow you to keep a bottle for a few days in the refrigerator, but I've found that the wine will begin to deteriorate after 24 to 48 hours. Incidentally, if you normally buy half-bottles, it makes much more sense to buy a 75-cl bottle and use the recorker. A full bottle is less expensive than two half-bottles, and the quality is much higher in the larger format.

5. Glassware is important, but ... I've noticed that U.S. wine magazines devote a lot of space to the proper glassware. In fact, I feel that many professionals and wine lovers have gone a bit overboard on this subject and sometimes pay more attention to the glassware than to the wine itself.

This is not to say that proper glassware won't enhance one's enjoyment of wine, for it will. For example, I recently participated in a tasting at the Franciscan Winery in Napa Valley (Franciscan has a portfolio of high-quality California wines), tasting wines in Reidel glasses against the same wines in standard glasses. Although I didn't see major differences in taste, the bouquet was much enhanced by the Riedel glasses.

In regard to champagne, the differences are somewhat less pronounced. The wines I tasted at Franciscan were young, powerful wines with strong bouquets as opposed to the more subtle aromas one finds with champagne. Still, this is a subject that merits exploration.

The most important aspect of selecting glassware for champagne is the shape of the glass. A tall narrow glass, whether it be the popular flute or the tulip shape, is ideal. Avoid the more bowl-shaped coupe style, which is attractive but not practical. The coupe is an open style that results in gas escaping too rapidly from the champagne. Inciden-

The best champagne re-corkers I have found (courtesy Champagne De Meric).

Typical champagne flutes (courtesy Champagne De Meric).

tally, the story that the coupe was shaped after Marie-Antoinette's breast is just a legend because the coupe dates back to the mid-seventeenth century.

Many professionals feel strongly that the tulip, with its inwardly tapering top, is superior to the flute because it does a better job of controlling the bubbles. Although I understand this theory, I've frankly found the difference between the tulip and the flute to be insignificant.

I mentioned the top-quality Austrian producer Reidel earlier. Although there is no question that Riedel produces glasses of excellent quality, their best products are quite expensive. I have glasses from a number of sources, but my favorite champagne glasses are made in Champagne by the Christalleries Royales de Champagne.

Regardless of your individual preferences, it is important to remember that outstanding champagne in a water glass is better than mediocre champagne in the best glasses. Look for good-quality glasses that fit your budget and taste, but don't worry if you use the inexpensive flutes available from a mass merchant. It is best to focus your resources on purchasing quality champagne rather than the best possible glassware.

One final note on glassware — never put champagne glasses in the dishwasher. Dishwasher detergents will leave a residue in the glass that will affect the appearance, smell, and taste of champagne. You may have experienced occasions where a glass of champagne seemed overly fizzy. This was probably due to soap residue in the glass. Glasses should always be washed by hand in hot water, using little or no soap or detergent, and dried thoroughly with a clean towel.

6. When it comes to pouring and tasting, slow is better. The secret to pouring champagne is to do it slowly. Pouring too quickly results in a large amount of foam and can lead to overflowing. In addition, before serving your guests or companions, first pour a very small amount for yourself to ensure that there have not been major problems with storage or cork quality.

If you are serving a few people, start by putting some in each glass (in Champagne, the custom is to serve women before men) and then add more to fill the glasses. Although it is easier to bring people already filled glasses, for a small group it tends to be more interesting if you fill the glasses in front of your guests. In addition, don't wrap the bottle in a towel or napkin. Let people see what they are drinking because explaining why you have chosen this particular champagne is part of the fun.

Now finally comes the part that you've been waiting for — the tasting. I won't go into all of the nuances of wine tasting because this information is available from many sources and by writers more knowledgeable on the subject than I am, but I do want to discuss a few points specific to the tasting of champagne.

As is true with all types of wine, there are a number of elements in the tasting of champagne. The first is visual. Champagne should not be pale and colorless. If it is, it's a sure sign of a champagne lacking in proper aging, although a blanc de blancs champagne will have a somewhat lighter hue than a champagne heavily based on the pinot grapes. At the same time, if the wine is dark brown you can be fairly certain that the bottle has been kept too long since disgorgement and it has turned to vinegar. Also, notice the bubbles. Small, very fine bubbles are a good sign, while somewhat larger bubbles tell you that this is probably a mass-produced, fifteen-month champagne. If there are very few bubbles, the wine is probably past its peak and possibly undrinkable.

The next step is the smell. There are many different bouquets of champagne, and one's preference is a matter of personal taste. I prefer the rich, nutty aromas that I find are associated with the best-quality champagnes, but your preference may lie with bouquets such as vanilla, spices, or a more flowery aroma.

The final step, of course, is to drink the champagne, leaving the wine in your mouth for a few seconds to fully explore the taste. Then ask yourself if you like this champagne, how it compares to others that you have tasted, and whether it is worth the price. Defining the exact components of the taste and bouquet can be fun, but if you don't like the champagne, none of this really matters.

Even if you are conducting a tasting to get an impression of a number of different champagnes, always swallow the wine — the finish is important. If you are drinking a better quality, more complex champagne, the taste will change somewhat as the wine is exposed to oxygen, so your first impression may differ from your final impression.

7. Champagne goes with almost everything. The art of matching wine and food is increasing in popularity across the globe. More than ever, chefs and sommeliers are being trained in this art, and some fine restaurants offer menus pairing different wines with different courses. This practice has encouraged both professionals and consumers to search out new wines, which I consider a very positive development.

The good news for champagne lovers is that champagne is perhaps the most versatile of all wines and matches up well with almost any type of food. Perhaps the only real exception are desert courses, especially chocolate, and even then one can choose a demi-sec champagne to accompany these dishes.

This is a surprise to many people who view champagne merely as an aperitif, or a way to begin a meal. Indeed, this is the image of champagne, but it is as a food wine that champagne truly shines because the combination with the meal serves to bring out the flavors and complexity of a top champagne. Champagne-only dinners are quite normal in the Champagne region, and the wine is successfully matched with a wide variety of dishes from vegetarian cuisine to spicy Asian courses.

Matching specific champagnes, or even specific types of champagne, with different dishes is a question of personal taste. Traditional wisdom has it that a blanc de blancs goes better with lighter dishes, while champagnes with more pinot noir and pinot meunier are best with more hearty dishes. I have not found this to be true, largely because one can't generalize for an entire category. For example, a 1993 Champagne Franck Bonville and a fifteen-month-old blanc de blancs from a mass producer are both made from chardonnay grapes, but they have little else in common.

One generalization I do believe is that older champagnes go extremely well with rich, flavorful dishes such as mushrooms. For example, a 1969 René Collard with a dish based on black truffles is a perfect combination; both the course and the wine are improved by the interaction.

Don't save your champagne for a party or for New Year's Eve. Try it with dinner. Keep track of how different champagnes go with different dishes so you can create combinations to match your taste. Then try a champagne-only dinner with some fellow wine lovers. They may be surprised at first, but I think you'll find they'll enjoy this different approach to food and wine pairing and appreciate your effort.

8. If you are a collector, champagne offers some interesting possibilities. I know I just said that champagne is a wine for drinking, not for collecting, because of its fragile nature after disgorgement. I am a collector by nature, but my entire permanent collection of champagne (bottles for saving rather than for drinking) consists of a bottle of Moët 1911 and a bottle of Bollinger 1929. Everything else I have is for drinking within the next few years.

However, there are a number of champagne-related collectible options. I know people who collect champagne labels and others who save one bottle (full or empty) of each kind of champagne they have tried. Others collect the different types of champagne recorkers, imprinted with the logo of different producers. Still others collect ice buckets from different producers, which make a very nice display item. Other collectibles include old posters, books about champagne, and various branded publicity items.

Perhaps the most interesting champagne collectible, however, is the plaque de muselet, the metal disk one finds over the cork. These disks, commonly known as capsules, are a very popular collectible in France. Although many producers still use generic plaques, more and more producers are branding these items with their name and logo. Often the plaques differ between the different products in a producer's line, often by color but sometimes also by design. There is even a price guide listing the various plaques and their estimated retail prices. Most are inexpensive, but some of the old and rare ones can sell for a few hundred dollars. These collectibles are sold in certain wine shops, by mail order, and at many flea markets in France.

There are many ways to collect plaques de muselets. Most people will simply buy or trade for as many as possible. My personal preference is to collect the plaques from different champagnes I have tried (I keep only different designs, not the color variations). These items can be put in a wall frame and make a very attractive display item.

One of the first things I did with De Meric was to discontinue the use of generic plaques in favor of branded ones. I plan to redesign the current version in the not-too-distant future to better reflect our new philosophy and production methods.

Appendix III: Sample Letters to Champagne Producers

Letter in English (to larger producers)

Dear Sir or Madame:

I am planning a trip to the Champagne region, and I would very much like to visit your cellars. I am a champagne lover, and I look forward to learning more about your products.

I will be in the region on [*date*]. Please let me know when would be a convenient time to schedule an appointment. There will be [number of persons] people in our party.

Thank you very much, and I look forward to seeing you.

Sincerely,
[name, address, fax, and e-mail]

Letter in French to smaller producers offering visits in English

Monsieur/Madame:

On visitera votre region le [day-month-year], et je me demande si nous pourrions prendre un rendez-vous pour une visite et dégustation à chez vous en anglais. On ne parle pas français. Nous serons [number of people] personnes.

Nous sommes des grands amateurs du champagne. J'ai trouvé votre nom dans le livre *The Art and Business of Champagne.*

Si c'est possible d'avoir un rendez-vous, pourriez-vous me dire à quelle heure vous préférez.

Je vous prie d'agréer l'expression de mes sentiments distingués.

[name, address, fax, and e-mail]

[rough translation]
We will visit your region, and I would like to make an appointment for a visit to your cellars and a tasting in English. We do not speak French. There will be [number of persons] people in our group.

We are champagne lovers. I found your name in the book *The Art and Business of Champagne.*

If a visit is possible, please let me know what time you prefer.

Sincerely,

Letter in French if coming with a guide or translator

Monsieur/Madame:

On visitera votre region le [day-month-year], et je me demande si nous pourrions prendre un rendez-vous pour une visite et dégustation à chez vous. Nous serons [number of people] personnes.

Nous sommes des grands amateurs du champagne. J'ai trouvé votre nom dans le livre *The Art and Business of Champagne.* Nous ne parlons pas français, mais on apporte un traducteur.

Si c'est possible d'avoir un rendez-vous, pourriez-vous me dire à quelle heure vous préférez.

Je vous prie d'agréer l'expression de mes sentiments distingués.

[name address, fax, and e-mail]

[same content, but explaining that you are bringing a guide]

Appendix IV:
Contact Information for Hotels, Restaurants, and Tourist Destinations

Hotels

Les Crayères, 64 Blvd. Vasnier, 51100 Reims.
Telephone: 011 333 2682 8080, fax: 011 333 2682 6552,
e-mail: crayeres@relaischateau.com

Grand Hotel des Templiers, 22 rue Templiers, 51100 Reims.
Telephone: 011 333 2688 5508, fax: 011 333 2647 8060,
e-mail: hotel.templiers@wanadoo.fr

Holiday Inn Garden Court, 46 rue Buirette, 51100 Reims.
Telephone: 011 333 2678 9999, fax: 011 333 2678 9990

Best Western Hotel de la Paix, 9 rue Buirette, 51100 Reims.
Telephone: 011 333 2640 0408, fax 011 333 2647 7504,
e-mail: info@bw-hotel-lapaix.com

New Europe Hotel, 29 rue Buirette, 51100 Reims.
Telephone: 011 333 2647 3939, fax 011 333 2640 1437,
e-mail: reimseurope@new-hotelcom

Royal Champagne, rte. N 2051, 51160 Champillon.
Telephone: 011 333 2652 8711, fax: 011 333 2652 8969,
e-mail: royalchampagne@wanadoo.fr

Auberge Le Relais, rte. N 3, 02850 Reuilly-Sauvigny.
Telephone 011 333 2370 3536, fax: 011 333 2370 2776,
e-mail: auberge.relais.de.reuilly@wanadoo.fr

Chateau de Fére, rte. D 967, 02130 Fère-En-Tardenois.
Telephone: 011 333 2382 2113, fax: 011 333 2382 3781,
e-mail: chateau.fere@wanadoo.fr

Hostellerie La Briqueterie, rte. de Sézanne, 51530 Vinay.
Telephone: 011 333 2659 9999, fax: 011 333 2659 9210

Hotel Campanile, Les Terres Rouges, 51530 Dizy.
Telephone: 011 333 2655 3366, fax: 011 333 2654 3167

Restaurants

Les Crayères, 64 Blvd. Vasnier, 51100 Reims.
Telephone: 011 333 2682 8080, fax: 011 333 2682 6552,
e-mail: crayeres@relaischateau.com

La Maison du Vigneron, rte. N 51, 51160 St.-Imoges.
Telephone: 011 333 2652 8800, fax: 011 333 2652 8603

Auberge Le Relais, rte. N 3, 02850 Reuilly-Sauvigny.
Telephone 011 333 2370 3536, fax: 011 333 2370 2776,
e-mail: auberge.relais.de.reuilly@wanadoo.fr

Les Cépages, 16 rue Fauvette, 51200 Epernay.
Telephone 011 333 2655 1693, fax: 011 333 2654 5130,
e-mail: lescepages@wandoo.fr

Restaurant Continental, 95 pl. Drouet D'Erlon, 51100 Reims.
Telephone 011 333 2647 0147, fax: 011 333 2640 9560,
e-mail: lecontinental-restaurant@wanadoo.fr

Le Mesnil, 51190 Le Mesnil-sur-Oger.
Telephone: 011 333 2657 9557, fax: 011 333 2657 7857

Les Berceaux, 13 rte Berceaux, 51200 Epernay.
Telephone: 011 333 2655 2884, fax: 011 333 2655 1036,
e-mail: les.berceaux@wanadoo.fr

Le Foch, 37 blvd. Foch, 51100 Reims.
Telephone: 011 333 2647 4822, fax: 011 333 2688 7822

Le Chardonnay, 184 ave. Epernay, 51100 Reims.
Telephone: 011 333 2606 0860, fax: 011 333 2605 8156

Royal Champagne, rte. N 2051, 51160 Champillon.
Telephone: 011 333 2652 8711, fax: 011 333 2652 8969,
e-mail: royalchampagne@wanadoo.fr

La Briqueterie, rte. de Sézanne, 51530 Vinay.
Telephone: 011 333 2659 9999, fax: 011 333 2659 9210

Hostellerie du Chateau, Chateau de Fére, rte. D 967, 02130 Fère-En-Tardenois. Telephone: 011 333 2382 2113, fax: 011 333 2382 3781,
e-mail: chateau.fere@wanadoo.fr

Hotel de La Poste, pl. Royer-Collard, 51300 Vitry-Le-François.
Telephone: 011 333 2674 0265, fax: 011 333 2674 5471

Le Grand Cerf, rte N 51, 51500 Montchenot.
Telephone: 011 333 2697 6007, fax: 011 333 2697 6424

Restaurant Jacky Michel, Hotel d'Angleterre, 19 pl. Mgr. Tissier, 51000 Chalons-en-Champagne.
Telephone: 011 333 2668 2151, fax: 011 333 2670 5167

Le Latin, 90 pl. Drouet d'Erlon, 51100 Reims.
Telephone: 011 333 2640 2006

Lys du Roy, 1 rte. Damery-Nogent, 51500 Sermiers.
Telephone: 011 333 2697 6611

Points of Interest

Office of Tourism, Marne Department, 13 bis rue Carnot, 51000 Chalons-en-Champagne.
Telephone: 011 333 2668 3752, fax: 011 333 2668 4645,
e-mail: cdt51@tourisme-en-champagne.com

Office of Tourism, Aube Department, 34 quai Dampierre, 10000 Troyes.
Telephone: 011 333 2542 5050, fax: 011 333 2542 5088,
e-mail: aube.champagne@wanadoo.fr

Office of Tourism, Epernay, 7 ave. de Champagne, B.P. 28, 51201 Epernay Cedex. Telephone: 011 333 2653 3300, fax: 011 333 2651 9522

Office of Tourism, Reims, 2 rue Guillaume de Machault, 51100 Reims. Telephone: 011 333 2677 4525, fax: 011 333 2677 4527

Office of Tourism, Chateau-Thierry, 11 rue Vallée, 02400 Chateau-Thierry. Telephone: 011 333 2383 1014, fax: 011 333 2383 1474

Office of Tourism, Bayel, 2 rue Belle Verrière, 10310 Bayel. Telephone: 011 333 2592 4268, fax: 011 333 2527 7206

Chateau Condé en Brie. Telephone 011 333 2382 4225

Musee de la Vigne et du Vin (wine museum), Champagne Launois Père & Fils, 2 ave. Eugène Guillaume, 51190 Le Mesnil-sur-Oger. Telephone: 011 333 2657 5015, fax: 011 333 2657 9782

Cristalleries Royale de Champagne, rue Belle Verrière, 10310 Bayel. Telephone: 011 333 2597 3766, fax: 011 333 2527 7206

Aube Cristal, Zone artisanale, 10310 Bayel. Telephone: 011 333 2592 0379, fax: 011 333 2592 0181

Train schedules and fares: www.sncf.com

Bibliography

Books

Baugier, Monfieur. *Memoires Historiques de la Province de Champagne*. Chalons, France: Claude Bouchard, 1721.

Bazin, Jean-François; Hulot, Mathilde, and Piot, Hélène. *Un Siècle de Millésimes*. Paris: Fleuris, 2001.

Bon, Christian, and Rigaux, Jacky. *Les Nouveaux Vignerons*. Dijon, France: Editions de Bourgogne, 2002.

Broadbent, Michael. *The Great Vintage Wine Book*. London: Mitchell Beazley, 1980.

Choiselle, Christiane, and Choiselle, Roland, and Thomas, Marcel. *La Grande Champagne*. Reims, France: Editions Matot-Braine, 1980.

Choiselle, Christiane, Choiselle, Roland, Clause, Georges, Dumenil, Claude, Fierobe, Nicole, Pape, Jean, Quérel, Georges, and Tamine, Michel. *Marne*. Paris: Editions Bonneton, 1998.

Clause, George, and Glatre, Eric. *Le Champagne Trois Siècles d'Histoire*. Paris: Stock, 1997.

de la Brosse, Benoit, and Coutant, Catherine. *Chefs de Caves de la Champagne*. Reims, France: Paysage, 1997.

de Rabaudy, Nicolas. *Champagne Le Guide*. Paris: Editions Hermé, 1997.

Edwards, Michael. *Champagne and Sparkling Wine*. London: Mitchell Beazley, 1998.

_____. *The Champagne Companion*. London: Apple Press, 1994.

Faith, Nicolas. *The Story of Champagne*. New York: Facts on File, 1989.

Fetter, Richard. *Dom Pérignon, Man and Myth*. Boulder, CO: Johnson Publishing, 1989.

Fredet, Dominique. *Un Siècle de Vendanges en Champagne*. Reims, France: Editions Dominique Fradet, 1998.

Garcia, André. *Les Vins de Champagne*. Paris: Presses Universitaires de France, 1997.

Germain, Bernard, and Stritt, Pascal. *Marne en Champagne*. Chalons-sur-Marne, France: Siloe, 1995.

Glatre, Eric. *Champagne Guide*. New York: Abbeville Press, 1999.

Glatre, Eric, and de la Chaize, Angélique. *Champagne*. Paris: Hoebeke, 2001.

Jahény, Jean-René. *Champagne*. Sommiers, France: Romain Pages Editions, 2000.

Juhlin, Richard. *Champagne, The Great Tasting*. Stockholm, Sweden: Methusalem, 2000.

Krug, Henri, and Krug Rémi. *L'Art du Champagne*. Paris: Editions Robert Laffont, 1979.

Lucas, Eileen. *The Eighteenth and Twenty-First Amendments*. Berkeley Heights, NJ: Enslow Publishers, 1998.

Mastrojanni, Michel. *Guide de l'Amateur de Champagne*. Paris: Solar, 2000.

Matthews, Patrick. *Real Wine*. London: Mitchell Beazley, 2000.

McNie, Maggie. *Champagne*. London: Farber and Farber, 1999.

Paulet-Gamet, and Henri; Paulet-Gamet, Jehanne. *Contes Champenois de Vignoble*. Reims, France: Editions du Lys de Reim, 1995.

Ray, Cyril. *Bollinger, Tradition of a Champagne Family*. London: Heinemann, 1971.

Redding, Cyrus. *The History and Description of Modern Wines*. London: Whittaker, Treacher, & Arnot, 1833.

Simon, André. *The History of Champagne*. London; Octopus Books Limited, 1971.

Stevenson, Tom. *Champagne*. London: Sotheby's Publications, 1986.

_____. *World Encyclopedia of Champagne and Sparkling Wine*. San Francisco: Wine Appreciation Guild, 1999.

Turnbull, James. *Champagne, Grandeur Nature*. Paris: Editions E/P/A, 1998.

Periodicals

La Champagne Viticole
Decanter Magazine
Guide Curien de la Champagne
Marne Hebo
La Revue du Champagne
La Revue du Vin de France

L'Union
Vins Magazine
The Wine Enthusiast
Wine News
The Wine Spectator

Index